BLACK WOMEN
PLAYWRIGHTS

STUDIES IN MODERN DRAMA
VOLUME 11
GARLAND REFERENCE LIBRARY OF THE HUMANITIES
VOLUME 2051

STUDIES IN MODERN DRAMA

KIMBALL KING, *Series Editor*

THE PINTER ETHIC
The Erotic Aesthetic
by Penelope Prentice

BARNESTORM
The Plays of Peter Barnes
by Bernard F. Dukore

NEW THEATRE VISTAS
Modern Movements
in International Theatre
edited by Judy Lee Oliva

DAVID MAMET'S
GLENGARRY GLEN ROSS
Text and Performance
edited by Leslie Kane

HOLLYWOOD ON STAGE
Playwrights Evaluate
the Culture Industry
edited by Kimball King

BLACK WOMEN PLAYWRIGHTS
Visions on the American Stage
edited by Carol P. Marsh-Lockett

BLACK WOMEN PLAYWRIGHTS
VISIONS ON THE AMERICAN STAGE

EDITED BY
CAROL P. MARSH-LOCKETT

GARLAND PUBLISHING, INC.
A MEMBER OF THE TAYLOR & FRANCIS GROUP
NEW YORK AND LONDON
1999

Library of Congress Cataloging-in-Publication Data

Black women playwrights : visions on the American stage / edited by Carol
   P. Marsh-Lockett.
         p.   cm. — (Garland reference library of the humanities ; v. 2051.
   Studies in modern drama ; v. 11)
      Includes bibliographical references and index.
      ISBN 0-8153-2746-3 (alk. paper)
      1. American drama—Afro-American authors—History and criticism.
   2. American drama—Women authors—History and criticism.   3. American
   drama—20th century—History and criticism.   4. American drama—19th
   century—History and criticism.   5. Women and literature—United States.
   6. Afro-American women in literature.   7. Afro-Americans in literature.
   I. Marsh-Lockett, Carol P.   II. Series: Garland reference library of the
   humanities ; vol. 2051.   III. Series: Garland reference library of the
   humanities. Studies in modern drama ; v. 11.
   PS338.N4B57   1999
   812.009'9287'08996073—dc21   98–42553
                                                                      CIP

Neal A. Lester's essay "'Filled with the Holy Ghost': Sexual Dimension and Di-
   mensions of Sexuality in the Theater of Ntozake Shange," first printed in
   Paintbrush: A Journal of Poetry and Translation 23 (Autumn 1996): 31–52.
   Used by permission.

Cover illustration, *Salamander,* created by Willie Jones through Art-at-Work,
   a youth program of the Fulton County Arts Council, Atlanta, Georgia.

Printed on acid-free, 250-year-life paper
Manufactured in the United States of America

Contents

Series Editor's Foreword — vii

Acknowledgments — ix

Critical Introduction
Other Scribbling Women: African American Female
      Dramatists
      Carol P. Marsh-Lockett — 3

Remaking the Minstrel: Pauline Hopkins's *Peculiar Sam* and
      the Post-Reconstruction Black Subject
      Martha Patterson — 13

Before the Strength, the Pain: Portraits of Elderly Black
      Women in Early Twentieth-Century Anti-Lynching
      Plays
      Trudier Harris — 25

Segregated Sisterhood: Anger, Racism, and Feminism in Alice
      Childress's *Florence* and *Wedding Band*
      LaVinia Delois Jennings — 43

"Sicker than a rabid dog": African American Women
      Playwrights Look at War
      Marilyn Elkins — 55

Mara, Angelina Grimké's Other Play and the Problems of
      Recovering Texts
      Christine R. Gray — 69

Black Male Subjectivity Deferred?: The Quest for Voice and
    Authority in Lorraine Hansberry's *A Raisin in the*
    Sun
    Keith Clark   87

The Desire/Authority Nexus in Contemporary African
    American Women's Drama
    Lovalerie King   113

Celebrating the (Extra)Ordinary: Alice Childress's
    Representation of Black Selfhood
    E. Barnsley Brown   131

The Discourse of Intercourse: Sexuality and Eroticism in
    African American Women's Drama
    Janice Lee Liddell   155

The Nightmare of History: Conceptions of Sexuality in
    Adrienne Kennedy's *Funnyhouse of a Negro*
    Carla J. McDonough   173

"Filled with the Holy Ghost": Sexual Dimension and
    Dimensions of Sexuality in the Theater of Ntozake
    Shange
    Neal A. Lester   193

Selected Bibliography   213
Contributors   219
Index   223

Series Editor's Foreword

Black Women Playwrights: Visions on the American Stage attempts to reveal the wide range and complexity of a critically neglected group of playwrights. Apart from Lorraine Hansberry, who wrote insightful but seldom confrontational plays about African American life from a female perspective, few African American women are well known as contributors to the stage. The present volume attempts to correct this oversight. The works of Alice Childress, Adrienne Kennedy, and Ntozake Shange represent three contemporary black dramatists who come readily to mind. However, the history of African American women writing plays has heretofore been incomplete. At the beginning of the century, Angel Grimké's *Rachel* exemplified the early lynching play. Marita Bonner in *The Purple Flower* described the futility of black life in America. So, too, did Georgia Douglas Johnson's *Blue Blood.* And Ruth Gaines Shelton and May Miller wrote folk plays in the 1920s. More recent contributions of writers like Alexis DeVeaux and Elaine Jackson are also discussed. The former marginalization of these writers is often as interesting sociologically as the perceptiveness of the critics who are currently reevaluating their dramatic achievements.

Professor Marsh-Lockett is ideally suited to the task of assembling a volume of essays on African American women playwrights. She received her B.A., M.A., and Ph.D. degrees from Howard University. She has published many articles in the *CLA Journal,* the *Dictionary of Literary Biography* and assorted book-length volumes. She is an associate professor at Georgia State University where she teaches African American, Caribbean, and postcolonial literature. Currently she is editing another volume for Garland, *New Critical Essays on*

Caribbean Literature: Caliban's Turn. Marsh-Lockett deserves credit
for bringing together in one volume so many neglected playwrights
who have finally been accorded the critical esteem they deserve.

Acknowledgments

This essay collection could not have come to fruition without support. I wish to thank students at Georgia State University in English 390J and English 486 for their enthusiastic response to drama written by African American women. Their insights sharpened my own thinking and underscored the need for this collection. I also wish to thank Georgia State University for support. The office of the Provost provided faculty development funds. The Research Enhancement Committee in the English Department provided support through summer awards. Many thanks go to my research assistants, Tiberiu Paskuy, Sabine Hollstein, Tammy Cole, and Sandra Neas for their willing spirits and splendid help at various stages. A special tribute goes to James Poulakos, who never failed to be present or to find teachable moments when computer tasks seemed daunting, and to Kimberly Weaver, who cheerfully volunteered her services just because she loves scholarship. Thanks go also to the contributing scholars who saw the necessity of this collection and readily agreed to participate in this project.

Finally, I must express my deepest appreciation to my husband, Harold, and to our children, Amanda and Joseph, for their love. They are my joy. The richness of our lives together enhances my work.

BLACK WOMEN
PLAYWRIGHTS

Critical Introduction
Other Scribbling Women:
African American Female Dramatists
Carol P. Marsh-Lockett

In his tidy little monograph, *An Anatomy of Drama* (1977), Martin Esslin writes,

> The theatre is the place where a nation thinks in front of itself. And in that context all sorts of matters assume political importance, for ultimately, there is a close link between the general beliefs of a society, its concept of proper behavior and good manners, its views of sexual morals, and the political climate of a nation. Changes in manners and mores may ultimately change the very temper of politics (101).

Esslin acknowledges that since theatrical portrayals can exert a potent influence on the manners and lifestyles of the times, "the theatre will inevitably be an instrument of social innovation and in that sense it is an institution subversive of the *status quo*" (104).

The tremendous irony of Esslin's text is that in his exploration of the "anatomy" of drama, his illustrations and models are overwhelmingly the works of white men, the stage which is his frame of reference being, therefore, a predominantly white male province. It is common knowledge, however, that power-based societal orchestrations masking as truths frequently have little to do with the actualities of any given situation or situations. Thus, inevitably, we have to contend with what Michel Foucault calls the "insurrection of subjugated knowledges." How we process theater history is no exception.

A frequently overlooked—at best marginalized—group of playwrights in the American theater world have been African American women. Typically, when we think of African American playwrights, Lorraine Hansberry, the first African American playwright to win the New York Drama Critics Award, comes to mind because of her spectacular success with *A Raisin in the Sun*, which, in 1959, was the first African American play ever to be produced on Broadway. *A Raisin in the Sun* is a comfortable family play with which all of America could identify, for in addition to its racial themes, the play also raises such issues as housing, the roles of women, marriage, child rearing, abortion, money, and employment. Yet few theater historians note the contribution of William Wells Brown, the first identified African American playwright whose 1858 play *The Escape: or a Leap for Freedom*, was the first in a long line of protest plays that addressed initially the horrors of slavery and then with the passage of time, the overall violation of African American civil rights. Originally read to white abolitionists, the play was finally performed in 1972 (Brown-Guillory 21). Later well-known protest plays are James Baldwin's *Blues for Mister Charlie*, Douglas Turner Ward's *Day of Absence*, Imamu Baraka's *Dutchman* and *The Slave*, and Charles Gordonne's *No Place to Be Somebody*. Even fewer scholars pay close attention to Pauline Hopkins's 1879 musical drama, *Slaves' Escape: or The Underground Railroad*. According to theater scholar Kathy Perkins, the play was performed by the Hopkins Colored Troubadours at the Oakland Garden, Boston, July 5, 1880, and was favorably reviewed in the *Boston Herald*. Hopkins's second play *Drama of Early Days* dramatized the biblical story of Daniel in the Lion's Den; however, to date, no one has located records of the play's performance. Given the combined variables of gender, race, and class, it is not surprising that Hopkins worked as a secretary while pursuing her craft as a writer and editor. The work for which she is best known is her novel *Contending Forces* (1899).

African American female playwrights who come readily to mind are Alice Childress, Adrienne Kennedy, and Ntozake Shange. Together with Hansberry, they dominate what little attention African American female dramatists have received. Childress's *Trouble in Mind* made theater history in 1955 as the first black play to win an Obie Award. In the play, Willetta, an actress, draws attention to racism in the theater by challenging an inherently racist script, which in turn, is undergirded by the racist assumptions of American society. Childress's best-known play, *Wedding Band*, broaches the taboo subject of interracial love in American society. Initially, staging was difficult, but it was eventually televised in 1973. Like Childress, Adrienne Kennedy won an Obie Award in 1964 for *Funnyhouse of a Negro*, which portrays the fragmented psyche of Sarah, a young African American woman who is unable to reconcile her African and European identities. The psychic cost attached to growing up black and female in America would surface again in 1971 with J. E. Franklin's *Black Girl* and Elaine Jackson's *Toe Jam*. This theme would finally receive major national theatrical attention with the performance of Ntozake Shange's 1974 Obie Award winning *for colored girls who have considered suicide when the rainbow is enuf*. In her deliberate blending of artistic norms and her flouting of the conventions of the English language, Shange explores the painful elements of the female experience and ultimately advocates that African American women seek empowerment from within themselves as opposed to external affirmation from a racist, sexist society.

Yet between Hopkins and Hansberry lies a long line of African American female playwrights whose works disturb the *status quo* and ultimately, in Esslin's words, prove "subversive." If they do not pose direct challenges to the *status quo* by publicly exposing in a distinct female rhetoric the horrors of racism and sexism in America, they decenter or destabilize prevailing white notions of the African American through an indifference to the power of white America. In other words, the subtext of the serious, comic, or folk tones of many of these plays is that African Americans have better things to do than constantly acknowledge and react to the evils of a white world. Unfortunately, many of the early plays languish in manuscript form, uncollected, unedited, unpublished, ignored in special collections like the Schomburg in New York City, the Moorland Spingarn Collection at Howard University in Washington, D. C., and the special collection at the Fisk University Library in Nashville, Tennessee.

Fortunately, because of increasing interest in African American women's drama, a relative few of these plays have been anthologized. A handful can be found in such collections of African American drama as James Hatch and Ted Shine's *Black Theater USA* and Darwin Turner's *Black Drama in America*. Kathy Perkins's *Black Female Playwrights: An Anthology of Plays Before 1950*; Margaret Wilkerson's *9 Plays by Black Women*; Elizabeth Brown-Guillory's *Wines in the Wilderness*, and Sydné Mahone's *Moon Struck and*

Touched by Sun are four anthologies of African American women's drama that have been published since 1989.

In her invaluable introduction to *Black Female Playwrights*, Perkins acknowledges that many of the early plays by African American women are flawed and challenge even veteran directors. Nevertheless, the plays are significant historical and cultural markers in that they document African American life after the turn of the century and African American women's responses to the times. Moreover, Perkins also indicates that these women wrote under artistically stressful circumstances generated by the variables of sex, race, and class. Rarely was an African American woman a formally trained playwright prior to 1950. Many were teachers whose plays were produced in schools and churches. Others also wrote poetry and fiction. Nonetheless, these early plays command respect.

In her introduction, Perkins notes also that in the early years, while their works differed, African American male and female playwrights wrote about similar issues. Frequently, she observes, those female playwrights who were educators wrote plays and pageants that celebrated the lives of great African Americans. We might conclude that male playwrights were less disposed to historical subject matter and the form of the pageant, preferring instead to confront contemporary social issues. Perkins observes that male playwrights set their works in Harlem and other large metropolitan areas. The women's plays employed both rural and urban settings but were often set inside the home with the action revolving around a traditionally female activity like sewing or cooking. Men were often either dead or away working. In addition, physical white presence was limited although racism informed the worlds of the plays. These early plays ascribe high value to marriage and family, which were constantly vulnerable to a racist superstructure. This was often a theme in a clearly defined body of "lynching plays."

Angelina Grimké's still widely-read and studied *Rachel* (1916), a carefully crafted work, exemplifies the early lynching play. In *Rachel*, the Lovings, a middle-class family, have moved from the South to New York City to escape racism, but Northern racism subverts the family's well-being. Rachel learns from her mother that her father and brother were lynched in the South, but life in the North is no better. Racism limits employment for Rachel and her brother, Tom, in spite of their substantial education. Rachel is also alienated by the cruelty of white schoolchildren towards their African American classmates. Therefore, she vows to remain unmarried and childless.

While it is significant that African American male and female playwrights both focused on survival in the wake of American racism, it is also interesting that W. E. B. Du Bois, one of the founders of the NAACP and Professors Alain Locke and Montgomery T. Gregory of Howard University were instrumental in the publication of many early plays by African American women. Under their influence, African American women had plays published and performed. Du Bois as editor of *Crisis* magazine and Charles S. Johnson of the Urban League, editor of *Opportunity* magazine, sponsored playwrighting contests that were judged by eminent white dramatists and critics in addition to Professors Gregory and Locke. In many instances, female contestants won these contests.

African American plays of this period, often referred to as "Native dramas," dealt authentically with African American life. As a part of the Little Negro theater movement in Harlem during the early 1920s, they provided viable alternatives to the prevailing superficial and stereotypical images of African Americans on the American stage exemplified by the implicit and explicit racism in the work of such dramatists as Eugene O'Neill and Paul Green. Native Dramas were of two types: "race" or propaganda plays, which explored issues of racial oppression and sought to evoke change, and folk plays, which simply depicted the African American experience without focusing on racial oppression. Exemplifying the "race" play is Marita Bonner's *The Purple Flower*, which advocates bloody revolution and portrays the futility of black life in America. Highly experimental in its form, the play won the *Crisis* prize in 1927 and anticipated the work of Adrienne Kennedy in the 1960s. Another example was Georgia Douglas Johnson's *Blue Blood*, winner of the 1926 *Opportunity* award, which treats miscegenation and white men's sexual exploitation of African American women. Examples of folk plays are Ruth Gaines Shelton's *The Church Fight* and May Miller's *Riding the Goat*. Shelton's play, which won the *Crisis* award in 1925, is a highly amusing morality play about ecclesiastical conflict in which characters have such names as Brother Judas, Brother Inquisitor, and Sister Take-It-Back. Miller's *Riding the Goat* (1925) is a delightful folk comedy that explores class conflict in a small African American community when its younger, highly-educated members encounter long standing cultural traditions. In addition to the works by Miller, Shelton, and Johnson, Du Bois,

Gregory, and Locke also facilitated the publication of plays by Myrtle Livingstone Smith, Zora Neale Hurston, and Eloise Bibb Thompson.

Plays by African American women up to 1950 treat themes such as lynching, rape and miscegenation, war, the disenfranchisement of black men who have fought for their country, the church and the religious experience, the need for birth control education, which by law, was not available to African American women, and concerns of color and caste. In its rhetoric, the drama focused outward and sometimes assumed a white presence in its audience. The drama demonstrated the double consciousness that Du Bois identified but also included distinctly female perspectives and concerns. In its composition and staging, it also satisfied Du Bois's recommendation that it should be by, about, for, and near African American people.

A significant turning point in African American women's drama occurred, however, in 1950. In her introduction to *9 Plays by Black Women*, Margaret Wilkerson notes that with Beah Richards' *A Black Woman Speaks*, a one-woman show first performed in 1950 for a white women's organization, Women for Peace, African American women's drama took a rhetorical turn. She holds that the plays then became more distinctly and aggressively female. They began to raise vexing issues, which nonetheless, served to open dialogue between African American and white women. *A Black Woman Speaks*, which won an Emmy Award in 1975, bluntly confronts white women's own oppression and their insidious collusion in the oppression of African American women and men. Lorraine Hansberry's unfinished *Toussaint* similarly approaches the oppressive role of a creole plantation mistress, imprisoned in gilded luxury in much the same way that Richards demonstrates, who is both physically cruel to and sexually exploitive of her female slave attendant, Destine.

In post-1950 plays, the candor also turns inward into the African American community and addresses the psychic dislocation that ensues when African American people in general and women in particular locate their center of power in norms and values alien to themselves, their roots, and their well being. These plays can be read and viewed as works which encode the intergenerational dysfunction resulting from the deep, painful cultural memory of the traumatic middle passage and slavery and the often-pathological coping mechanisms in the absence of an alternative African spiritual centeredness amongst dislocated Africans. In other words, the plays put before America the disordered responses accounted for by well-known African American scholars as

Molefi Asante, Na'im Akbar, Gerald Jackson, and others. More specifically, they dramatize the impact of America on African American women, an impact which finds its theoretical frame in the writings of scholars such as Angela Davis, Paula Giddings, Patricia Hill Collins, Barbara Smith, and bell hooks. Alexis DeVeaux's *The Tapestry* (1986) shows the near- destruction that the central character, Jet, experiences when she is torn between the demands of her narcissistic lover, Axis, the shallowness and dependency of her disloyal friend, Lavender, and her own need to pass the bar exam so that she can render meaningful service to the African American community. Jet is saved only by the psychic tug of her black roots. Elaine Jackson's *Paper Dolls* (1983) explores the beauty myth and cultural humiliation to which African American women sometimes subscribe. Returning at points to the form of the minstrel show, the play dramatizes that the more African American women focus on becoming what they are not, the more difficulty they have with what they are. P. J. Gibson's *Brown Silk and Magenta Sunsets* (1985) inverts the myth of the neutered African American mother who constantly demonstrates strong, self-sacrificial devotion to family. In this instance, Lena Larsen Salvinoni has been centered in her sexuality throughout her life and enmeshed in her own memory of her affair with Roland, an older musician with whom she has had a daughter and a son. In the world of the play, she is the alcoholic widow of a wealthy Italian who cannot escape the damage that her self- centeredness wrought in her past. She has an affair with a younger man, who, the play implies, could be the son she abandoned several years before. Not invested in anything meaningful, let down by her hedonistic personal history, and completely without a community, Lena commits suicide. Similarly, increasingly well-known Atlanta playwright Pearl Cleage's recent work *Blues for an Alabama Sky* signifies on the concept of the New Negro as it looks at the other side of the Harlem that was in vogue. Key Harlem players, Langston Hughes and Josephine Baker, are only points of reference in the dramatic world which explores free love, interracial sex, homosexuality, abortion, and religious fundamentalism which rationalizes even murder in an otherwise glorious Harlem. In the same vein, Cleage's most recently published play, *Flyin' West* (1992), dramatizes the under-examined saga of African Americans who, under the provisions of the Homestead Act of 1860, fled the South for western states. More specifically, *Flyin' West* tells the story of five African American women who struggle to keep their land in the all-black town of Nicodemus, Kansas. The play also examines African American women's experiences during slavery, miscegenation and its accompanying pathologies, spousal abuse, intra-group betrayal, and African American female autonomy.

This collection of critical essays seeks to contribute to the relatively scant and disparate existing scholarship on African American women's drama. These essays address issues which have historically bedeviled the psyches and have had deep and lasting impacts on the lives of African Americans. Essays on the dramatists whose work is examined here indicate much about the politics of the theater and play publication in addition to the position of the African American woman as "Other" in the margin-center paradigm. A survey of these essays will indicate that very few African American women's plays have experienced mainstream publication and production. By far, as indicated by the balance or seeming lack thereof in this collection, most attention has been focused on Lorraine Hansberry, Alice Childress, Adrienne Kennedy, and Ntozake Shange. Yet African American women continue to write honest, beautifully crafted plays which, sadly, frequently do not progress beyond staged readings or performances in university, local, or at best regional theaters.

The issues treated in these plays fall into two broad categories. The first is public discourse in which the essayists furnish discussions of how the dramatists confront the external realities of African American life through their art. Martha Patterson discusses Pauline Hopkins's use of the double-edged nature of the minstrel show to address the external definition of African Americans in the hostile climate of the Post-Reconstruction era. Trudier Harris discusses the strength and vulnerability that characterize African American womanhood in those dramas which focus on the horrors of lynching. LaVinia Jennings continues a discussion begun by Beah Richards in *A Black Woman Speaks*. In her discussion of the plays of Alice Childress, Jennings examines the tensions existing in America between African American and white women resulting from a legacy of slavery and oppression in which white women derived vicarious power from white men over African American women. Marilyn Elkins shows how selected African American female dramatists portray the impact of war on the African American community in general and on African American women in particular. Finally in this group of essays, Christine Gray's discussion of Angelina Grimké's unpublished manuscript *Mara* challenges the designated final draft and conventional reading of *Mara*. In so doing,

Gray addresses the politics contextualizing African American literary scholarship and production.

The second group of essays present private explorations in the African American community. Often these musings involve the question of identity, an issue which has historically tormented the souls of dislocated Africans. This question often finds expression at the core of African American and Caribbean literature in the question of "Who am I?" as opposed to white American and other settler literature which at its core raises the question "Why am I here?" Keith Clark examines Lorraine Hansberry's problematic construction of African American male agency in *A Raisin in the Sun.* In a closely related essay, Lovalerie King discusses the theme of African American self-definition in contemporary African American women's drama. Similarly, E. Barnsley Brown examines Alice Childress's construction of African American selfhood through her use of a black æsthetic within the frame of realistic drama. Such an achievement, according to Brown, enabled Childress to reach both African American and white audiences.

The issue of African American identity and selfhood in the African American community, more specifically African American female identity, is frequently enmeshed in constructs of sexuality embedded in the psychosocial/ psychocultural history of America which developed and codified a sub-human sexual identity for African Americans in order to rationalize slavery and its residual social, political, and economic oppression. Where the African American man was constructed as a brute and a potential rapist, the African American woman was constructed as a whore. The remaining three essays within this second group effectively probe and deconstruct the myth of anti-social and morally inappropriate African American sexuality that ultimately reinforces the notion of white superiority. In an historical survey of selected plays by African American women, Janice Liddell shows how the playwrights under discussion covertly or overtly use sex and sexuality to respond to the racial and gender oppression of African American women. Carla McDonough analyzes how Adrienne Kennedy employs sexuality as a theme in her portrayal of the fractured psyche of Sarah in *Funnyhouse of a Negro.* She concludes that Sarah's condition is a product not of self-hatred, as earlier interpretations of the play have posited, but of a colonial construct in which white power seeks to secure its centrality by displacing its own sexual energy upon all black people. Finally, Neal Lester's discussion of Ntozake Shange's plays demonstrates how Shange has destabilized white patriarchal definitions of African American female sexuality and has advocated for the African American woman's control over her own sexuality as a significant component of her empowerment.

Clearly, the work of African American female dramatists gives the nation reason and opportunity to think in front of itself. In the literary canon, these dramatists are daughters of Sycorax and sisters of Caliban. In the world of theater, they are forced to confront Prospero as gate keeper and to compete against both Miranda and Caliban for precious few opportunities. In that peculiar relationship that exists among the playwright, the reader, the audience, the stage, and the text, their plays emerge as womanist visions of African American and by implication all of American life. They challenge the prevailing externally prescribed notions of the world according to African American women who in Nathaniel Hawthorne's discourse would be yet another "damned mob of scribbling women." To date, there is only one extended critical study of this fascinating body of work. Much more work must be done.

WORKS CITED

Brown-Guillory, Elizabeth. *Their Place on the Stage*. New York: Greenwood P, 1988.

———. *Wines in the Wilderness: Plays by African American Women from the Harlem Renaissance to the Present*. New York: Greenwood P, 1990.

Esslin, Martin. *An Anatomy of Drama*. New York: Hill and Wang, 1977.

Hatch, James, and Ted Shine, eds. *Black Theater USA: Forty-Five Plays by Black American*. New York: Free, 1974.

Mahone, Sydné. *Moon Struck and Touched by Sun*. New York: Theatre Communications Group, 1994.

Perkins, Kathy. *Black Female Playwrights: An Anthology of Plays Before 1950*. Bloomington: Indiana UP, 1990.

Turner, Darwin. *Black Drama in America*. 2nd ed. Washington, D. C.: Howard UP, 1994.

Wilkerson, Margaret, ed. *9 Plays by Black Women*. New York: New American Library, 1986.

Remaking the Minstrel
Pauline Hopkins's *Peculiar Sam* and the Post-Reconstruction Black Subject

Martha Patterson

On July 5, 1880, Pauline Hopkins's three-act play, *Slaves' Escape: or The Underground Railroad*, was performed in Boston's Oakland Garden and was greeted with almost uniformly favorable reviews.[1] The cast included Hopkins herself, her mother, stepfather, the nationally-known Hyers Sisters, and a chorus of over sixty (Shockley 23). Originally titled *Peculiar Sam, or The Underground Railroad* and consisting of four acts, Hopkins's short comedic play depicts a successful escape along the underground railroad and culminates in the news of the black male protagonist's accomplishments, thereby promoting a black social mobility and agency increasingly attacked following Reconstruction. In order to sanction this passage into upward mobility, however, Hopkins often presents her black performers as spectacles, entertainers seemingly always ready to amuse a white audience. Her play features buffoonish stereotypes of black characters, a caricatured black vernacular, and laments for the security of the "ole plantation"—all features of the popular minstrel tradition. As perhaps the greatest disseminator of racist images in the nineteenth century, the minstrel show is a necessary if implausible site for Hopkins's revision. Hopkins works to subvert the racist ideology of the dominant minstrel show tradition by granting subjectivity and social mobility to those characters who resist appropriation by the slave master. While the protagonist, Peculiar Sam, may conclude his performance "dancing to 'Golden Slippers,'" the audience is reminded that this performed "bufoonishness" enabled him to thwart the treachery of the slave master and the overseer. Sam appears, then, as a classic trickster figure or, to use a term which Henry Louis Gates, Jr. has deftly theorized, a kind of Signifying Monkey, who employs an "ironic reversal of a received racist image of the black as simianlike . . . ever punning, ever troping, ever embodying the ambiguities of language" (52). By creating subject positions for some of her black characters and by reminding her primarily white audience of the "performativity" of the black male protagonist's buffoonery, Hopkins signifies upon the racist tropes of white minstrelsy.

Considering the fact that many of the political gains made by African Americans during Reconstruction were lost in the 1870s and the consequent black exodus from the South in 1879, it is not surprising that Hopkins would celebrate an analogous journey to freedom in the face of racist oppression. While more ex-Confederates regained control of the South's state legislatures as they returned home and worked to overturn Reconstruction legislation, more border states became Democratic. Southern congressmen won enough northern support to repeal the Southern Homestead Act of 1866, effectively eliminating hopes for the promised "40 acres and a mule." Hoping to appease white Democratic Southerners and responding to a new Democratically controlled congress, President Hayes withdrew federal troops in 1877, and in 1878 the use of armed forces to insure fair elections was forbidden (Franklin 258). Although the Ku Klux Klan was officially outlawed in 1871, racist violence and intimidation, especially of black property owners, continued to grow. Disclosures of corruption scandals in Republican governments also helped to hasten the overthrow of radical Reconstruction (Franklin 260). Hopkins critiques this political shift and the North's growing refusal to insure civil rights for black Americans by essentially rewriting Reconstruction's history in her play. She ends her work with Peculiar Sam's joyous announcement that he is to be Ohio's next congressman because his "friends in Cincinnati have stood by [him] nobly" (120). In the election of 1867, however, Ohio voters had overwhelmingly rejected measures insuring black suffrage (Gillette 9). And in the mid-1870s, the state was increasingly voting Democratic in opposition to the Republican-sponsored Civil Rights Bill (Gillette 242).

Hopkins gives herself the role of Virginia, "the plantation nightingale," in order to disavow this state's leading role in the reversion to conservative Democratic politics. Hopkins's Virginia, whom "white folks love . . . best, of all/ The young mulatto girls" (103), is both a reminder of the painful legacy of slavery and the bourgeois potential of black women. While Virginia embodies white privilege as she is brought "up like a lady" in the "big house," she affirms her black identity most powerfully when she marries the black male protagonist, Peculiar Sam, who leads the slaves to freedom. Centrally positioned on stage singing jubilee songs, Virginia becomes an icon of black bourgeois womanhood to be admired by her primarily white audience.

According to one contemporary reviewer, Hopkins's play was based on the Anna Madah Hyers and Emma Louise Hyers's production of *Out of Bondage* (1876) about the aftermath of emancipation.[2] Adapted by the sisters from a drama by white playwright Rev. Joseph Bradford, the play was the first musical drama to be produced by a black company and "signaled the beginning of the transition from minstrelsy to Black musical comedy" (Tanner 26). Leo Hamalian and James Hatch argue in *The Roots of African-American Drama: An Anthology of Early Plays, 1858-1938* that Hopkins may have been influenced by William Wells Brown's *The Escape: or, A Leap for Freedom* (1858), a drama which was published but never performed. In its construction of the mischievous female character, Juno, *Peculiar Sam* also shows parallels to Harriet Beecher Stowe's *Uncle Tom's Cabin* (1852); one anonymous reviewer, in fact, directly compares Juno to Topsy. Certainly, Hopkins's play comes from a long tradition of anti-slavery melodramas—like *Uncle Tom's Cabin* and Dion Boucicault's *The Octoroon* (1859)—which worked to attract Northern white audiences with diverse political allegiances by denouncing the cruelty of the slave auctioneer and overseer while romanticizing the plantation system.

Newspaper reviews of *Slaves' Escape*, which Hopkins collected in a scrapbook, document a fairly grand and successful production. By 1880 both the Hyers Sisters and Sam Lucas had national reputations, and their combination with the locally successful Hopkins Colored Troubadours insured a large audience.[3] One review stated, "The attendance at this well-known place of amusement yesterday was probably as large as ever seen here, and it is estimated that 10,000 persons visited the garden during the day and evening" (Reviews). Acknowledging the popularity of the Fisk Jubilee Singers, who were touring throughout the 1870s, the Hopkins Colored Troubadours performed jubilee songs both during and after their performances. Complementary variety entertainment in accordance with the Independence Day celebrations served both to link African American freedom with the freedom of the country while reinforcing a conception of black life as buffoonish spectacle. One publicity announcement promised: "After the evening performance will be presented the COTTON PLANTATION SCENE on the lawn, with Sam Lucas in his specialities and the entire company in a GRAND PLANTATION FESTIVAL with a working representation of the boats Robert E. Lee and the Natchez on the Mississippi river" (Reviews).

The fact that Hopkins positions her famous black acting troupe both as spectacles within a pageant and agents signifying upon white power structures reflects the changing styles of both black and white minstrel show traditions. According to Eric Lott in *Love and Theft: Blackface Minstrelsy and the American Working Class*, early blackface minstrel shows performed by white actors betrayed both a fascination and repulsion with black experience, especially as they worked to foreground the sexual potency of black men: "Minstrel performers often attempted to repress through ridicule the real interest in black cultural practices they nonetheless betrayed—minstrelsy's mixed erotic economy of celebration and exploitation, what Homi Bhabha would call its 'ambivalence'" (6). These shows featured an interlocutor who introduced the entertainers and served as the butt of the endman's jokes. According to Carl Wittke, in his nostalgic *Tambo and Bones: A History of the American Minstrel Stage*, "Endmen were expected to cultivate an eccentric vocabulary, full of bad grammar, faulty pronunciation and a kind of bombastic ignorance"(142). Superstitious and fearful, the endman was the focus of much of the audience's laughter. In the first part of the show, the performers positioned themselves in a semi-circle, reciting ballads, playing the banjo, or performing comic acts. Popular settings for this first part included slave cabins, river boats, and cotton fields. In the second part of the show, the olio, introduced after 1850, actors performed variety entertainment, with every member of the company performing a dance at some point on center stage. Until the mid-1870s, according to Robert Toll in *Blacking Up: The Minstrel Show in Nineteenth-Century America*, the content of black minstrel shows was quite similar to that of white shows. As white minstrel shows increasingly became burlesque or variety shows with broad, middle-brow themes, black minstrel shows specialized in representations of African American life on the plantation, often with direct or indirect critiques of the power wielded by the white master (Toll 234). Throughout the course of *Peculiar Sam*, for example, Hopkins works to change the role of endman and interlocutor, thereby subverting expectations that the black man as buffoon is a stable concept.

While most black troupes advertised themselves as "original or genuine plantation minstrels" and worked to attract a primarily black working-class audience, most white-managed troupes worked to unify a politically diverse electorate. According to Alexander Saxton, in *The Rise and Fall of the White Republic: Class Politics and Mass Culture in Nineteenth-Century America*, the antebellum minstrel shows "propagandized metaphorically the alliance of urban working people with the planter interest in the South" (165). David Roediger notes in *The Wages of Whiteness: Race and the Making of the American Working Class* that "minstrelsy made a contribution to a sense of popular whiteness among workers across lines of ethnicity, religion and skill. It achieved a common symbolic language—a unity—that could not be realized by racist crowds, by political parties or by labor unions" (127). In *This Grotesque Essence: Plays from the American Minstrel Stage*, Gary Engle stresses that as minstrel shows create clownish scapegoats, they serve to unify a white electorate anxious about their own social mobility (xxviii).

Hopkins, however, works to forge an alliance between her white and black audience by stressing their common dependence on a fluctuating marketplace, a marketplace still suffering residual effects from the Panic of 1873. This project, in addition to the more prosaic goal of making a profit, necessitated a broad marketing strategy. Although Boston's black population in the late 1870s was relatively small, the prominence of all the black actors involved would have insured a large turnout. *Slaves' Escape* was advertised as a "great musical drama" in one advertisement, while one reviewer promised a "grand sacred jubilee concert" following the main performance (Reviews).[4] By stressing the more "serious" jubilee nature of many of the group's performances while promising great visual spectacle, Hopkins works to appeal to both working and middle-class audiences.

Hopkins offers a site of potential resistance to conservative Democratic politics in part by negotiating a place for middle-class black women and men in dominant bourgeois culture, albeit at the expense of subjecting the black underclass to moments of ridicule. *Peculiar Sam* begins with Sam, Pete, and Pomp dancing to banjo music, a non-diagetic display characteristic of minstrel performances, where the "savage" energy of the black male performer is highlighted. As the music increases in intensity, Sam, who has many of the characteristics of the traditional minstrel endman, dances into a kind of sexualized frenzy, finally exclaiming, "Take kar dar, de spirits a movin' in me, Ise comin'"(101). As Lott points out, displays such as these demonstrate that "'black' figures were there to be looked at, shaped to the demands of desire; they were screens on which audience fantasy could rest, and while this purpose might have had a host of different effects, its fundamental outcome was to secure the position of white spectators as superior, controlling figures" (140-141).

That security, however, is threatened by Sam's peculiarity, his refusal to remain in slavery, his ability to successfully masquerade, and finally his social ambition. He is in love with Jinny, the "plantation nightingale," a persona reminiscent of P.T. Barnum's enormously popular "Swedish nightingale," Jenny Lind, and played by Hopkins herself, in the 1880 production. To Sam, Mammy, and sister Juno's great dismay, Jinny has been forced by the plantation master to marry Jim the overseer. Jinny, who does not speak in the parodic black vernacular and who according to Mammy has been brought up "like a lady" by being accorded the privileges of house service, is desired by both men. "Ah! Jinny is a simple chile," sings Sam, "Wif pretty shini' curls,/ An' white folks love her best, of all/The young mulatto girls/Tell her to wait a little while,/Tell her in hope to wait,/For I will surely break the chain,/That binds her to the gate"(103). As Jinny connotes whiteness, she reiterates the racist stereotype that black men desire white women. As a mulatto, however, she is a reminder of the rape of black women by white men in the plantation household. Jinny is continually presented as an icon on stage—Hopkins's stage directions require that Jinny often be centrally framed by other characters— reminding the audience of both the "tragic" legacy and the bourgeois potential of black women.

Jinny is most dangerous as she serves to spur the ambitions of her black suitors, inspiring Sam to exclaim, "We's all gwin to Canidy"(105). Sam reminds the audience not only of the duplicity of the slave master—"An' den they tells ho kin' dey is, an' how satisfied we is, an' den thar dogs an' horses"—but also of the biblically sanctioned imperative of escape—"when am dat time comin' dat yous tol me 'bout eber since I was knee high to a crickey, when am Moses gwine to lead us forsook niggers fro' de Red Sea?" (102-103). While Mammy promises the Lord's intervention, she's fearful of any direct escape measures. She, Jinny, and Juno are nostalgic for the security of plantation slavery, a romanticization of plantation life ever present in earlier minstrel performances to bolster anti-abolitionist sentiment and solidify a conservative political base among ethnically diverse audiences.

When Sam confronts Jim, the man to whom Jinny has been married against her will, they fight each other in a farcical melee. Hopkins directs the actors to "spar with their fists. Two of three times. JIM butts at SAM, but misses him, SAM passing over his head in careless manner. Make this set-to as comical as possible"(106). Jim brandishes a whip, which Sam confiscates and "flourishes. . . as if to strike [Jim] with it"(106). Hopkins both disavows and reminds her audience of these instruments of slave torture, instruments increasingly being taken up against African Americans in the post-Reconstruction South. To provide space for her black male protagonists in dominant white culture, Hopkins must first emasculate them. She constructs these black men as childishly unthreatening—furnished with instruments of violence, they are unable to use them; Sam finally drops the whip in disgust and Jim wails, "Ise gone dead, Ise gone dead" when struck by Sam.

Virginia provides the anchor in all this confusion. As Sam leaves the stage to prepare for the escape, Jinny suggests, "Let's sing again before we leave our old home" (108), providing another extended pause in the narrative action of the play. The editorial comments state, "*I should think* 'Home, Sweet Home' *well sung by the soprano might be a decided hit. . . .*" While longing for her southern home and representing it, Virginia becomes tragic as she continually reminds her audience why she is leaving, thereby denying the paternalistic visions of slave culture which the dominant minstrel tradition celebrated. As a star vehicle for Hopkins, Jinny's aspect demands that her audience recognize her as a suffering, genteel black woman.

While the last scene in Act I is framed by Virginia's laments for "Home Sweet Home" and Mammy's tearful farewell to the "ole home, de place whar my chillern war born, an'my ole man am buried," such a frame cannot contain the signifying threat of Sam's tricksterism (108). Before the chorus can sing its final refrain of "Home Sweet Home," Sam returns on stage dressed as a "gentleman overseer," *"flourising* [sic] [a] *whip"* and adopting the master's dialect. His family, in fact, mistakes him for the "Marse" and Sam's sister Juno exclaims, "What a peccoliar fellar you is! Look jes like a gemman" (108). In a classic signifying gesture, Juno voices Sam's threat to the white master as a mere peculiarity or personal eccentricity.

This focus on disguise and tricksterism continues in Act II when the protagonists approach a cabin on the underground railroad run by the apprehensive Caesar. Misrecognizing Sam and calling him "one ob dem tricksy m'latter fellars," Caesar initially denies the family entrance. When Jim comes to the cabin looking for the escaped slaves, Sam adopts yet another voice. These series of disguises foreground the performativity of the hero's previous actions and the constructedness of the plot. Denied agency in a performance of caricatured blackness, Sam is able to regain agency and ultimately the master's money by playing a master. Thinking Sam is providing legitimate information about the escaped Mammy, Juno, and Jinny, Jim pays Sam a dollar.

A fiscal transaction at the expense of the slave owner works finally to bring Jim into the community of the protagonists. After Jim catches on to Sam's ruse, Jim appears as a ghost, initially frightening Sam, until Sam discovers Jim's identity and demands the master's hundred dollars in Jim's possession. While ghost apparitions were common in minstrel shows, often as parodies of *Hamlet,* this instance may be in reference to the hooded vestments of the Klan and serves as a critique of blacks who made alliances with white property owners for financial gain. The fiscal stake in the narrative is important, not only as it foregrounds the ultimate dupe, the slave owner who has lost his money and his slaves but also as it reminds Hopkins's audience that freedom depends not only on physical escape from poor working conditions but also just payment for work performed but on the formation of necessary alliances against an exploitive labor system.

When Sam returns to the group bringing Jim, Sam gives Juno the responsibility of guarding him, giving her yet another symbol of the master's authority, his gun. Upon first seeing the gun Juno had exclaimed, "Why I kno's all 'bout shootin' dat gun. I used to go up inter Misses room an' shoot dat ol'gun at de bedstead, an' Marse he, he, Marse an' Misse wonder how dat bedstead kamed full o'holes"(116). The fact that Juno has destroyed the bedstead suggests the domestic and sexual turbulence caused in the master's household by slavery. While the "Marse an' Misse" increasingly become disempowered as the butt of jokes, Hopkins works to undermine the sentimental notions of the "ole plantation" some of her characters endorse. At the end of the scene, Sam dons a disguise once again, this time *dressed as an old man,* " and the group continues on their journey leaving Jim behind.

These revolts against the master's authority culminate in Act III when Sam reveals he had directly stolen the master's money and used some of that money to buy poison for the master's dogs: "He hab plenty ob money an' I thought I'd done nuff to 'sarve some ob it, an' I jes helped mysel' to a pocket full. An' wif some ob it I bought de stuff wh' fixed dem dogs; 'deed I did, kase dis chile am no fool" (118). "Money," Sam declares "'s ebery man's frien,'" a statement which encourages the working-class members of Hopkins's audience to identify with the characters as employees, subject to the potential treachery, greed, and whims of their employers.

Act IV changes the scene to Canada after the war. Mammy and Caesar are married now—"Jinny a singist, Juno a school marm; an'las'but not leas', dat boy, dat pecoolar Sam, eddicated an' gwine to de United States Congress." While Mammy still longs for the plantation and Caesar wants to be buried at "ol' Marser's feet, under the de 'Nolin tree," they are clearly marked products of an earlier generation. Sam bursts into the scene and announces that he has been successfully elected because "My friends in Cincinnati have stood by me nobly"—a clear reminder to post-Reconstruction audiences that such allegiances no longer occur. All are still anxious, however, because Jim has not been found and still poses a threat to Virginia. Finally, Jim appears and informs the group that there is no reason to fear that he will "mislest" Jinny because he has a wife and twins— named Jinny and Sam—and has become an attorney. While reminding audiences of the Post-Reconstruction racist stereotype of the black male as sexual threat, Hopkins disavows it by assuring audiences that opportunities for upward mobility mean a greater commitment to personal and social order. In traditional comic form, Jim is forgiven and included in the subsequent Christmas wedding celebration of Sam and Jinny. While Jim still speaks in the caricatured black vernacular, Juno virtually loses hers and Sam loses his entirely in this last act. These dialect changes not only reflect the protagonists' social mobility, they also reinforce Hopkins's commitment to the trickster voice. Jim may remain an object of laughter for the largely white audience of Hopkins's play, but that laughter will be uncomfortable at best when he reveals that "arter that ol' Lincoln sent his sogers down dar, an' Marse he runned 'way an' seein' he didn't stop for his valuables, I propitiated 'em to my private uses" (122). The verbal word play of "propitiated"/"appropriated" suggests Jim's savvy opportunism will continue when he claims his authority as "one ob de pillows ob de Massatoosetts bar" (123). Sam's voice likewise promises future signifying on the white master and the system of oppression his authority represents. Sam finally announces to the audience, "Ladies and gentlemen, I hope you will excuse me for laying aside the dignity of an elected M. C., and allow me to appear before you once more as peculiar Sam of the old underground railroad" (123). Such a shift signals Sam's transformation from the minstrel show's endman to interlocutor, a re-positioning which suggests his control of the performance all along. Even Hopkins's final stage directions—"SAM *dancing to 'Golden Slippers,' remainder happy*"—remind her audience and readers that while she may repeat aspects of the minstrel tradition, she continually revises them. By choosing this particular song by the prominent black songwriter, James Bland, instead of his popular "Carry Me Back to Old Virginny"(1878), she celebrates yet again new beginnings over nostalgia.

NOTES

1. In *The Roots of African American Drama: An Anthology of Early Plays 1858-1938*, Leo Hamalian and James V. Hatch note that Hopkins wrote at least two earlier plays, *Aristocracy* and *Winona* (1878). According to Eileen Southern in the *Biographical Dictionary of Afro-American and African Musicians*, Hopkins also wrote *Urlina, the African Princess*. Performed in 1879 by the Hyers Sisters at the Bush Theatre in SanFrancisco, *Urlina* is set in Africa "'where a usurping king has banished the princess Urlina, rightful successor to the throne'" (Hill in Tanner 26). To my knowledge, these earlier plays are not extant.

2. In an essay entitled, "Famous Women of the Negro Race. Phenomenal Vocalists," which Pauline Hopkins wrote for *The Colored American Magazine* in 1901, she praised the ground-breaking work of the Hyers Sisters' performance in "Out of Bondage": They next appeared in "Out of Bondage," a four-act musical comedy, written for the sisters by Mr. Joseph B. Bradford, of Boston, under the management of Redpath's Bureau. This play was but a skeleton sketch, designed to show off the musical ability of the performers. But it served its purpose and gave impetus to study and careful cultivation of the musical gifts of talented musicians who desired to adopt the lyric stage as a profession. The introduction of this drama, in which, for the first time, all the characters were represented by colored people, marks an era in the progress of the race. Never, until undertaken by these ladies, was it thought possible for Negroes to appear in the legitimate drama, albeit soubrette parts were the ones they portrayed. (51). The handwritten manuscript of "Out of Bondage" is located in the Rare Book Collection, Library of Congress, Washington, D.C.,

according to James V. Hatch and Omanii Abdullah, *Black Playwrights 1823-1977* as cited in Jo Tanner's *Dusky Maidens* (139 n. 35).

    3. *See Robert Toll's Blacking Up: The Minstrel Show in Nineteenth Century America* for a brief description of the careers of Emma Louise Hyers, Anna Madah Hyers, and Sam Lucas (210, 217).

    4. Toll notes that the Fisk Jubilee Singers adopted their title of "Jubilee Singers" only after being "mistaken" for minstrels during their first northern tour (236).

WORKS CITED

Engle, Gary D. *This Grotesque Essence: Plays from the American Minstrel Stage.* Baton Rouge: Louisiana SUP, 1978.

Franklin, John Hope. *From Slavery to Freedom: A History of Negro Americans.* New York: Knopf, 1980.

Gates, Henry Louis, Jr. *The Signifying Monkey: A Theory of African-American Literary Criticism.* New York: Oxford UP, 1988.

Gillette, William. *Retreat from Reconstruction: 1869-1879.* Baton Rouge: Louisiana SUP, 1979.

Hamalian, Leo, and James V. Hatch, eds. *The Roots of African American Drama: An Anthology of Early Plays, 1858-1938.* Detroit: Wayne State UP, 1991.

Hopkins, Pauline. *Peculiar Sam, or The Underground Railroad. The Roots of African American Drama: An Anthology of Early Plays, 1858-1938.* Ed. Leo Hamalian and James V. Hatch. Detroit: Wayne State UP, 1991.

Lott, Eric. *Love and Theft: Blackface Minstrelsy and the American Working Class.* New York: Oxford UP, 1993.

Peterson, Jr., Bernard L. *Early Black American Playwrights and Dramatic Writers: A Biographical Directory and Catalog of Plays, Films, and Broadcasting cripts.* Westport: Greenwood, 1991.

Reviews. Scrapbook, Pauline E. Hopkins Papers, Fisk University Library, Nashville.

Roediger, David R. *The Wages of Whiteness: Race and the Making of the American Working Class.* New York: Verso, 1991.

Saxton, Alexander. *The Rise and Fall of the White Republic: Class Politics and Mass Culture in Nineteenth-Century America.* New York: Verso, 1990.

Shockley, Ann Allen. "Pauline Elizabeth Hopkins: A Biographical Excursion into Obscurity." *Phylon* 33 (1972): 22-26.

Southern, Eileen. *Biograhpical Dictionary of Afro-American and African Musicians.* Westport: Greenwood, 1982.

Tanner, Jo A. *Dusky Maidens: The Odyssey of the Early Black Dramatic Actress.* Westport: Greenwood, 1992.

Toll, Robert C. *Blacking Up: The Minstrel Show in Nineteenth-Century America.* New York: Oxford UP, 1974.

Wittke, Carl. *Tambo and Bones: A History of the American Minstrel Stage.* New York: Greenwood, 1968.

Before the Strength, the Pain
Portraits of Elderly Black Women in Early Twentieth-Century Anti-Lynching Plays
Trudier Harris

Lynching is a theme usually identified with African American male writers, one that focuses primarily on male characters. These characters either suffer long and die heroically by way of a leisurely lynching and/or burning, or they have their lives snuffed out immediately and gruesomely with a quick hanging. Black women are usually background figures to the major characters and action. The few black women writers who treat lynching treat it gingerly; they summarize dramatic action in fiction or describe actions that occur offstage or a long time before the current action in drama. In contrast to most male writers, women writers focus on the black female characters who feel the impact of the lynching of their husbands, sons, and fathers. Indeed, a minor genre developed in early twentieth-century African American drama in which black women playwrights repeatedly portray families, now women headed, who have lost beloved males to lynching or where discussion of a possible lynching provides the raison d'être for the play. Yet, unlike what would become stereotyped portraits of strong, resilient black women by mid-twentieth century, these playwrights depict black women who are in pain, ineffectual, and often unable to hold their families or their own bodies together. Their bodies reflect the lynching crises they endure as well as the general unhealthy state of American society that prevailed at the point of their creation. Lynching as a theme and black women in physical and psychological pain, then, become the dual forces driving several of these early plays, including Angelina

Grimké's *Rachel*, Mary Burrill's *Aftermath*, and Georgia Douglas Johnson's *A Sunday Morning in the South* and *Blue-Eyed Black Boy*.

A GENRE WITHIN A GENRE

One of the historical embarrassments in the development of the United States is that it is a country where, for many decades, lynching became a national pastime. In a country that claimed liberty, equality, and justice for all, black men, women, and children, especially in the last decade of the nineteenth century, were taken from their homes or chased down like animals, mutilated by the cutting off of ears, gouging out of eyes, castration, or other knife carvings into their flesh, and lynched, burned, shot, or a combination of all three. It is also an historical, national embarrassment that no federal law against lynching could ever be passed in this country, though the Dyer Anti-Lynching bill was several times presented in Congress.

History has been detailed in recording the efforts of those involved in the anti-lynching campaign, whether it was Ida B. Wells-Barnett taking a stand in Memphis, Tennessee, in the 1880s or writing in T. Thomas Fortune's *New York Age* or the *Chicago InterOcean* in the 1890s. Well known are the statistics that W.E.B. Du Bois recounted in the *Crisis* magazine; equally well known are the stories of how Walter White, a black man light enough to pass for white, did so and "investigated lynchings." For several decades the NAACP kept records of the numbers of lynchings committed in this country, and white women, such as Jessie Daniel Ames, organized to try to stop white men from lynching black men in the name and so-called honor of white women. The record in literature is equally clear: many black male creators of fiction and poetry, along with a few of their female counterparts, graphically depicted lynching as one of the major threats to black survival and community cohesiveness.[1]

The subordination that black women writers experienced in relation to males in fiction and poetry, however, was not duplicated in drama. Black women created a subgenre within drama as well as within literature that treats lynching and added women's voices to communicating an artistic response, a sustained vein of protest, to the barbaric practice of lynching. It is striking that most of these plays were never staged, though Georgia Douglas Johnson submitted several for consideration by drama groups sponsored by the Works Progress Administration.[2] Not only would production costs and "stageability" decrease opportunities for presentation of such plays, but the theme,while crucial, was extremely controversial. In the post-war, pre-Depression years of the twentieth century, a period when race relations were certainly strained, it would have been difficult at best to highlight, in living drama, one of the most volatile points of contention between the races.

While lynching might have been the national pastime, everybody wanted to ignore it. Just as the causes for lynching were a part of the national mythology (black men were usually assumed to have raped white women), so too were the conceptions that white Americans held of themselves. They were the best of the best, ever democratic and just; indeed, perhaps God tossed out the mold when he created them. For such persons to alter those perceptions sufficiently to allow them to accept depictions of their crueler sides, and in fact to ask them to recognize those tendencies and do something about them was too much for history or literature to bear—especially not in a dramatic mode, for one of the primary reasons for attending theaters is to obtain relief from the problems that beset one every day.

Equally relevant to stageability is the fact that drama, by its very nature of presentation before audiences, complicates the manner and method of development of the theme of lynching. Whereas Richard Wright in "Between the World and Me" or "Big Boy Leaves Home" could depict black men who were tarred and feathered and whose skin was slowly burned from their bodies, Angelina Grimké in *Rachel* (1916) had to choose another course of action. *Rachel*, a rather long three-act play set in New York in the first decade of the twentieth century, centers upon the Loving family: mother Mary, brother Thomas (Tom), and daughter Rachel. Although she celebrates the anniversary—October 16th—of the deaths, Mrs. Loving keeps from her two surviving children the fact that their father and brother were lynched ten years before in the South, which means that they were killed in the 1890s, the peak years for lynching in the United States and about which Wells-Barnett wrote (the husband was killed for writing an editorial, in the manner of Wells-Barnett, denouncing the lynching of another black man, and the son, as was true of many historical family counterparts, was just a convenient addition to the crowd's thirst for blood). Finally revealing that family history, Mrs. Loving discovers that Rachel cannot recover from it. Rachel becomes overly sensitized to the plight of black children, including a little black boy whom she adopts after his parents die of smallpox. Obsessively fearful that the child, Jimmy Mason, will grow up and be psychologically and economically if not physically lynched, Rachel determines to protect him as best she can, and she vows never to bear children rather than watch them grow up and gather the scars that will eventually destroy them. She consequently rejects the marriage proposal of John Strong, a family friend. A story about being weighed down by one's history, the play is a more long, drawn-out discussion of life and its consequences than a dramatic rendering of lynching; protest comes through the depiction of the long-term destructive consequences of lynching upon the family of the lynching victims.

In anti-lynching dramas by black women playwrights, therefore, speech and thought take the place of action.[3] In *Rachel*, the horror of lynching must be created imaginatively through the power of words and the actors and actresses' abilities to make that power felt, for certainly no hanging by the neck until dead—not even symbolic—could occur on stage. And the play becomes a story of forced segregation, for at the time the play was written and first produced, it would have been practically impossible to conceive of a scene in which white people would have been willing to play the villainous perpetrators of such atrocities against African Americans.

The play also highlights the difference between black male and female treatment of lynching. Grimké confines her play to the domestic sphere, as opposed to the open, outdoor spaces in which most lynching occurs in fiction and poetry. Indeed, Grimké's set is almost claustrophobic in its sameness, and perhaps, through a stretch of the imagination, that in and of itself could be viewed as an objective correlative of the psychological damage that lynching as the specific evil and racism as the general evil cause the characters in the play. A single room dominates the stage, with the walls painted green—even the window has a green shade. Furniture, paintings, flowers, a piano, and a sewing-machine crowd the set. The room reflects the cluttered state of Rachel's mind as well as the general imprisonment that she and Tom feel, being black and cramped in job opportunities—in spite of their stellar educations for that period (the play occurs between the time Rachel is eighteen and twenty-two; Tom is a year older).

Mary P. Burrill's *Aftermath* (1919) shares themes and characters with Grimké's *Rachel*. Briefly, the play, set in South Carolina, focuses on the eighty-year-old Mam (short for "Mammy") Sue; her mostly obedient, sixteen-year-old granddaughter Millie; her frightened, eighteen year-old grandson, Lonnie; and her progressively militant older grandson, John. Returned from fighting in World War I, John learns that his father has been lynched and burned (Millie has kept this knowledge from him for six months before his return and tries to continue the charade when he arrives home). With the bravery that the war has inspired in him (he has won several medals) and with warm memories of being treated like a man in Paris, John takes his service revolver, thrusts his lieutenant's gun in Lonnie's hand, and, at play's end, goes disastrously out to avenge his father's death. Like Grimké's *Rachel*, Burrill's *Aftermath* is equally confining physically and psychologically. Characters carry the psychological weight of knowing that American justice does not apply to black people, that goodness in humanity is irrelevant, that the space of a tiny cabin is all the world allowed to those born black in the American South. John asserts that "beyon' a certain point prayers ain't no good!" (63), and he names revenge for his father's death as one of those times: "This ain't no time fu' preachers or prayers!" (65). We see his anger and feel his outrage, but we are not privy to his revenge; just as his father's death has taken place offstage, so his potential revenge is confined to that arena.

It is more the psychological than the physical damage of lynching that black women dramatists portray. A portion of this focus can certainly be explained by genre, but a portion of it is perhaps also tied to gender. African American women throughout their literary encounters with lynching seem less willing to confront the actual bodily destruction that occurs during the executions. Alice Walker's "The Flowers" (1973) is a typical example. In that short short story, a young girl comes upon a place in the woods where a black man has been lynched and views the remains of his destruction and its method. What she thinks is the root of a rose is "*the rotted remains of a noose, a bit of shredding plowline, now blending benignly into the soil. Around an overhanging limb of a great spreading oak clung another piece. Frayed, rotten, bleached, and frazzled—barely there—but spinning restlessly in the breeze*" (120). While Margaret Walker shows the lynching of two women in *Jubilee* (1966), she does not focus in graphic detail on the murders. She shifts focus from the women being lynched to those reacting to the lynching: "There were some who declared that they actually heard the women's necks pop as they fell through the trap, but this might have been a gross exaggeration. Under the stress of the moment one could hear almost anything. Vyry was shaking and shuddering and her teeth were clattering in her head" (103). The time lapse effect in the passage is also a mediating device; commentary moves from the moment of occurrence to a point in the future when collected memories related tales about the incident. Walker thereby modifies horror by distancing her readers from the lynching as well as from Vyry's reaction. It has been only recently, in Toni Morrison's *Beloved* (1987), that a black woman writer has allowed her readers and her characters to see, feel, and respond—without mediation—to the graphic destruction of a black male body in a lynching/burning. When Schoolteacher captures Sixo and burns him, his death is compared to "cooking hominy. . . . His feet are cooking; the cloth of his trousers smokes" (226). And even this description is not as painfully graphic as those found in the works of several black male writers.

For most black women writers, the focus in lynching stories is almost always after the fact of lynching, as Burrill's play *Aftermath* aptly reflects in its title. Burrill directs her attention toward the effects that the loss of a father or brother or cousin has upon the lives of the characters in the play, male and female. John is exceptional in that he discusses the possibility of his own lynching and seems to manage his own transformation into a militant. That action, however, is more ideal than real, and it is appropriate that the play ends at the moment John decides to take his army pistol and confront the whites who have lynched and burned his father, for history clearly suggests that militant action against offending whites would not only lead to the death of the black man but those of his family as well. Most of the black male characters, like Tom Loving in *Rachel*, ultimately seem to falter from outrage into inertia.

Black women playwrights, then, seem more interested in the effect of lynching upon hearth, home, and mind instead of body (gouging out eyes or chopping off ears, hands, and feet), but the works by these women seem more pessimistic than those by their male counterparts. As Kathy Perkins has pointed out, Rachel's decision to allow her future to cave in to racism is, in effect, a call for genocide.[4] But it also might be viewed as self-indulgent. Here is a beautiful woman who has had privilege beyond what her lynched father and brother could have imagined, yet she is willing to insult the memory of their deaths by deliberately conceding to spiritual annihilation. The melodramatic language of the play would seem to support this particular interpretation. Rachel asserts after her mother's story:

> Then, everywhere, everywhere, through the South, there are hundreds
> of dark mothers who live in fear, terrible, suffocating fear, whose rest

by night is broken, and whose joy by day in their babies on their hearts is three parts—pain. Oh, I know this is true—for this is the way I should feel, if I were little Jimmy's mother. How horrible! Why—it would be more merciful—strangle the little things at birth. And so this nation—this white Christian nation—has deliberately set its curse upon the most beautiful—the most holy thing in life— motherhood! Why—it—makes—you doubt—God! (149)[5]

Rachel's speech is one of many in which the consequences of lynching are rehearsed throughout the play; even when the word "lynching" is not used, it is clearly the impetus to the emotional turmoil that Rachel experiences.

Georgia Douglas Johnson's presentations in *A Sunday Morning in the South* (1925) and *Blue-Eyed Black Boy* (circa 1930) similarly recognize the trend set by other black women playwrights— conversation about lynching becomes the basis of action. However, that is more so in the latter Johnson play than in the former. In *A Sunday Morning in the South*, an elderly black grandmother, Sue Jones, is sitting eating breakfast with her grandsons, Tom and Bossie Griggs, and a neighbor when a policeman brusquely enters her cabin to question Tom's whereabouts on the evening before. A young white woman has been attacked, and Tom fits the description. A second officer brings the young woman into the cabin to coach her identification of Tom, whereupon he is taken out and summarily lynched. Before breakfast has been interrupted, conversation in the play has centered upon the attacked young lady, with Sue and her neighbor Matilda advocating "the law" handling the matter, even as they recognize that men can be falsely accused and punished. Tom voices his desire to study law in order to become an agent of change for his community. Conversation ends abruptly with the accusation and death. Nonetheless, it is noteworthy that Johnson conceived a play in which two white males and a white female actually appear on stage. That is as close to dramatic action as any of the plays comes, for the dominant mode remains conversational and rhetorical.

In *Blue-Eyed Black Boy*, another elderly black mother, Mrs. Waters, sits waiting with her daughter Rebecca for her hard-working son Jack to come home from work. Exemplary in his efforts to care for his mother and sister, Jack is the epitome of goodness. Then, an abrupt transition: the news comes that Jack has brushed against a young white woman on the street, argued with her, and that she has had him jailed.

A mob gathers to lynch him. Rebecca's fiancee, Dr. Tom Grey, manages to get to the governor and prevent the lynching in the proverbial nick of time. The mixed-blood young black man about whom the discussion takes place never appears on the stage. The on-stage characters look through a window and report the actions of the mob to each other and the audience. Violence is in the outside realm; the domestic sphere contains the emotional energy expended in reaction to it. Johnson, therefore, joins Grimké and Burrill in distancing herself from the physical horrors of lynching. She puts words between herself and the brutality in an effort to be able to stomach the topic about which she writes. An appropriate analogy is the theme of incest as it has been treated by two other African American writers. In Alice Walker's *The Color Purple* (1982), there is nothing between the reader and the fact that Celie is raped by her stepfather. Readers must confront the horror even as Celie feels it, at the moment she experiences it. By contrast, consider Jim Trueblood's account of having sex with his daughter in Ralph Ellison's *Invisible Man* (1952). We get the story from the narrator, who recounts meeting Jim Trueblood many years before, and who then summarizes the tale or nightmare that Trueblood asserts occurred many months before that; the language the narrator and Trueblood use to relate the incident is so couched in surrealistic overtones and Freudian symbolic references that we must peel through several layers before we actually get to what happened.

A similar kind of distancing occurs with the plays of Grimké, Burrill, and Johnson. African American women playwrights could almost be accused of disguising the horrors that serve as the impetus to their works. Either through language, or pretensions to gentility, or psychological blocks against the horror of their own potential creativity, these women shy away from directly treating the issue of lynching, so much so that in the case of *Rachel* and *Aftermath*, we might ask whether these are truly anti-lynching plays, or if we might correctly place the focus somewhere else.

Yet for all their technical and dramatic flaws, the plays come out more on the side of contribution than detraction from African American literature. They encourage viewing African American female creativity in a different light, sometimes questioning its ultimate intent but appreciating the efforts of black women playwrights in the ongoing battle against lynching. While questions remain about the ways in which these playwrights elected to make their voices heard, it is clear that they deserve their place among those historically who tried to get the nation and the world to see that lynching was never justified, that it was a blot upon the American character, and that all people of good will should have joined together to put an end to it. The real tragedy is that their message was so minimally heeded.

DECREPIT OLD BLACK WOMEN

The dominance of the portrait of Mama Lena Younger in Lorraine Hansberry's *A Raisin in the Sun* (1959) might easily lead those unfamiliar with early twentieth-century female African American dramatists to conclude that strong black matriarchal figures are prominent on that earlier literary landscape as well. Such is not the case. Most of these plays have a repetitive number of aging, nearly decrepit black women characters. Indeed, their physical infirmities seem to suggest the general powerlessness of the situations in which they find themselves. Undone by racism and menial work, these women are stick figures in comparison to Mama Lena. And they whine and pray more often than not. They have neither the spiritual fortitude nor the physical stamina that would suggest a stereotypical notion of strong black women. Yet they are frequently heads of households and, from the existence of their (often biracial) offspring, have previously been sexual beings. These figures are easily precursors to Hansberry's Mama Lena Younger, but without her physical or psychological strength. With this cadre of nurturing, long-suffering women, these playwrights have added to the stereotypes of mammy figures that would dot the literary landscape for many decades to come. Not nearly as grand as William Faulkner's Dilsey, in their supportive, self-sacrificing roles, they clearly are a less than admirable type, reduced to praying or depending on the "quality" white folks to rescue their threatened loved ones.

With almost all these women, there seems to be a gap between their chronological age and their psychological age. Since they have teenage or adolescent children, given the life expectancy and child-bearing stages in the early twentieth century, they are relatively not that old. Yet they sound as if they are the rock of ages. Their voices are stereotypically old as they are simultaneously not stereotypically strong. Wrapping these women in the aura and mannerisms of the elderly, in spite of their chronological ages, reflects a perception of black female representation that influenced these playwrights in spite of themselves. They perceived of black female characters from the point of view of predominant (white) popular imagination and literature. And black women from this perspective are examples of asexual, self-sacrificing, and family-oriented women but not particularly powerful within their communities and certainly not within the larger society.

Grimké's Mary Loving is the epitome of the long-suffering, nurturing black mother who gives all for her children. For ten years, she bears the knowledge that her husband and oldest son have been lynched because she does not wish to cause distress to her surviving offspring.[6] This overprotection has caused her to age beyond her sixty years. Yet she keeps hinting that there is something she must tell Tom and Rachel, which suggests that she is less comfortable with the role of isolated burden bearer than some of her literary descendants would be. Still, it is only with much trepidation that she shifts the burden from her own shoulders to Tom and Rachel. That revelation begins Mrs. Loving's physical deterioration; by tying bodily discomfort with the fact and memory of lynching, Grimké anticipates the other black women playwrights who would allow health problems to loom much larger with the female characters in their texts.

Immediately after sharing the story of the lynching with Rachel and Tom, Mrs. Loving begins to reflect physically her psychological condition. At the beginning of Act II, after Jimmy Mason has come to live with the Lovings, Mrs. Loving is described as "bent and worn-looking" when she appears in a doorway; "she limps a trifle" (153). We then learn that she has rheumatism, which is apparently becoming progressively worse because she uses liniment to treat it (there had been no mention of any impairment in Act I). In response to Tom's assertion that she is not old, Mrs. Loving counters: "Oh! yes, I am, dearie. It's sixty long years since I was born; and I am much older [than] that, much older" (154). The obvious implication is that she has been carrying too many heavy burdens. She limps through Act II, but other concerns take over Act III.

Indeed, Rachel, at age twenty-two, becomes *the* weary and sick black woman in the last act of the play. Her world-weariness makes her much older in some ways than her mother, for Mrs. Loving has to try to encourage Rachel to look to the future in spite of the problems in the present. Mrs. Loving, like the other mothers and grandmothers, will attempt to turn her child to God, but Rachel is not particularly receptive to religious comfort. After hearing of children, including Jimmy, experiencing the psychological warping of racism, Rachel initially faints, then takes to her bed for four days before the physical ill health transfers to permanent psychological deterioration. The play ends with

Rachel in a noticeably unstable mental condition, perhaps even suicidal.

Burrill's Mam Sue in *Aftermath* is, at eighty, chronologically the oldest of the women and understandably slowed down. Burrill nonetheless presents her as if she were on her very last leg. The description of Mam Sue, as descriptions of most of the women do, draws special attention to her infirmity. Pictured at play's opening as busily sewing, with a red bandanna on her head, *"Mam Sue is very old. Her ebony face is seamed with wrinkles; and in her bleared, watery eyes there is a world-old sorrow"* (57). In addition to the infirmity of age, Mam Sue suffers from an unspecified ailment of the knee, for which she needs liniment at regular intervals. When John arrives home, Mam Sue is described as *"hobbling painfully to meet him"* (61). The reason for Mam Sue's injury is not specified, but it significantly alters her ability to move and identifies her as another of the ineffectual black women in these early plays.

Another factor in her weak portrait is the lack of control Mam Sue has over her granddaughter Millie in crucial matters. Certainly Millie seems to be respectful enough, but she refuses, in spite of Mam Sue's admonitions to the contrary, to write and inform John of his father's death. The moral superiority that Mama Lena Younger wields over Beneatha is lacking in the relationship here. Mam Sue prays fervently and indeed there is a scene, which anticipates the famous exchange between Beneatha and Mama Lena, in which she chides Millie's seeming lack of faith. Nonetheless, Mam Sue, unlike Mama Lena, is finally unable to bring her will to bear upon her grandchildren. The very force of any potential will she has is questioned, for John, like Millie, will not heed her advice to turn to God instead of to violence. As John prepares to rush out to avenge his father's death, Mam Sue can only *"piteously"* lament: "Ohn, mah honey, hon' yuh go do nothin' to bring sin on yo' soul! Pray to de good Lawd to tek all dis fiery feelin' out'n yo' heart! Wait 'tel Brudder Moseby [the preacher] come back—he's gwine to pray—" (65). Mam Sue's words ring as hollow as the stage direction suggests, and they are ultimately as ineffectual as the liniment she uses on her knee.

In *A Sunday Morning in the South*, the grandmother, Sue Jones, is yet another stereotypically elderly black woman. Johnson uses imagery commensurate with that to be found in any racist text of the period: *"As the curtain rises Sue Jones is seen putting the breakfast on the kitchen table. She wears a red bandanna handkerchief on her grey head, a big blue gingham apron tied around her waist and big wide old lady comfort shoes. She uses a stick as she has a sore leg, and moves about with a stoop and a limp as she goes back and forth from the stove to the table*" (31). A stereotypically mammy-like servant, Sue Jones is incapable of offering any real assistance when her grandson is accused of attacking a white woman.

An injury to her leg will prevent Sue, as it will prevent Mrs. Waters in *Blue-Eyed Black Boy*, from rising to her own feet to get help from her "good" white folks. She sends Matilda to the white woman, Miss Vilet, whom she nursed as a child and who is the daughter of a local judge because Mrs. Waters herself "can't go quick" (36). She hopes they will prevent the intended lynching. Unfortunately, these substitute actors begin their journey too late, for the lynchers kill Tom Griggs practically before Matilda and Bossie can get out into the street. The helplessness of the situation is reflected in Sue's bodily movements before and during her short wait: "Sue. (*shaking nervously from side to side as she leans on her cane for support*) Oh my god, whut kin I do?" (35). Once she dispatches her messengers, she still feels helpless: "*Sue rocks back and forth in chair, head buried in her apron*" (36). Prayers that her neighbor Liza sends up to "bring this po orphan back to his ole cripple grannie safe and sound, do Jesus!" (35) do not offset the social snares in which Tom has been caught, but they do highlight—yet again—the physically impaired state of these elderly women and their inability, in spite of everyday nurturing, to help their offspring in crisis situations.

Since this is a Sunday morning, and the church is nearby, various songs are heard during the course of the play. When the emotional intensity increases after Tom is taken away, the songs reflect the helplessness of the situation. "Alas, and did my savior bleed/And did my sovereign die" (36) is essentially a foreshadowing of Tom's death, for the innocent will not be saved. "I must tell Jesus, I cannot bear my burdens alone" (37) positions Sue to deal with her loss, for shortly after the song is heard, she learns that Tom has been lynched. There is no consolation to be found, however, either before or after the tragedy, for the news of Tom's murder precipitates Sue's fatal heart attack.

Her foot injury and her heart—the physical immobility and the love for her grandson—pinpoint the pain inherent in the portrayals of these decrepit elderly black women. How Sue Jones hurt her foot is never made clear, and her weak heart is only mentioned as she sits waiting for Matilda and Bossie to return with news of Tom. Her condition makes it increasingly clear that these black women playwrights manipulate illness for its symbolic power, a power that extends beyond the familial into the social and the racial. The same is true of Johnson's second play.

Johnson's Mrs. Waters in *Blue-Eyed Black Boy* dotes on her son and is perhaps a little too proud of the position he holds within the family as well as within the community. That pride is a part of her ill health, for she and her daughter Rebecca comment with equal pleasure on Jack's blue eyes, and Rebecca wishes that she had been born with them. Informed that her son has been arrested, Mrs. Waters asserts: "My God—it ain't so—he ain't what brushed up against no lady, my boy ain't. He's, he's a gentleman, that what he is" (49). Pride in the eyes inherited from a white father extends to adoption of the most valued trait in that father: he is a gentleman. Mrs. Waters forgets that such a designation can never be bestowed upon a black boy, even if he does have blue eyes. The weakness of identifying with Southern white blood and mores that can create as well as destroy a blue-eyed black boy is a weakness in self-identification comparable to Mrs. Waters's pronounced physical injury to her foot.

Mrs. Waters's foot is as much a central focus in the play as is the possible lynching of her son Jack. When the play opens, "*Mrs. Waters is discovered seated in a large rocker with her left foot bandaged and resting on a low stool*" (47). The circumstances and fact of her injury—she has stuck "an old rusty nail" in her foot—are far less important than its physical symbolism in the play. Mrs. Waters, the presumably nurturing mother, is hindered in this role by the injury to her foot; the strength that would come to be identified with black female characters is thus undermined. When news comes that Jack is threatened, therefore, she must rely upon others to effect assistance for him. By taking away the potential for easy physical movement from Mrs. Waters, Johnson further transforms her play from action to speech and thought.

When Mrs. Waters directs Rebecca to run into her room and return with "that little tin box out of the left hand side of the tray in my trunk" (49), she is also exposing the vulnerability that undermines her strength. That trunk contains a ring apparently given to her by Jack's father, who is now the governor of the state. Giving the ring to Dr. Grey, her second substitute in action, Mrs. Waters admonishes him to carry the ring to Governor Tinkhem's house, and "just give him the ring and say, Pauline sent this, she says they going to lynch her son born 21 years ago, mind you say twenty-one years ago—then say—listen close—look in his eyes—and you'll save him" (50). Pauline Waters's injured foot prevents her from getting the box containing the ring as well as from running to the governor's house to seeks his aid in saving her son. Sexual weakness—probably not her own fault—and physical powerlessness combine to place Pauline's family at the mercy of an offstage white governor, who, like the blue-eyed black boy, never appears in the play.

The foot injury, then, becomes symptomatic of the position of the elderly black woman. It increases Pauline's ineffectualness and reduces her moral strength. Because she is not in route to the governor but must wait agitatedly to hear from Dr. Grey, Pauline seems to doubt the Christian belief that she tries to pass on to Rebecca: "Trust in God daughter—I've got faith in him, faith in—in the Governor—he won't fail" (50). With as much faith in the earthly and the heavenly father of her child, Pauline Waters continues to pray. The fact that her son is saved could be attributed to either "Father." Such ambiguity of faith during crisis moments is certainly atypical of the stereotypically strong black women. It seems yet again that Mrs. Waters's physical injury is the tear in the fabric of her faith as well as her social situation in America.

THE ELDERLY BLACK FEMALE BODY AS METAPHOR

American mythology precludes any concentration on black female bodies as having iconic value, except when that value reinforces popular conceptions of black women's places in the society or when that value is negatively complimentary. A black woman's face can grace a box of pancake mix because that image is one that soothes the populace and suggests that black women, as cooks, are nurturing and supportive of the white status quo. Black women could similarly be identified with other cleaning products, but none—for most of American history—could be expected to grace shampoo bottles, or appear in lingerie ads, or saunter across movie announcements. All of these images would suggest that black women had an *appealing* sexual side rather than being limited to the muddied sexuality identified with bearing children for their raping slave masters. And *youth* is always essential in the representation of any bodily images designed for popular consumption in America.

Perhaps inadvertently, but nonetheless noticeably, playwrights Angelina Grimké, Mary P. Burrill, and Georgia Douglas Johnson suggest that the poor condition of the bodies of the elderly black women who appear in their plays reflects the state of ill health of the larger racist American society. These playwrights initially undermine notions of representation by using primarily elderly black women and subtly transforming the ways in which they are usually perceived. These women finally are ineffectual at nurturing, but they are very effective in showing how sick their society really is. They thereby gain symbolic value even as their bodies deteriorate or as they die, that value exceeds the fact of their ill health.

The bodies of these black women are the sites upon which these playwrights explore the development of racism in America. Black women not only worked the fields during slavery, but they had their bodies invaded by the seed of white men. That invasion—and the offspring issuing therefrom—cast them in the peculiar position of being liaisons between violation, denial, and public rejection by the men who forced themselves upon them and loving the children born of those forced unions. Their bodies in ill health became symptomatic of the ill health of a country founded upon the power that exploited and then usually rejected the products of that exploitation. The seed that entered black women's bodies, if born male, became the further site for racist destruction by white men who considered all black men potential rapists of white women. Weakness in the bodies of these black women, therefore, is the objective correlative of the society's most potent poisons. And it is the physical manifestation of the psychological damage done to women who could make little claim upon their violators.

For all their symbolic power, the bodies of these black women also suggest something about their creators. Certainly these characters work well to explore ideas about the consequences of lynching, but their depictions also comment on how these relatively young and vibrant black women playwrights perceived their elder sisters. While Grimké makes an effort to individualize her description of such women, Burrill and Johnson are guilty of the worst kind of stereotyping of black women in clothing, appearance, speech, and the regularity with which their characters call on "de Lawd." Head scarves and aprons abound, the women are more dottering than not, and the dialect that Burrill and Johnson use—no matter how realistic—is descended from the plantation tradition. Strikingly, in *Blue-Eyed Black Boy*, where the governor intervenes to save Pauline Waters's son, the dialect is less pronounced, which almost implicitly suggests that Pauline is a cut above the other women by virtue of having slept with a white man who became a governor. Therefore, while these playwrights might have been daring in their treatment of lynching and transformative in important ways in their use of black female bodies, they were surprisingly traditional in some features of their portraits of their major characters. They appear to have accepted notions of class and color prevalent among African Americans in the early twentieth century. Well-educated characters like Rachel and her mother (although we get no information on how the latter came by her skills) speak in wonderfully exalted tones, in nearly perfect standard English; the other, generally illiterate women, must struggle with the dialect of the masses. There is a class factor inherent in these descriptions, then, that separated the playwrights by education and "breeding" from most of the characters they created.

Even as the characters call on the Lord, however, their praying postures are suspect, for Christianity does not fare well in these plays. As Frederick Douglass indicted practitioners of Christianity in his narrative, so most of these characters indict a so-called Christian country for its barbaric practice of lynching. When Christianity ultimately holds sway in one of the dramas, it is not an easy domination. Characters call on God as quickly as they call on human beings. At times, their cries to God ring without conviction, and it is clear that habit rather than belief informs their actions. In this trend, Grimké, Burrill, and Johnson are far ahead of their immediate descendants, for it would be well into the 1960s and 1970s before many African American writers generally parted ways with Christianity.

It could be argued that reclaiming one's fate from Christian strictures and supplications recenters it in the body. If divine intervention is not forthcoming, then only human possibility exists. When that human possibility is impaired, as with the bodies of these women, outcomes are bleak at the very least. Only one of these plays, therefore, ends on an optimistic tone or even remotely presages a future. Rachel is on the brink of suicide at the end of *Rachel*, John and Lonnie set out for certain death in *Aftermath*, and Sue Jones actually dies in *A Sunday Morning in the South*. Only in *Blue-Eyed Black Boy* does help come in time, and the play ends before any extended value can be placed on that source of help—though it certainly suffices for the moment. The black female body in ill health, therefore, is not only a metaphor for American racism but a sympathetic response to the continuing destruction of the black male body.

NOTES

1.   For more detailed discussion of lynching, the advocates against it, writers who treat it, the stylized pattern it frequently took, and its impact upon black communities, see Trudier Harris, *Exorcising Blackness: Historical and Literary Lynching and Burning Rituals* (Bloomington: Indiana UP, 1984).

2.   In a paper presented at the Association for Theatre in Higher Education annual meeting in Atlanta, Georgia, on August 3, 1992, drama scholar Winona Fletcher discussed the difficulties Johnson had in getting her plays staged, especially in trying to win over evaluators who were at times almost as illiterate as they were hostile. I should note as well that the length of Johnson's plays—roughly seven pages each—might also have influenced staging decisions.

3.   Drama scholar Kathy A. Perkins and I discussed this feature of the play when we shared a panel at the annual meeting of the Association for Theatre in Higher Education in Atlanta, Georgia, on August 3, 1992.

4.   Paper presented at the Association for Theatre in Higher Education annual meeting, Altanta, Georgia, August 3, 1992.

5.   It is noteworthy that a third anti-lynching play, *Safe*, which Johnson also wrote in the early 1930s, centers upon a young black mother actually killing her newborn son. She gives birth against the backdrop of a mob taking a young black man to be lynched and against his cries for leniency. When she learns that her child is male, which means that he is potentially subject to the same fate, she chokes him to death rather than allow him to grow up with the possibility hanging over his head.

6.   Mrs. Loving also desires that Tom be a "*gentleman*," the same desire that Mrs. Waters has for her son Jack in *Blue-Eyed Black Boy*, where the implications of that designation have equal tones of a pathetic adoption of values from the society that oppresses these men.

WORKS CITED OR CONSULTED

Grimké, Angelina Weld. *Selected Works of Angelina Weld Grimké*. Ed. Carolivia Herron. New York: Oxford UP, 1991.

Harris, Trudier. *Exorcising Blackness: Historical and Literary Lynching and Burning Rituals*. Bloomington: Indiana UP, 1984.

Morrison, Toni. *Beloved*. New York: Knopf, 1987.

Perkins, Kathy A., ed. *Black Female Playwrights: An Anthology of Plays Before 1950*. Bloomington: Indiana UP, 1989.

———. "Antilynch Plays by Mary P. Burrill and Angelina Weld Grimké." Unpublished paper presented at the annual meeting of the Association for Theatre in Higher Education. Atlanta, Georgia, 3 August 1992.

Stephens, Judith. "Anti-Lynch Plays by African American Women: Race, Gender, and Social Protest in American Drama." *African American Review* 26 (1992): 329-339.

Walker, Alice. *In Love and Trouble: Stories of Black Women*. New York: Harcourt, 1973.

Walker, Margaret. *Jubilee*. New York: Houghton, 1966.

Segregated Sisterhood

Anger, Racism, and Feminism in Alice Childress's *Florence* and *Wedding Band.*[1]

LaVinia Delois Jennings

In most critical discussions of the first phase of Alice Childress's writing career, the period between 1949 and 1968, the interracial conflicts in her works overshadow and displace the gender conflicts. As gendered texts, the scripts of *Florence* (1949) and *Wedding Band* (1966) delineate through characterization, plot, and theme socio-psychological complexities uniquely female in insight and experience. The black female protagonists in these dramas exercise their right to self-actualization, to resist the conventions of motherhood, and to renounce other-imposed images and definitions of themselves. As evolving black women, they demand public and private equality in the arts, in the work place, and in love. Childress, politically aware of the racial, social, and power dissonance present among women, deliberately enacts the black woman-white woman segregated sisterhood dialectic as her first frontier for dramatic exploration. In doing so, she profiles women confronting women about the roles, choices, differences, hypocrisies, and racism of women. Within her depictions, black female characters use anger and defiance as means of exorcising psychic hostilities that American's history of white racism, as unseen signifier, breeds between white and black, between non-colored women and women of color.[2] Two of Childress's other works during this period also depict subtle and direct displays of racially provoked black female anger. In the integrationist drama, *Trouble in Mind* (1955), however, Wiletta Mayer unleashes pent-up anger at the theater's white patriarchy that persists in staging false images of blackness. And in *Like One of the Family . . . Conversations from a Domestic's Life* (1956), a collection of sixty-two short monologues, Mildred Johnson resists stereotyping by the white women who hire her for day work. Collectively, the major works of Childress's early playwriting are dramas of revolution, protest, or accusation, generally centering on violent verbal and physical confrontation between blacks and whites. The positioning of these plays within this dramatic enclosure prefigures the revolutionary drama of Sonia Sanchez, Barbara Molette, Martie Charles, Ntozake Shange, LeRoi Jones (Imamu Amiri Baraka), and Ed Bullins of the mid-1960s and 1970s.

Because African American women have historically been victims of white female as well as male racism, classism, and sexism, their writings not infrequently utilize anger to articulate tensional differences between themselves and white women. In her keynote address entitled "The Uses of Anger: Women Responding to Racism," Audre Lorde made the following cogent statement to the National Women's Studies Association conference in 1981:

> Women responding to racism means women responding to anger; the anger of exclusion, of unquestioned privilege, of racial distortions, of silence, ill-use, stereotyping, defensiveness, misnaming, betrayal, and co-optation. . . . Any discussion among women about racism must include the recognition and the use of anger. . . . Most women have not developed tools for facing anger constructively. CR [Consciousness Raising] groups in the past, largely white, dealt with how to express anger, usually at the world of men. And these groups were made up of white women who shared the terms of their oppression. There was usually little attempt to articulate the genuine differences between women, such as those of race, color, age, class, and sexual identity. There was no apparent need at that time to examine the contradictions of self, woman as oppressor. There was work on expressing anger, but very little on anger directed against each other. No tools were developed to deal with other women's anger except to avoid it, deflect it, or flee from it under a blanket of guilt. (124)

Validating Lorde's assertion as well as Childress's dramatic charge, literary and social critics such as bell hooks[3] and Hazel Carby cite that white women have not realized their implication in the oppression of black women from the slavery era to the racially divided women's movements of the late nineteenth and twentieth centuries. They point out that white women, especially of bourgeois status, have denied their culpability and felt justified in responding to ensuing black female rage with reciprocal anger. Rarely has their work treated the more pressing issues precipitating the anger.

The plots of *Florence* and *Wedding Band* pit black women directly against white women who, placing color over a common sisterhood, replicate the racist behavior and exclusionary practices of white patriarchy. As further amplification of this, Childress illustrates how white women in positions of power fail to make a difference with regard to gender because of racial bias. Significantly, moments of racially based anger culminate in epiphanies. Both plays climax in black female protagonists unleashing pent-up hostility at racist white women which leads to the alteration of their own psychic bases. Mama Whitney and Julia Augustine, the protagonists of these dramas, realize that they are responsible not for altering the psyches of their oppressors but for the management of their own. For Childress's female characters, anger, as Carol Tavris's study of the emotions states, "is as much a political matter as a biological one. The decision to get angry has powerful consequences," and has "an emphatic message: *Pay attention to me. I don't like what you are doing. Restore my pride. You're in my way. Danger. Give me justice*" (45).

Foremost, anger in Childress's drama does not exist solely for the sake of anger. It transforms. Her encoding of anger deconstructs its perception as a disruptive, useless principle and converts it into a constructive liberating force capable of imparting growth, vision, voice, and change. As psychoanalysts theorize, vocalizing anger can have constructive as well as deconstructive potential, and seemingly women have the most difficulty identifying and positively tapping into what has traditionally been for them a suppressed emotion. One reason for this is that American culture, like many patriarchal cultures, mandates that women deny their anger and aggression lest they convey the perception that they are unfeminine or hysterical. Harriet Goldhor Lerner, psychologist at the Menninger Foundation, states that taboos against women feeling and expressing anger are so powerful that women have a difficult time knowing when they are angry. Often women silence and shut off their anger, Lerner continues, because they feel that the display of emotion is useless and will be sacrificed to no gain or that it is better to practice "de-selfing"—to "betray and sacrifice the self in order to preserve harmony with others" (2-3). Once they

locate their anger, Childress's women discover that to continue de-
selfing to preserve harmony is impossible. Silent submission and
emotional distancing are styles of managing anger that do not work.
Their initial polite compliance is merely a defense against a rage that
reveals itself only in traumatic situations when all defenses break down.
Their anger serves as signpost that important emotional issues of their
lives need examination and resolution, that too much of themselves—
their beliefs, values, desires, or ambitions—is being compromised
(Lerner 10-11).

Florence launches Childress's indictment of white women as
principal practitioners of racism and classism against members of their
own gender. Her structuring of the race/gender hierarchy adheres to the
traditional pecking order that Zora Neale Hurston, Toni Morrison, and
other black women writers discuss which positions white women over
blacks and places black women at the bottom of the power-deference
rung. In her study of racism and sexism, Diane K. Lewis states,

> white women have not only been given deference, they have also had
> some access to power and authority. While they themselves lacked
> authority in the dominant society, they have had a route to power
> through their kinship and marital ties with men (e.g., fathers,
> husbands, and sons) who do exercise authority in the public sphere.
> Moreover, white women, as members of the dominant group,
> formerly held both considerable authority and power vis-à-vis the
> subordinate racial group. (536)

The initial deference that the protagonist of *Florence* shows mirrors this
power/authority/race matrix.

Set in a train station racially segregated by a railing, Mama
Whitney, with cardboard suitcase in hand, is on her way north to
retrieve her daughter Florence, a young mother and widow who has
fled the racist South to pursue her dream of becoming a dramatic
actress and singer. Since her departure, Florence, unwilling to concede
defeat by discrimination and in dire financial straits, has been able to
obtain only two acting jobs—one in a black production and the other as
a domestic in a white play. Mama is ambivalent about foiling
Florence's ambition but her other daughter, Marge, has convinced her
the failure is for Florence's own good since Florence has "notions a
Negro woman don't need" (*Florence* 8). Besides, from Marge's
perspective, Florence should be home taking care of her young son,

Ted, instead of leaving Mama and herself strapped with her maternal duty.

While Mama waits for her train, "a well dressed" white woman "wearing furs and carrying a small, expensive overnight bag" breezes in and introduces herself as "Mrs. Carter." From across the railing, the two women engage in conversation about Mrs. Carter's brother's unsuccessful book, *Lost My Lonely Way*, a story about a tragic mulatta who would rather be dead than have one drop of black blood. Mrs. Carter adamantly defends her brother's biased plot, but Mama refutes its validity by offering up testimonies of blacks of mixed ancestry that she personally knows who have not tried to kill themselves because they have African blood.

The conversation stalls until Mrs. Carter apologetically rekindles their exchange, asserting that she has liberal sensibilities. When she discovers Mama's reason for traveling to New York, Mrs. Carter reveals that she, too, is an actress and knows many influential people in the theater. Belief in Mrs. Carter's self-proclaimed liberalism and promising theater contracts prompts Mama to petition her aid in securing theater employment for Florence. Expressing her moral obligation to help obtain Florence "security," Mrs. Carter gives Mama the telephone number of Melba Rugby, the director of an upcoming Broadway musical who is in need of a maid. Mrs. Carter offers to contact Rugby personally to recommend Florence, stating, "I'll just tell her no heavy washing or ironing . . . just cleaning and a little cooking . . . does she cook?" (*Florence* 45).

Mrs. Carter's unexpected racial condescension provokes Mama's rage: she clutches Mrs. Carter's wrist tightly causing her discomfort. Intimidated by Mama's unexpected aggressiveness, Mrs. Carter, once she is freed, retreats to the "White ladies" room. Mama's rage signifies an epiphany. Instead of going to New York, she sends Florence the check which was to have paid for her daughter's return fare along with the encouraging message: "Keep trying" (47).

Although it is apparent that the white woman racially stereotypes Florence by suggesting that she seek employment as a maid instead of following her aspirations to become an actress, the bourgeois Mrs. Carter exhibits racism and classism throughout her conversation with Mama. First, as southern racist-classist manners and linguistic deference dictate, Mrs. Carter introduces herself by marital title and patronymic, yet never asks Mama's surname or Christian name. Failing to address Mama by any name, she requests that Mama dispense with the formality of calling her "Mam" but does not invite true informality by offering her less formal first name. Second, in the discussion of the tragic mulatta, Mrs. Carter invokes white patriarchal and racial authority by implying that a white male, in this case her brother, knows more about the emotions and experiences of black people in general and black women in particular than a black woman does. Third, Mrs. Carter, stereotyping blacks, responds "pleasantly" to hearing of Florence's aspirations as a singer; "Your people have such a gift. I love spirituals" (43), she comments. Nevertheless, she resists the thought that Florence might be excellent for a part in Melba Rugby's upcoming New York musical. She herself has had nominal success in a male-controlled theater but is still unwilling to help another woman. If Rugby is of a similar racist mindset, she is nothing more than a full-blown composite of Mrs. Carter. Described as a "most versatile woman" who "[w]rites, directs, acts . . . [and does] everything," Rugby is capable of empowering theater women of all colors but apparently may choose to imitate the racist, sexist exclusions of her male peers. Last, Mrs. Carter projects class bias in her interpretation of "security" for Florence. Working long hours cleaning, cooking, washing, and serving as the primary caregiver for the children of another household in exchange for a single room, meals that must be eaten alone in the kitchen, low wages, separations from her own family, and limited leisure time surely is not the way that Mrs. Carter defines "security" for herself.

The ventilation of Mama's anger allows her to revise her racial orientation, which, until the moment she clutches Mrs. Carter's wrist, has been ideologically flawed. Previously she has deferred to women in Mrs. Carter's class partly because *de jure* and *de facto* segregation have mandated that she do so and partly because she has been socially brainwashed into believing that women of Mrs. Carter's social status, since they had more, knew more, and were reputed to be more, were indeed more, and more meant better. Mama has also erroneously superimposed her own truly liberal sensibilities upon all women. Now, for perhaps the first time, she sees clearly the moral blindness, the social ambiguities, and the intellectual immaturity of the Mrs. Carters of the world. To underscore the moment of her psychic illumination, childress has Mama sit quietly and stare straight ahead for several seconds.

Mama's past method of coping with racial strife has been to endure whatever comes. Falling on a psychological continuum between Marge and Florence, she initially is capable of neither passive acceptance nor active resistance to white racism. When Mrs. Carter condescendingly offers to help Florence obtain work as a maid, Mama's consciousness, perhaps for the first time, expands, bringing long-suppressed anger to the surface. She must act as the empowerer of her daughter instead of relying on another who is in a position of strength but who is unwilling to look beyond class and racial difference to help. Paralleling her physical journey, Mama undergoes a psychological journey which, as Deborah E. McDowell asserts, is for black female characters unlike the implicitly socio-political journeys taken by black male characters in the works of African American male writers. Hers is a personal journey, a journey in which she "is in a state of becoming 'part of an evolutionary spiral, moving from victimization to consciousness'" (McDowell 194).

Breaking respectful silence, Mama angrily pulls Mrs. Carter off balance, reproaching her with the diminutive "child!" (*Florence* 46), quite the antithesis of her earlier respectful "Mam." Her anger unlocks her understanding and locates her voice—"You better get over on the other side of that rail" (46), she commands Mrs. Carter—and serves as a catalyst for her personal change. No longer indecisive about the role she must play in effecting Florence's dream, she chooses to empower her daughter, realizing that she cannot rely on gender kinship to assist her. As a woman aiding and empowering a woman, Mama is the figurative "sister" of the play. The literal sister, Marge, reinforcing white patriarchy and disdainful of her biological sister's strivings, constructs an ideologically flawed sisterhood as well.

A similar pattern of conflict, anger, confrontation, and epiphany occurs in *Wedding Band*. Beyond interracial, heterosexual relations and black women's rights, the plays primary assault, as Catherine Wiley asserts, is against the segregated of black women and white women during the WWI-era of South Carolina (the period of the play) and across America today: "Childress's play can be read today as a history lesson pointed at white women to remind them and us, and in 1966 or now, that our vision of sisterly equality has always left some sisters out" (187). The tension between Julia Augustine, a thirty-five-year-old seamstress who has been conducting a ten-year miscegenetic relationship with Herman, a forty-year-old white baker, and Herman's mother, a woman who hates not only blacks but her own impoverished German background, detonates an anger which heightens Julia's awareness of her true relation to women inside and outside her race.

Julia silences herself in order to preserve harmony in her interracial relationship. Herman instructs Julia to tolerate his mother and sister,

Annabelle, when they arrive at her house to transport him home under the cover of darkness when he falls sick with the influenza that is ravaging the country. But the bigotry that Herman's mother exhibits foils Julia's attempt to erase her true emotions from the first face-to-face encounter with her common-law mother-in-law whom she knows refers to her as "nigger."

A white supremacist, Herman's mother renders Julia invisible when she enters the black backyard community in which Julia resides. "[A]ssuming" the airs of "quality" and "calm well-being," the fifty-seven-year-old mother of Herman surveys the backyard with cold detachment (*Wedding Band* 45). Looking past Julia, she fails to acknowledge her as she enters her house and immediately concocts a tale to explain Herman's presence in a black woman's bed: "My son comes to deliver baked goods and the influenza strikes him down. Sickness, it's the war" (*Wedding Band* 45). Racial biases fuel her condescending rhetoric as she moves, quite rapidly, from one racist assumption to another. Herman's mother invokes the black female sexual myth to explain why her son cohabits with Julia. When Julia innocently remarks that even in sickness she knows what Herman wants her to do for him, she wryly retorts with sexual innuendo: "I'm sure you know what he wants." She then tells Julia that she "ought to learn how to keep her dress down" (*Wedding Band* 46). Her racial imaginings conceives the idea that Julia has "hoo-dooed" Herman (47). Since Herman's mother is convinced that all black people steal, she alleges that the bakery's profits have suffered because of Julia's thievery. Intent on burning her son's clothing in Julia's possession, she insinuates that the contamination of a black woman is more virulent than the influenza. To Herman's mother, Julia is a pestilence, an irrefutable sign that she has incurred God's wrath. Ignorant of the power of love—she even announces that she "don't know nothin' about it"—she offers to buy Julia off: "Take it [money that Herman has given Julia earlier] and go. It's never too late to undo a mistake. I'll add more to it. (*She puts the money on the dresser*)" (48, 46).

Participating in her own castigation, silencing, and erasure proves intolerable for Julia once her temper is roused. Herman's delirious recitation of the Calhoun speech proclaiming people's inequality and Herman's mother's rhetorical challenge of "Who you think you are?" (*Wedding Band* 51) set her off . An angered Julia responds,

I'm your damn daughter-in-law, you old bitch! . . . The black thing
who bought a hot water bottle to put on your sick, white self when
rheumaticism threw you flat on your back . . . who bought flannel
gowns to warm your pale, mean body. He never ran up and down
King Street shoppin' for you . . . I bought what he took home to
you . . . the lace curtain in your parlor . . . the shirt-waist you
wearin'—I made them. . . . If I wasn't black with all-a Carolina
'gainst me I'd be mistress of your house! Annabelle, you'd be
married livin' in Brooklyn, New York . . . and I'd be waitin' on
Frieda . . . cookin' your meals. (51)

The two women's lives have intersected indirectly on numerous
occasions, and were it not for the barrier erected by race, their physical
meeting would be radically different. Julia's words provoke a shouting
match between the two women but do not destabilize Herman's
mother's sense of superiority. "I'm as high over you as Mount Everest
over the sea. White reigns supreme. . . . I'm white, you can't change
that" (51), she proclaims as she and Annabelle depart with a fever-
delirious Herman.

The expression of repressed anger for allowing her own oppression
liberates Julia. Julia's angry exchange with Herman's mother activates
her voice, crystallizes a realistic view of her ten-year relationship with
Herman, and facilitates a communal nexus with Mattie, Lula, and
Fanny, the black women of the backyard. Herman's mother reminds
Julia that no matter where she goes, her status as a black woman will
remain unchanged. Fleeing to the north may lead to the changing of her
last name if she marries Herman but the racial past and ancestry that
she shares with black women and all African Americans are her
permanent legacy. Julia has not worn the mask of self-effacement, but
she has for love's sake voluntarily worn the mask of silence and
abdicated control over her life. To complete the psychological journey
that anger begins, she must now reclaim control. When Herman's
mother and Annabelle return to retrieve Herman a second time from
Julia's house, Julia *"silently stares at them, studying, each WOMAN,
seeing them with new eyes. She is going through that rising process
wherein she must reject them as the molders and dictators of her life.
'Nobody comes in my house'"* (65), she commands. Marge Jennet
Price-Hendricks points out that "as Julia assumes control, she discovers
her 'voice' and she realizes that she need not fear to speak. Hers is a
black woman's voice, shaped by history as she begins to make

connections between her gender and her race. Childress makes quite
clear that women should never fear their own voice, for the silence
'hurts'" (194).

A continuing cycle of racism and a segregated sisterhood between
black and white women are evident in *Wedding Band* but perhaps, as
Childress's optimistic ending subtly hints, not necessarily eternal.
Among women from the old school of America's segregationist
politics, the success in effecting an integrated women's cooperative and
community will prove the most problematic and perhaps the most
disappointing. Women like Herman's mother, carrying their own class
baggage about self, are hardest to reach. Hatred of her own ethnicity
exacerbates her hatred of blackness. Julia's and her exchange of racial
epithets, "Black, sassy nigger" and "Kraut, knuckle-eater, and red
neck" (*Wedding Band* 50), conjures serious reservations concerning the
relaxing of tensions between the next generation of black and white
women which Teeta, Mattie's daughter, and Princess, the little white
girl for whom Mattie serves as a nanny, represent. In an earlier scene
the young girls have already made racist notions a part of their play
discourse. While the two jump rope they chant "Ching, ching, china-
man eat dead rat. . . . Knock him in the head with a baseball bat"
(*Wedding Band* 22). Even at her young age, Princess (as her name
implies) expects linguistic deference from her black playmate:

> *Princess.*   You wanta jump?
> *Teeta.*   Yes.
> *Princess.*   Say "Yes, Mam." (*Wedding Band* 22-23)

Annabelle, the literal "sister" in the play, is the character who
embodies hope for the future of interracial sisterhood (Wiley 195). Not
without faults, she has not, however, been cut off from the potential to
love as has been her mother. She does not condone her mother's racism
and expresses relief that before her father died he "changed his mind
about the Klan" (*Wedding Band* 47). Furthermore, her mother's
"makin' a spectacle" (46) of herself with Julia shames her. Annabelle
disapproves of her brother's relationship largely for selfish reasons—
Herman will not marry the white widow with whom they have tried to
match him; therefore, she cannot marry her boyfriend Walter and move
north. She holds both Julia and Herman responsible for their ten-year
affair and is willing peacefully to share her view. She tells Julia, "I'm
sorry . . . so sorry it had to be this way. I can't leave with you thinkin' I

uphold Herman, and blame you. I say a man is responsible for his own behavior" (49).

At the play's conclusion, Julia bars Herman's mother and Annabelle from her house so that Herman may die peacefully in her arms. Yet after her mother exits, Annabelle remains, moving closer to the house to listen to Julia's final words to her brother. In her forward movement and quiet listening to Julia reside optimism for the future relationship between black and white women. Unlike her mother whose racism provokes her to respond to Julia by engaging in name calling, Annabelle is open to what the black woman has to say. As Catherine Wiley suggests, Julia's curtain speech directed to the dying Herman can also be applied to the two remaining women on stage. Annabelle's willingness to listen to Julia signifies that "perhaps Julia and Annabelle will someday be on their way to mutual respect. . . . Sisterhood, especially from the point of view of white women learning to understand black women, begins with listening, not to what one wants to hear but to what is being said" (Wiley 196).

The anger vented in *Wedding Band* is not as subtle as that displayed earlier in *Florence*, yet both presentations indicate that regardless of intensity anger resides often at the periphery, if not at the core, of many women's interracial exchanges. Exploding the common sisterhood myth and solidarity rhetoric of shared and equal victimization among all women, Childress exposes a feminist issue in dire need of address and redress. In the meantime, her early drama admonishes angry black women to take charge of their rage to empower themselves and others in their communities.

NOTES

1. Paper originally presented at the MLA Convention, New York, December 1992.

2. Nancie Caraway, *Segregated Sisterhood, Racism and the Politics of American Feminism* (Knoxville: The U of Tennessee P, 1991), 3. Caraway refers to "white racism" as the "unseen signifier . . . which has segregated Black and white feminists and silences the former."

3. bell hooks. *Ain't I a Woman: Black Women and Feminism* (Boston: South End P, 1981).

WORKS CITED

Caraway, Nancie. *Segregated Sisterhood, Racism and the Politics of American Feminism*. Knoxville: The U of Tennessee P, 1991.

Childress, Alice. *Florence, Masses and Mainstream*. 3 October 1950. 34-47.

———. *Wedding Band: A Love/Hate Story in Black and White*. New York: Samuel French, 1973.

hooks, bell. *Ain't I a Woman: Black Women and Feminism*. Boston: South End, 1981.

Lerner, Harriet Goldhor. *Dance of Anger*. New York: Harper, 1985.

Lewis, Diane K. "A Response to Inequality: Black Women, Racism, and Sexism." In *Issues in Feminism: A First Course in Women's Studies*. Ed. Sheila Ruth. Boston: Houghton Mifflin, 1980. 532-551.

Lorde, Audre. "The Uses of Anger: Women Responding to Racism." In *Sister Outsider*. Freedom, CA: Crossing, 1984. 124-133.

McDowell, Deborah E. "New Directions for Black Feminist Criticism." In *The New Feminist Criticism*, ed. Elaine Showalter. New York: Pantheon, 1985.

Price-Hendricks, Marge Jennet. "The Roaring Girls: A Study of the 17th Century Feminism and the Development of Feminist Drama," Dissertation, University of California, Riverside, 1987.

Tavris, Carol. *Anger, The Misunderstood Emotion*. New York: Simon, 1982.

Wiley, Catherine. "Whose Name, Whose Protection: Reading Alice Childress's Wedding Band." *Modern American Drama: The Female Canon*. Ed. June Schlueter. Rutherford: Fairleigh Dickinson UP, 1990. 184-197.

"Sicker than a rabid dog"
African American Women Playwrights Look at War
Marilyn Elkins

Writing about the battlefield has traditionally been a male's prerogative. In his preface to *Men at War* (1942), Ernest Hemingway states that his sons can now possess "the book" that contains "the truth about war as near as we can come by it," since these "best" stories show what "other men that we are a part of had gone through" (xxvii, xi). That Hemingway felt threatened by any invasion of this masculine turf is evident in his response to Willa Cather's front-line scene in *One of Ours*. Writing to Edmund Wilson, Hemingway dismisses this scene as a "Catherized" version of the battle scene in *Birth of a Nation*. He says that the "poor woman had to get her war experience somewhere" (118), articulating a common misconception: men consider stories about war as their gender's specialty, a no-woman's land that can be infiltrated neither by woman's experience nor imagination. Yet African American women invade this traditionally masculine turf with great success, skillfully infiltrating this bastion of male prerogative.

Their treatment of war is double-edged. African American women counterpoint the nation's declared international conflicts with its undeclared racial war at home: the war that black women living in a predominantly white racist culture know intimately. To speak about this experience crosses lines that are dangerous. After all, African American women playwrights are almost triply othered when the subject is war: writing, itself, has often been viewed as the venue of whites; playwrighting has traditionally been regarded as a man's profession; and war is decidedly a masculine subject.

Nonetheless, African American women have insisted on raising their voices in protest against the wars in African American history and on demonstrating their ability to write about such forbidden subjects. While their works frequently underscore the inherent irony of an African American fighting for freedom abroad when he or she has been denied that same freedom at home and in the armed services as well (until 1948 blacks were segregated within the armed forces "except for 2,500 who saw briefly integrated service for three months in the spring of 1945" (Stillman 5), they are also keenly aware of the material and economic interests that fuel such wars and continually question their underlying validity. Thus, they often attack the idea and concepts of war itself. Their portrayal of these complexities renders their perspective on war uniquely valuable for its interrogatory quality.

In her treatment of the Civil War, then, it is not surprising that Lorraine Hansberry chooses a soldier who is without identifiable regionalism to serve as her narrator for *The Drinking Gourd*; he explains the confrontation in terms of economic factors and suggests that the driving force behind slavery and the Civil War itself is solely the acquisition of material goods. His measured, straightforward description of the practice of slavery and the war that is being fought around it is more chilling than a more emotional one might have been. The dispassionate reporting suggests the war's true absurdity: that a "civilized" country could have allowed the conditions leading to this war to exist.

Written for television, which relies heavily upon dialogue—a form at which Hansberry excels—the play was never produced. It follows much of what would seem to be requisite screen writing format, and one wonders why it has been ignored by those seeking material for production. After her success with *A Raisin in the Sun*, Hansberry would seem to be a natural to write for America's most popular media. But her portrayal of the Civil War and the underlying greed of white Americans who fought on both sides of the conflict must have made the project somewhat suspect for the major networks. Hansberry begins her play with a quotation from Alexander H. Stephens, the Vice-President of the Confederacy: "Our new government is founded upon the great truth that the Negro is not equal to the white man—that slavery is his natural and normal condition" (714). While her epithet underscores that the Civil War as fought by southerners was certainly fought for wrong reasons, the play itself argues that white northerners were fighting for objectives that were only slightly less base in terms of their innate self-interest and greed. The soldier-narrator quickly points out that "cotton seed, Europe, Africa, the New World, and Cotton . . . have all gotten mixed up together to make trouble" (714), emphasizing the role of economics in what is supposed to be a war fought over civil liberties. For the narrator, the war seems to be fought over the labor force, which is necessary to give meaning to the intersection of the cotton seed and the earth—labor he describes as so cheap that it is more cost efficient to "work a man to death and buy another one" rather than treat the first man more fairly (715).

Bearing the primary burden for exposition, the narrator explains the methods used for ensuring the success of slavery as well. He points out that Africans who were imported to serve as labor were from different parts of Africa and, therefore, often unable to communicate. Traders and planters purposely combined these people in such a manner to prevent insurrection through their lack of a common language; the soldier-narrator explains that the laws enacted to prevent their becoming literate in the language of their new land were a continuance of this policy. Keeping the slaves separated from each other and from the greater populace by keeping them illiterate was a planned aspect of slavery from its very inception.

In its portrayal of southern whites, the play uses heavy irony to illustrate the lack of knowledge such men actually had about the conditions and mentality of the slaves who lived on their plantations. Everett, the son of a successful white planter, suggests that if the southern cause begins to fail, the Rebels can always "arm the blacks," and that they will join in the fight for the Confederacy. His father, Hiram, has no such fantasy and "salutes" his son for his lack of logic and inability to see that the "idea that you can give somebody a gun and make him fight for what he's trying like blazes to run away from in the first place" (719) is illogical and impractical. Looked at from the perspective of the play—a time when African Americans were still living in a country with conditions from which they often wanted to run away from but for which they were fully expected to fight in the event of war—these lines seem particularly resonant.

A self-made man southern style, Hiram came into the county where he now owns a prosperous plantation with four slaves and fifty dollars. He has managed to accomplish his great economic success in thirty-five years, and he is willing to fight to the death to defend the fortune he has made from the labor of his slaves. Yet his son is the real villain of the play: he insists that the country really needs "some decent legislation . . . to reopen the African slave trade" so that the plantation can yield the profits it once produced; as it is currently run by his father, he describes it as "a resort for slaves" where they work only nine-and-a half-hour days (721). One idea emerges clearly from their arguments: slavery is no longer as profitable as it once was, and the war is partly being waged to reclaim the right to continue to import cheaper labor from Africa.

The play closes just as the war begins. But the soldier, speaking in an epilogue, insists that slavery was allowed to end because it had become "a drag on the great industrial nation" that American wanted to become (735). When the soldier picks up his rifle to join the fray, he insists that he is fighting against slavery because its continuance would cost "our political and economic future" (735), implying that Northern whites are not fighting because of morality. He admits that slavery has already cost "much of our soul" (735); this loss, however, did not prompt whites to take up arms.

Hansberry's critique of those who fought in this war seems to indicate that they were not fighting to free the Negro but were fighting to ensure their own economic futures. She suggests that what appears to be white altruism is always motivated by greed—even when it appears to be constructed around the sympathetic ideals of freedom. The play argues that altruism is rare—if not altogether nonexistent; when the issue is war, the issue is economics. Hansberry's play sounds a note that had already received similar treatment in a work by one of her literary foremothers. In one of the earliest plays to deal with the complexity of the African American's dilemma about joining his country's struggles, "Mine Eyes Have Seen" (1918), Alice Dunbar-Nelson dramatizes the competing issues for the young male who is drafted. Certainly, she does not treat the issue of the black soldier who would fight to defend a system that enslaves him with the same level of absurdity as Hansberry: she does not argue that the African American who joins in the World War I cause is as misguided as an African American who would fight for the Confederacy. However, she does raise the issue, one that remains as almost as absurd, of the legitimacy of fighting for a country that does not provide equal treatment for all its citizens. By providing her protagonist, Chris, with additional demands upon his loyalty, she gives him an opportunity to refuse to serve in WWI through the possibility of a justifiable exemption. If he goes to war, he will be deserting his needy family to participate in a battle for a country that has allowed his father's murderer to go unpunished and which has denied him any social justice. For Chris, his sister and invalid brother are the "cause" that needs him, but Dan and Lucy remind him that he is also obligated to carry on the good name of the race; if he asks for this exemption, he risks being seen as cowardly. This assumption would also, he knows, reflect on all male members of his race.

This issue—the recurring need to prove African American manhood—is a focal point of the play. While Chris points out that the white children who are dying are no different from "our little black babies" who are being thrown in the flames by "our fellow countrymen" who he suggests are reminiscent of "the worshippers of Moloch" without the excuse of a religious rite (176), he eventually seems unable to resist the call to battle because Julia points out that "it is our country—our race" (177). This pronouncement coincides with the music of a passing band that is playing "The Battle Hymn of the Republic," and his sister's pleas. The sentimental appeal of the legitimate battle cause represented by the music juxtaposes Chris's own pronouncement that no man should have to suffer the indignity of being called a "slacker and a weakling" (177). When he hears the music, Chris squares his shoulders and admits that his eyes have also "seen the glory." This statement becomes the metaphorical announcement of his decision to enlist. The symbolism is clear both for his family and for the audience. That Dunbar-Nelson intends us to find Chris's decision correct and honorable is also clear. When Lucy speaks of being able to get on without Chris's help and concludes with her pronouncement of pride at his decision, the audience is clearly intended to concur.

This one-act treatment of the complicated dilemma with its frequent use of gaming metaphors suggests that the theme of war and the choice to participate in it takes on "chancier" ramifications when the man making that choice is African American. If he refuses to fight, he can, in effect, register his resistance to the prejudice he is daily asked to endure, but his refusal also seems to confirm white prejudices about his general worthiness and manliness. Dunbar-Nelson's approval of Chris's decision to join is complicated; she allows the audience to understand his dilemma and to understand its unfairness. Therefore, her appeal for black enlistment is certainly more qualified than some of those which were offered in the contemporary commentaries for *Crisis* magazine. Many of these strongly advocated black participation in the war because the editor, W. E. B. Du Bois, hoped that black participation in the defeat of an avowedly racist enemy would allow

African Americans to make important gains on racial fronts at home.[1]
The June 1920 issue of *Crisis* carried a play by Joseph Seamon Cotter
in which two American soldiers, one white and one black, die hand in
hand, wondering why they have been unable to live in such closeness at
home. The chance of this occurring on the battlefield was highly
unlikely; Jim Crow practices were the rule for African Americans on
both sides of the Atlantic. Contrasted with these male visions of war as
a venue through which the African American could prove his
worthiness, redeem his manhood, and be accepted by white society,
Dunbar-Nelson's play scarcely seems sentimental. Her frequent use of
tropes of chance help undercut its apparent sentimental appeals.

Dunbar-Nelson's gaming metaphors parallel the war metaphors
which women writers frequently adopt even when they write about the
African American struggle for equality. The war metaphors become a
dramatic lexicon that demonstrates the private pain that results from
public hypocrisy. Nowhere does this lexicon speak with greater
resonance than in Adrienne Kennedy's *A Rat's Mass* (1965). By
combining the images of Nazism and incest, she paints a moving
portrait of the consequences of prejudice for young children. Although
the war is confined to the metaphorical, the metaphor is essential for
illuminating the African American struggle.

In Kennedy's surrealistic play, Brother and Sister Rat have animal
characteristics: he combines a rat's head and tail with a human body,
while she has a human head and a rat's tail and belly. These
characteristics seem to symbolize the animal-like characteristics that
prejudiced whites arbitrarily assign to people of African descent. In his
hallucinations, Brother Rat envisions Nazis who surround the dying
baby that seems to be the result of his incestual act with his sister.
Symbolically, the Nazis represent Rosemary and white America—
enforcers of white, preconceived ideas about black Americans. Because
Brother and Sister Rat want to please their white friend Rosemary, they
are unable to refuse to act in the stereotypical ways that she,
representative of whites in general, expects and demands. Sitting on top
of the slide, exalted as a white Goddess, Rosemary demands that these
two perform the sexual act that she wants but is too inhibited to
demand. In a perverted, voyeuristic manner, Rosemary—"the first girl
[they] ever fell in love with" tells them that if they love her, they will
do what she wants.

Following the literal action of the play sometimes proves difficult
as is often true in Kennedy's drama. But Kay, Sister Rat, seems to have

become pregnant by Blake, Brother Rat. As a result of the guilt they now feel for their innocent act (innocent because it is conducted at the suggestion of one whose Catholicism would seem to indicate she is versed in the study of sin and, therefore, not one who should insist that her friends commit an specifically forbidden act), they believe they have been literally enveloped by rats. Thus, the physicality of their rat-like appearance is also symbolic. They refer to their time of innocence, their lack of knowledge and guilt prior to the incestuous act on the slide, as the time "when we were young before the War, and Rosemary our best friend" (86). Kay seems uncertain of what has transpired, asking "What were those things she made us do while she watched?" (87). The brother wants to be a Nazi so that he can kill his sister, his partner in guilt.

With the lines—"Before rat blood came onto the slide we sailed. We did not swing in chains before blood, we sang with Rosemary. Now I must go to battle"—Blake (Brother Rat) seems to suggest that white Americans also entrap black Americans to fight their wars as a way of redeeming themselves from the crimes that white Americans have insisted black Americans perform (87). When Rosemary speaks, her statement is not ambiguous. She declares that "the Nazis will get you on the battlefield" (87), implying that wars are also a legal method by which white Americans commit black genocide.

Blake appeals to the Great Caesars—representatives of other, more victorious warriors—to wait until he can once again be as he was before encountering "Rosemary with the worms in her hair" (88-89). The brother and sister finally predict a just war that will produce a real spring as its aftermath. This war will occur when they grow up and hang their persecutors so that they can walk again through the trees and innocence that they seem to be allowed only when they are free of the white oppression represented by Rosemary and Nazis. Blake suggests that his freedom can only come from putting a bullet in his head, and then his "battle will be done" (90). Blake's internalization of Rosemary and society's projected recriminations and false accusations has become what he calls "the secret of his battlefield" (90).

In the battlefield of black America, "God is hanging and shooting us," the "rats" argue (91), and everywhere they go they seem to step in each other's blood. When Rosemary explains that her greatest grief was the life that Kay and Blake shared together, the play also suggests that whites participate in this genocide because of a jealous reaction to what they perceive as blacks' greater ability to feel and respond to life.

Sending young black men off to die at the hands of the Nazis seems one way of eliminating the source of this jealousy and of avoiding recognizing their own shortcomings.

The play terminates with the extermination of the rats. Rosemary calls this death her wedding to Blake. This death struggle is the only marriage that is reserved for white and black America. The Nazis arrive, marching, bearing shotguns, and Brother and Sister Rat realize that they will soon become "headless" in a place that no longer contains "sounds of shooting in the distance" (92). When the procession of soldiers fires on the brother and sister, they—after attempting to scamper to safety—are felled by the shots. When the curtain falls, only Rosemary remains standing and inviolate. This bleak vision seems to argue that whites will prevail and eliminate African Americans, unless they hang their oppressors from trees. In the world of the play, America is itself a battlefield, and African American men and women must join the battle to survive. They are under attack and must arm themselves appropriately or disappear. The play argues convincingly against any success of ameliorating this undeclared war between the races.

The war that Kennedy describes is psychological as well. The reification of Rosemary and her whiteness, her supposed superiority that allows her to command others to perform the deeds she wishes to witness without running the risks of participation, her continued appeal to Blake even after he is aware of her duplicity, and her power suggest the colonization process and its full sway over the African American self-concept. Rosemary's complicity in the deaths is evident in both her actions and, symbolically, in the worms in her hair; they mark her as a carrier of death and decay for people such as Kay and Blake.

This play treats war as inevitable, as a natural part of the black condition—and one that the best of intentions and home lives cannot prevent blacks from joining. Blake and Kay have not grown up in an urban wasteland, but in the supposedly more idyllic world of a "midwestern neighborhood" of "Italians, Negroes and Jews," where even Holy Communion dresses and the Catechism fail to teach the Rosemarys the moral lessons that they would need to refuse to accept their part in this war of persecution. Blake and Kay have loving parents who have tried to protect them, and while these children would seem to be far away from the urban battlefields of gang wars and drive-by shootings, they are, nonetheless, unsafe because of the institutionalized war against African Americans.

All of the writers discussed thus far seem to demonstrate that the victims of war are often found far from its battlefields. But no playwright shows how direct such victimization can be in a more convincing manner than Ntozake Shange. The lady in red's description of beau willie's war-damaged psyche in *for colored girls who have considered suicide/ when the rainbow is enuf* illustrates that the psychologically wounded who survive wars often return to vent their hurt and anger on those who have remained at home. When beau willie drops his children to their death, it becomes clear that the greatest victims of war are often found far from its official battlefields.

The description of beau willie is that of someone who is having a psychotic breakdown. He has stopped worrying about cleanliness: "lil specks of somethin from tween his toes or the biscuits from the day before ran in the sweat that tucked the sheet into his limbs" (55). He seems to be almost catatonic, like "an ol frozen bundle of chicken" (55). He leaves his bed only to search for wine or water to drink and waits for friends who will possibly bring him "some blow or some shit/ anythin" (55). The narrator, the lady in red, repeats that there is no air, indicating the claustrophobic atmosphere of the room and the relationship between the couple.

The lights beau willie sees in the alleys remind him of search lights in Vietnam, and he retreats under the covers to wait for an "all clear." The narrator implies that crystal is sympathetic, but beau willie is unable to accept her sympathy and insists that nothing is wrong with him. When the narrator delivers the lines "any niggah wanna kill Vietnamese children more n stay home & raise his own is sicker than a rabid dog" (55), we realize that she is repeating crystal's response, but she also seems to be making a judgment that is her own and perhaps that of Shange as well. Using street vernacular to capture the intensity and emotion of the scene, Shange's diction reverberates with the tension between the couple and the war that beau willie has brought home with him.

That this tension is new to the couple is also clear; it's "how their thing had been goin since he got back" (55). Beau willie has returned with a deep cynicism that makes him suspicious of everyone—even crystal's role as mother and the legitimacy of his children. The couple have been together since she was thirteen, but his war experience has taught him to distrust her, just as it has undermined his belief in himself.

Crazy, denied veterans benefits to go to school, and placed in remedial classes, beau willie has little to feel good about. He turns his anger toward the only safe victims, crystal and their children. The intense craziness of his behavior is also captured in the frenzied language of the narrator: "so he wen to get the high chair/ & lil kwame waz in it/ & beau waz beatin crystal with the high chair & her son" (57). The soldier uses any weapon that is necessary for his survival, and beau willie has simply taken this edict to its extreme in civilian form.

By alternating the versions of the story from that of crystal to that of beau willie, Shange lets the audience enter inside the tortured world of beau willie. He sees his own behavior as logical, maintaining that all he really wanted to do was marry her so he can "be a man in the house" (57). This plea illustrates that war has failed to provide the promised feeling of manhood and acceptance for its black soldiers. Beau willie has been rejected upon his return and is unable to hold his job as a taxi driver because the war has left him fragile and paranoid, convinced that his customers are out to kill him for $15. His tour in Vietnam has left him even less prepared to compete for the symbols of manhood that he needs to feel worthy.

He also has the crazy man's ability to charm and dispel distrust in his would-be victims. He charms his daughter and uses her to convince crystal that he can be trusted; suddenly he oozes kindness, and this proves fatal because crystal finds this treatment so irresistible. When the narrator describes his holding the children out of the window, the audience is already prepared for the disaster that will follow, for we have been unconvinced by his show of tenderness and distrust his intentions. The sudden flat "& he dropped em," nonetheless, takes us by surprise. The audience is stunned, realizing that the two young children have joined the many Vietnamese children as innocent victims of war. If beau willie thought he would gain respect and a place in American society by risking his life in Vietnam, he has certainly been sadly disappointed. This disappointment is directed at those who are closest to him and those who are even more vulnerable than he.

Most of these playwrights have dealt with wars that do not reflect the personal interest and freedom of black participants; Hansberry never looks at the black soldiers who were fighting for the union army, so she is unable to give us the kind of fervor captured in the film *Glory*. But the playwright Anna Deavere Smith looks at war that is fought for one's own freedom and suggests that such wars call for a different response.

In her work *Piano*, published as a work in process, Smith places this struggle on a large sugarcane plantation outside Santiago de Cuba in Cuba in 1898, shortly before the Spanish American war. Her main female character, Susanna, a Cuban woman of Congolese descent who is employed as a maid in the household of wealthy Spanish aristocrats, is actively involved in the fight to rid her country of this foreign influence. Her employers are unaware of her activities.

Susanna disguises herself and her activities by wearing highly starched uniforms and appearing to be the perfect, dedicated servant. She keeps her hair in a tight bun and makes every effort to downplay her African features. When she first appears in the play's manuscript, she seems to be fully under the sway of her Castilian-speaking employers, particularly Alicia. But slowly Smith reveals the subterfuge that Susanna is employing to keep her employers unaware while she manages to subvert Alicia's loyalty to both her husband and the Spanish cause.

Smith first develops Susanna's power over her employer by showing us how Susanna is able to persuade Alicia to ignore her husband's rules and allow the young, as-yet-unnamed Rosa to be fed in exchange for work. Alicia's reliance upon Susanna for companionship and approval is quickly apparent.

Another part of Susanna's disguise seems to be the rather rough treatment that she gives to Rosa once she is hired. When the young girl masters her lessons in washing the floor that surrounds the piano, Susanna rewards her by calling her "good little criollito mulatto" and tells her that she can see how well she is doing and how smart she is. The young girl has a natural ability to play the piano; just by watching her employer, she is soon able to create music that she manages to play when she is not being watched. Carlito discovers her talent and asks her to accompany him as he plays his violin.

Alicia, who really has very little talent with the piano, has even less at running her household. She depends upon Susanna for everything—even for giving orders to the cook, and she accepts without question the stories about her ancestors that Susanna passes along to her. The family falsely assumes that Susanna will protect them from the revolution. When Eduardo's brother, a Spanish Army General, arrives as part of the war effort, he insists on being served Spanish food, and Alicia is unable to find a cook who can provide the Anadalusian specialties he demands. His cultural imperialism extends beyond food; he is upset when Alicia and her son perform German and American music, insisting that true music is written by Spanish composers and asking Carlito to play a zarzuela or flamenco. When Carlito responds that a violin is not the same as a guitar, Smith underscores the stupidity of colonial elitism that assumes that one culture's music is easily imposed upon another and that one reacts negatively to all food and art that is not one's own. Antonio eventually cables to his headquarters to send a cook because he cannot—or will not—eat African food. He decides that he should have affairs only with Indians because "you can plant something with the Indians. But the Africans. You can forget it. Willful out of stubbornness and ignorance . . . I would not waste my seed on an African" (20). General Antonio has been rounding up people and placing them into *reconcentrados* and attacking the insurrectionists at every opportunity.

It is appropriate then that Chan, the Cuban Chinese cook who prepares African recipes that have been in Alicia's family for years, is the soldier in the Cuban liberation forces who kidnaps Carlito and holds him for ransom. Carlito is aware of his uncle's unsavory character, calling him "a monster" who is "greedy like a hound" and "disgusting like a pig," a man "who boasts about the things that thieves boast of" (15). He sees Susanna as "a queen of her people" who will keep him safe. His observations, words of wisdom from a child, are also meant to criticize the character of soldiers, such as Antonio who fight wars for their personal greed rather than for any democratic ideals and to celebrate strong women such as Susanna whose actions are built upon a principle of caring. Carlito also understands that Rosa has musical talent and insists that she develop that ability by giving her lessons. He is also more aware than his father and uncle and is undeceived by Susanna and Alicia who pretend to shop when they are actually attending African ceremonies.

With their house seized as a military headquarters and their son kidnapped, Alicia and Eduardo begin to realize just how costly their fantasy life has been. Alicia begins whispering "Cuba Libre," and the audience realizes that her sympathies have been with the Cubans is this struggle. In her newly liberated state, she tells her husband that he can no longer use his power over her to illustrate his manliness and suggests that he "wrestle" with his brother instead. She calls him "a cuckold to [his] brother's bloodthirsty ambition," a weak man who "can't get [his] honor to rise" (36). She is upset that her house that has been "a friend to the Indians, the Africans, the diplomats, the composers, the intellectuals" will now become the military headquarters for a cause that is mercenary in its thrust.

The play ends with a woman, Susanna, killing the General as "the servant of Chango and Santa Barbara" (52). Clearly, she has struck a blow for the liberation of her people; her cause is a just one. Smith's portrayal of the unsavory general allows the audience to applaud the manner of his death and the female courage that is evident in Susanna's character.

These five plays suggest that African American women are less likely than their male counterparts to see war as an opportunity for African American men to prove their worth and manhood. The women's plays are more concerned with the issue behind the war and whether or not it represents a cause worth dying for. Lorraine Hansberry suggests that whites have always been unwilling to die for the rights of blacks and asks us to consider why blacks have been expected to make such sacrifices for whites. By focusing on the Civil War and reminding us that the Union was moved more by economic concerns than by its concern for liberating African Americans, she underscores the historical marginality of African American males. Alice Dunbar-Nelson's earlier vision was somewhat more optimistic, perhaps reflecting the hopes of African Americans who volunteered for service in WWI with the idea that their battle worthiness would allow their fellow Americans to recognize and accept their black manhood. If her vision seems naive today, it is still important as a reflection of African Americans' continued aspirations following the collapse of Reconstruction. Adrienne Kennedy takes Hansberry's bleak vision farther, showing through her symbolic language that America's wars, in reality, often function as a convenient form of black genocide. She asks her audience to recognize that the real war is the war between blacks and whites in America. Ntozake Shange elucidates the way in which the battlefields of wars fought on foreign soils intrude into the most private and personal of spheres of American life. War can prove equally deadly for the families of returning soldiers. Only Anna Deavere Smith presents a situation in which blacks are fighting for their own liberation and, therefore, are making a wise decision in risking their lives. So that fighting for one's liberty cannot be confused with the issues of manhood, Smith presents us with a woman who is willing to go to battle—a woman who emerges victorious through a combination of artifice and physical courage. Yet Smith also shows us that even the justified struggle for freedom has human costs that often seem prohibitive.

Triply othered, these five women playwrights manage, nevertheless, to employ their artistic voices to speak out against the woe that is war. Their compelling voices insist that we concur with their judgments, and they illustrate that African American women can cross the battle lines of race and gender to stake out new claims for their voices. Their plays that explore the cost and pain of war become sophisticated weapons aimed at the senseless loss of African American life as a result of America's materialist and racist national culture.

NOTES

1. For a thorough discussion of Du Bois's complicated reaction to black participation in WWI, see Michel Fabre's essay "W. E. B. Du Bois and World War I."

WORKS CITED

Dunbar-Nelson, Alice. "Mine Eyes Have Seen." *Black Theater USA: 45 Plays by Black Americans, 1847-1974*. Ed. James V. Hatch. New York: Macmillan, 1974. 173-178.

Fabre, Michel. *From Harlem to Paris: Black American Writers in France, 1840-1980*. Urbana, IL: U of Illinois P, 1991.

Hansberry, Lorraine. *The Drinking Gourd. Black Theater USA: 45 Plays by Black Americans, 1847-1974*. Eds. James Hatch and Ted Shine. New York: Free, 1974. 713-736.

Hemingway, Ernest, ed. *Men at War: The Best Stories of All Time*. New York: Crown, 1942.

Kennedy, Adrienne. "A Rat's Mass." *New Black Playwrights*. Ed. William Couch, Jr. New York: Avon, 1970. 83-92.

Shange, Ntozake. *for colored girls who have considered suicide when the rainbow is enough*. New York: Macmillan, 1977.

Smith, Anna Deavere. *Piano*. New York: Theatre Communications Group, 1989.

Stillman, Richard J. *Integration of the Negro in the U. S. Armed Forces*. New York: Praeger, 1968.

Wilson, Edmund. *The Shores of Light: A Chronicle of the Twenties and Thirties*. New York: Farrar, 1952.

Mara, Angelina Grimké's Other Play and the Problems of Recovering Texts

Christine R. Gray

Researchers who work with primary texts that have remained unpublished serve two roles for their readers. They function as reporters and as interpreters. As a reporter, a researcher informs her audience of what she has discovered and perhaps how she came across the material. Objectively, the researcher describes the contents of what has been uncovered, its form, and perhaps its state or condition. In this role, a researcher is neutral, acting only as a conduit between the text she has located and the reader. Or, as textual analyst James Thorpe writes, "The role of textual criticism is to provide essential mediation between the author and his audience" (50). In her other role, that of interpreter, the same researcher comments on the document by placing it within the context of other materials by the same writer. She may point out various themes and concerns in the text and subtext as they relate to the time in which the piece was written. She might also evaluate the text aesthetically and formally and go on to use it as a piece of evidence, so to speak, in supporting her assertion that the work is part of, or reflects a specific tradition.

If, as the reporter, the researcher has, however, either overlooked or been unaware of other versions of the text, then, quite obviously, the interpretation will be incomplete, skewed—one might say flawed—for it has not taken into account the other drafts of the work. Consequently, we as readers do not learn of the evolution of the text, that is, the process it went through as it became what appears to be the final text.

We are not informed of, as textual scholar Ralph G. Williams writes, its "versional stages" (45). And we as readers are the poorer for this gap, for we do not learn of, for example, the options the writer considered, the growth of the document in its embryonic stages and shapes. For it is the entire text—in all its forms, changes, deletions, emendations—that gives us some insight, albeit limited and perhaps uncertain, into the mind of the author during the composing process. As textual critic G. Thomas Tanselle has noted, a researcher "cannot simply accept any text that is convenient but must take some pains to investigate the textual history of the work" (30).

In doing recovery work, researchers must often leaf patiently through papers and scraps in their attempts to reconstruct a text. This sifting makes the process of recovery painstaking, for each page—its contents and its physicality even—may reveal clues to assembling a whole text or to the possibility of establishing such. The process of reconstructing the text places a greater burden on the researcher than if the work were available to readers in some form, however marred. Instead, as Thorpe avers, the researcher as the mediator must be precise and fully aware of the multiple aspects of the document before issuing commentary or interpretation.

It is the act of reporting and subsequent interpreting that I wish to address here. I do so in relation to *Mara*, an obscure play written by an African American woman in the early part of the twentieth century. This play serves as an example of the many problems that can arise as primary African American documents and texts that are being recovered, reported on, and interpreted are either misread or read only in part. Those who have commented on *Mara* have based their interpretations on the draft of the play labelled "complete" by its repository library, the Moorland Spingarn Research Center (MSRC) at Howard University.[1] Their commentary on this play allows us to realize the errors in interpretation and the gaps in information that result when a researcher assumes that "complete draft" is the same as "final draft."[2] The errors that arise from limiting oneself to only a designated "complete draft" are magnified by the fact that the play discussed herein was neither published nor produced; in shaping their opinions, readers are, therefore, dependent on the commentaries of these writers for their knowledge of this play.

* * *

Research on the best-known plays written during the "New Negro Renaissance" often explores what have been called "kitchen table plays." Written by African American women, these one-act dramas focus on the concerns of female characters over passing, miscegenation, poverty, and child rearing. African American dramatists of the early twentieth century also chose lynching as a topic; these plays addressed the threat and reality of death by hanging by whites to control a black community.[3] Angelina Grimké (1880-1958), a Washingtonian by birth, is usually credited with laying the foundation for subsequent African American dramatists. Believed to have written the first lynching play, *Rachel*, she has been called "the mother of black drama."[4]

Although notice has been given to Angelina Grimké's poetry, her two plays, *Rachel* and *Mara*, have received relatively scant attention. Of the two, *Rachel*, no doubt because it was published and produced, has received more critical notice. First performed in March 1916 in Washington, D.C., *Rachel*, presumably written in 1915-16, was presented as the NAACP's response to the film *Birth of a Nation*, which played in that city in 1915. Although important in the history of American drama and in race relations in America, the play was not widely produced; instead, as Gloria Hull points out in her chapter on Grimké in *Color, Sex, and Poetry*, "It required publishing *Rachel* [in 1920] to make it the consciousness-raising instrument that Grimké wished it to be . . . . As a book, *Rachel* commanded considerably more attention" (120- 21).

Although no one in *Rachel* is lynched during the play, the piece fits within this tradition because it highlights the effect death by hanging has on the title character and her brother. To a large extent the course of the play is determined by Rachel's learning of these violent deaths. After hearing that her father and brother were lynched several years earlier, Rachel, a young African American woman, vows never to marry, for she does not want to bring children into a world where the possibility of such ruthlessness exists.

Several scholars who have written on *Rachel* have mentioned what is believed to be Grimké's only other play, *Mara*. Gloria Hull, Claudia Tate, and Jeanne-Marie Miller agree that *Mara* is a lynching play. Tate speaks of *Mara* as evidence that Grimké was "obsessed with lynching" (217); Miller points out the "brutal lynchings of the family" (518); and Hull writes of lynching as "the subject" of *Mara* (124). All three seem to have based their claim that *Mara* is a play in the lynching tradition on a photocopied draft of the play that the MSRC has labeled as "complete."

There are, in fact, several versions of *Mara*, none of which was designated as final by Grimké and none of which was produced. From the box holding the *Mara* papers, two versions or drafts can be sorted out that we might call "dominant." That is, although there are various versions and revisions of the play, only two of them form two complete manuscripts. For simplicity in discussing these two versions, I have labelled these two manuscripts the lynching version and the romance version. It is only the lynching version of *Mara* that seems to have been read by these scholars, for they neither note, discuss, nor allude to the changes in plot found among the papers of the other versions. In relying only on one draft of the play, the few scholars who have written on *Mara* have used the play as an example of Grimké's involvement with plays in the lynching tradition. Based on what the MSRC has designated as the "complete play," Grimké, it seems, *did* write *Mara* as another lynching play, in the same tradition as *Rachel*. A closer examination of the balance of the drafts and pages in the *Mara* file, however, raises a question about this assumption: Although the MSRC may have marked one draft as complete, is it necessarily Grimké's final manuscript, the one scholars should rely on, in discussing *Mara*? In going to the other folders, one comes across evidence suggesting otherwise.

Scholarly attention paid to and recovery work carried out on the work of Grimké and other pioneering African American female playwrights have increased over the past several years. That these and other scholars have not delved into the *Mara* file is not, however, surprising. Through even a cursory glance at the *Mara* papers, a researcher is forewarned of the complications and questions that the file contains. The contents of the Act One folder alone hold such a jumble of papers that a determination of which draft is final is, at best, highly improbable: the box of *Mara* papers contains Act I, scene one; Act I, scene one, copy two; Act I, scene two, revision; and Act I, "odd sections." Further, within each of the other folders are pages marked "insert," while other pages have numerous notes in the margins. This panoply of parts and pastiches is true of each of the four acts for each of the play's two main versions. In addition, the *Mara* holdings include four revisions of the play and then, finally, the photocopied "complete draft." The confusing state of these papers may go toward explaining why *Mara* lies, still in holograph form, in folders and fragments in the Moorland Spingarn Research Center.

As supported by the various manuscripts, Grimké must have struggled with the writing of *Mara*. The several folders of the play offer parts of various plots, maybe three or four—anyone reading through the entire file box would agree that the number is difficult to determine. Formally, the play texts make up, almost literally, a quilt of confusing patches and pages, few of which can be easily sewn together. For example, the types of paper on which Grimké wrote the play vary widely. Some paper has a linen finish; some is plain typing paper; some is pulp paper; some pages are of a twenty-pound weight paper, while others are onion skin; some pages have yellowed with age, while others have not. Parts of the play are on paper lined in either blue or turquoise, while other pages are unlined. Some pages of the manuscript are written in either blue, brown, or black inks; other pages are written in pencil. In several instances, the handwriting is small and faint; on other pages a large, thick scrawl reaches from margin to margin. Some pages are held together with rusty pins. Marginalia, inserts, revisions, parts of copies, crossed-out paragraphs, changes in the names of characters, new scenes and revised scenes, and the deletion of characters add further to the frustrations that a researcher faces in wrestling with *Mara*. How can such a collection be assembled into a comprehensible text? Is a satisfactory reconstruction even possible?

Perhaps the first question to attempt to answer in unpacking *Mara* concerns the date of the play's composition. The date is significant, I believe, for by establishing it we are able to link the plays *Rachel* and *Mara* and thereby gain further insight into the composition of *Mara*. Hull remarks that the play "should probably be dated sometime in the early to middle 1920s" (124). Drawing apparently from Hull's research, Tate suggests "some time around 1920" as the date (217). In her essay on Angelina Grimké, Miller omits dating *Mara* altogether; the MSRC does not offer a date for the play.

In excavating the *Mara* file—that is, in going beyond the MSRC's "complete draft"—one finds abundant evidence that the play was written several years earlier than has been thought, possibly between 1915 and 1917. Written on the backs of various miscellaneous draft pages are short essays and poems in Grimké's handwriting. A poem and an essay focus on Grimké's concern for African American soldiers leaving for Europe to fight in World War I, which the United States entered in 1917. Another page is an unfinished essay on the distortion

of African American history found in textbooks and the effect this
might have on students, black and white. This would no doubt have
been of concern to Grimké, who was teaching English at Dunbar High
School at the time. One page of a draft has, amidst the lines of the play,
a set of initials and a date typed with a red ribbon: FWC 10/19/15.
Centered on that same page is "Miss Grimké." Perhaps this was a cover
sheet from a student's paper that she had used as scrap for her draft of
Mara.

In relation to the play's date perhaps the most interesting
discoveries in the *Mara* file are remnants from an early version of
Rachel. In her initial drafts of this play, Rachel, the play's title
character, was named Janet. Several scraps of paper in the *Mara* file
have this same name, a feature which indicates that composition of
Mara may have begun as early as 1915, when Grimké was writing
Rachel. Indeed, at one point in the play Grimké gives, presumably by
mistake, the lines intended for the character Mara to a character named
Janet. Furthermore, a poem that Grimké included in *Rachel* is found
among the *Mara* papers. Entitled "In Twilight," the eight-line verse is
recited by Rachel in the third, and final, act of that play. These
fragments of evidence suggest that there is a greater connection
between these two plays than has previously been considered, and that
connection may lie within a drama competition in 1915.

A curious and unexplored area for research is the NAACP's drama
contest, which was announced in *Crisis*, its journal, in March 1915. The
organization had hoped to reach a white audience via the stage as a way
of defusing possible racial tensions from that autumn's showing of the
controversial *Birth of a Nation* in Washington. In subsequent issues of
the magazine, the contest was never again mentioned, nor has this
writer located any letters or follow-up announcements on the contest in
the NAACP files between 1914 and 1917. It is not known, therefore,
with which plays, if any, *Rachel* competed. One cannot help but raise
an eyebrow, however, on learning that Archibald Grimké, Angelina
Grimké's father, was the head of the Washington branch of the NAACP
at the time of the contest. It does not seem too far-fetched to suggest
that he had a hand in the selection of *Rachel*, his daughter's own
submission, as the contest winner.[5] Relying on the evidence of the
names from *Rachel*, the poem, and the dated material found in the
Mara files, it seems highly possible that *Mara* was one of Angelina
Grimké's early drafts as she created her entry for the contest, the one
for which *Rachel* was selected. Perhaps her father dissuaded her from

submitting *Mara* in that—whether the romance or the lynching version—it would not appeal to a white audience.

In addition to its being the first African American lynching play, *Rachel* is noteworthy for avoiding a tradition popular on American stages black or white in the early twentieth century: black stereotypes.[6] Her main characters do not speak in dialect; the black character is not the butt of the humor, and the actions and plot are not dependent on superstition, the image of the happy plantation, or ignorance. They display no elements of folk ways or culture. Instead, her characters speak in standard English, and their homes reflect aspirations to bourgeois levels of taste—servants, dinner parties, paintings by European artists, pianos, and books, for example. Further, her characters differ also from plays by her contemporaries in that they are not flat. Instead, Grimké's characters are three dimensional in that they reveal their thoughts, fears, and anxieties and, thereby, a depth rare in plays either portraying African Americans or written by African Americans up to that time.

Grimké did break away from her predecessors and her contemporaries writing for the African American stage. She was not, however, able to divorce her work from elements of romance and melodrama. Both are woven thickly into the texts of the romance version of *Mara*. In *Domestic Allegories of Political Desire*, Tate writes of texts at the turn of the century that convey a political agenda through the seemingly inoffensive form of the novel and of the "genteel" female characters who fill those pages. *Mara* is similar to *Rachel* in this respect, for both characters use ornate language and are imaginative, sensitive, and given to emotional outbursts. They appear to be educated and, considering their surroundings, are what would be considered genteel, refined. They reflect the Victorian taste and propriety popular in the latter part of the nineteenth and first decade of the twentieth centuries.

Initially, *Mara* seems to connect two traditions in the writing of African American women, lynching plays and the genteel tradition. In her essay "Angelina Grimké: Playwright and Poet," Miller remarks on "Grimké's use of black genteel characters, whose refinement is in glaring contrast to the cruelties waged against them solely because of their race" (519). Tate, too, writes of Grimké's reliance on the genteel tradition of the nineteenth century to bolster her own reading of *Mara* as a lynching play.

I question, however, Tate's placement of *Mara* within the tradition of lynching plays. If one reads only what the MSRC has designated as a "complete draft," *Mara* is indeed a lynching play. The three main characters—Mara, her mother, and her father—are presumably lynched off stage at the play's close. If, however, as Tanselle suggests, researchers "take some pains" to review the versional texts, the play and questions of the playwright's intention become much richer and exceedingly complex. In fact, the play moves in a different direction and becomes, thus, part of a different tradition, that of Victorian melodrama. In reading the alternate text, the romance version, one can ascertain that *Mara* is not necessarily about race at all. It is, instead, shaped as a nineteenth-century romantic melodrama. If, as Jerome McGann has noted, "Every text . . . is a social text" and is thereby "a material event or set of events, a point in time" (2-3), the romance version of *Mara* should be considered more closely than it has heretofore been. Overlooked in favor of the lynching version of the play, the romance version reflects Grimké's tastes and background, her "point in time," more accurately, it seems, than the lynching version.

The two dominant versions of *Mara* merit consideration. In Act I, scene two, both versions, differing from one another only in the names of minor characters, have similar plots. In both, Mara dances joyfully in the moonlight as Lester Carew, a wealthy, young white man, spies on her over the wall surrounding her family's estate. Noticing him, she pauses, and, as Grimké writes, "stands still—as if drawn by some irresistible force she goes toward him." Mara, who has been sheltered her entire eighteen years, asks him a series of childlike questions: Is he a giant because he can look over the ten-foot wall? Does he work in a circus? Have people told him that he's beautiful? Mara tells him that he may be evil, for, she says, her mother has told her that things that are beautiful may be so. She tells him that the wall surrounding the Cedars, the family estate, was built to keep out evil and to keep in good. After learning from her who else lives on the property, Carew asks to be let in. When she doesn't have the key, he prepares to leave and says he will return only if she promises not to tell anyone of his visit.

In Act II, one week has passed. Here the portrayal of Mara in the romance version differs significantly from that of the "complete draft." In the romance draft, she is heavily involved with Carew. Rather than rejecting his advances, she welcomes them. Indeed, she seems even coy and flirtatious. Waiting for her to come out at night, Carew hides in the shrubbery as he watches the house. He whistles "several beautiful bird notes" to get Mara's attention. Unlike the lynching version, Mara voices her resentment of the wall that surrounds the family estate. She tells Martha, the maid, that she is upset by her father's insistence that she remain indoors:

> The dark is so big, so black and I'm so so little. . . . Am I wicked? Don't you think [my father] treats me as though I were a prisoner? Am I not a prisoner? . . . All I can do is stand at the window and look at the beauty of it all until it hurts. Every simple thing out there calls and calls, calls me all day. . . .

Martha gives her permission to go outside briefly. Still hiding, Carew repeats the bird note as Mara walks outside in the dark toward the sound. They meet and look at each other. As she opens her mouth, he places his fingers to his lips. She moves toward him slowly until they are face to face:

> *Carew*: Did you want me to come?
> *Mara*: Yes. How did you get over the wall?
> *Carew*: You have forgotten that I am a dream. Is there any boundary to
> dreams? . . . If you were sound asleep in that little white bed of yours and I came, would you be surprised?
> *Mara*: No, you have come so often since I saw you a week ago.
> *Carew*: I have come often?
> *Mara*: I haven't been able to think or to dream of anything but you.

Grimké writes that Mara "tries to read his soul and evidently sees sincerity in his eyes and smiles up at him tremulously, wistfully, happily."

> *Carew*: Don't you know that at the least sound dreams disappear—vanish. I have wanted you so—I know you can't understand that.
> *Mara*: I can understand. I have thought of you.
> *Carew*: Much?
> *Mara*: Yes. . . . When I have not been thinking of you, you have been just behind every thought.

She sits beside him and he asks if she comes out every night at this time.

Carew: You were made for moonlight—only you are more beautiful.

He asks to see her birthday ring as a pretense for holding her hand.

Carew: You begrudge me these few minutes of holding your hand. In your dreams haven't I ever touched you?
Mara: No, no, you mustn't.
Carew: When I come to you in your dreams, I am not satisfied with just this. And you do not resist me then when I do this [kisses the tip of her hand]. You turn to me and smile, Mara, isn't that so?
Mara: Oh, how do you know?
Carew: Mara, can't you guess. It's because your beautiful soul and mine are one. Don't you know it?
Mara: Yes.

She offers him her hand, which he kisses as well as her bare forearm and shoulder. When she draws away he accuses her of not caring for him. "Here's my hair," she tells him. Grimké describes the scene: "Carew draws her to him and kisses her hair and places a hand on either side of her face and raises it to him and looks into her eyes. She relaxes and sighs. He kisses her lids and then her mouth."

Carew: I wish I might be with you always here just like this. Don't you?
Mara: Yes.
Carew: Shall I return tomorrow night?
Mara: Oh yes, please.
He reminds her that she mustn't tell her father of his visits. Before he leaves, he tells her to wait a week to tell her father.
Mara: You will come tomorrow night?
Carew: Yes, and every night, shall I.
Mara: Oh, yes.

In this version, Grimké has shifted the focus of her play. No longer is the play about the features to which critics have pointed. That is, the play from this scene forward is not centered on race, lynching, the revenge Mara's father seeks for both the death of his enslaved mother and for Mara's rape. Instead, the play focusses on the awakening of Mara's sexuality. Indeed, the title of this version at one point was *Lust*. Dreamlike, protected, naive, Mara is beguiled by a young man of much experience. She seems to be attracted to him but skittish about this, her first encounter with a man. She is presented as a fragile, trusting young woman, one who is carried away by her imagination. As Grimké writes in her head notes to one draft, Mara is "innocent and ignorant of the world." In the lynching version, her breakdown, or derangement, in Acts III and IV are brought about by an implied sexual contact with Carew. As the draft of the romance version reveals, however, Mara encourages Carew's advances.

The MSRC's lynching version focuses on Richard Marston's settling of a debt for his mother's rape and death. Mara's madness is caused by the lust of the white man, Lester Carew. In Act III, Mara wanders outside during a thunderstorm and returns bedraggled; she has, presumably, been raped by Carew. Seeking revenge for this rape, Richard Marston fires a pistol and kills Carew. This deed leads to the lynching of the entire Marston family. In the romance version of the play, Mr. Marston's mother is not murdered but sold. Further, Mara is not raped but flirts with and lusts for Carew, the white man, as much as he does for her.

In Tate's interpretation, the Marston family is "walled off from the rest of the community in response to the prior murder of Mr. Marston's mother." She comments further that the wall cannot prevent a "lusting white man who rapes Mara on her eighteenth birthday" (217). In the text scholars have relied on, Marston's mother was beaten to death as Marston, a child at the time, heard her screams. In Grimké's headnote to one of the other play texts, however, Marston's mother was sold after his birth when the senior Carew tired of her sexually. She died of mistreatment but not in front of Marston or on that plantation, as Tate has written.

The final scenes of the two versions also have striking differences. In the lynching version, a gang of white men batter in the front door of the Marston home. Richard Marston sits in a chair silently. Ellen Marston stands between him and the angry crowd. The couple is dragged out of the house, presumably to be lynched. Mara, appearing at the top of the stairs, calmly witnesses this. Carrying a lily, a symbol for purity, against her heart and a lighted candle, she slowly descends the stairs. She seems oblivious to the tension and her impending death. As she comes down the stairs, she sings Elaine's Song from Tennyson's "Lancelot and Elaine" in his long poem *Idylls of the King*. Still in a deranged state, Mara, "in a soft wonderful voice," says "Death—I follow." Several men seize her and carry her out, where she is presumably hanged. One can only wonder how scholars could have overlooked these curious features of the play, for these elements are in the lynching version about which Tate, Hull, and Miller have written and which they have, presumably, read.[7] In their comments on the plays, why have these scholars not pointed out the peculiar mention of Lancelot in the manuscript?

The romance version is not as subtle in its reliance on Tennyson's poem "Lancelot and Elaine," for it contains numerous allusions to the British poet's popular poem. Tennyson's Elaine is a young woman who has been shielded from the world by her father. She has spent her life in a distant tower; she has never been in love nor even been exposed to the possibility of romance. Having lost his way, Lancelot arrives at the remote castle, where he meets Elaine. She imagines herself in love with him; he does not, however, return her affection. Heartbroken, she asks that on her death her body be placed on a bier in a lake and that both a lily and a letter professing her love for Lancelot are to be placed in her hands. She then dies of unrequited love for Lancelot.

The similarities between Tennyson's poem and Grimké's romance version of *Mara* are both fascinating and jarring. When meeting with Carew, Mara calls herself Elaine and says that Carew is Lancelot. As she tells her mother, "I am Elaine." She refers to the note that Elaine was holding at her death and asks if her mother has seen it. She later asks where the lilies are and says that she, Mara, must get a lily for Elaine. She remarks to her father that after Elaine "died out there [in the garden], she told me to come and bring her a lily." She tells her nursemaid that Lancelot will arrive presently and that she "shall be beautiful in his sight." She states that she "should be wearing lilies but for some reason [she] may not wear them any more." She then remarks that she "shall be dead soon."

In the romance version's final act, Mara descends the stairs to meet the waiting mob as she sings "The Song of Love and Death" from Tennyson's poem and carries a lily.[8] Grimké describes Mara as looking "like a spirit" with the "light of the candle cast[ing] a delicate golden radiance over her face—all trouble, care, perplexity have left it—it is full of wonderful, calm expectancy." Her final words before she dies are "Oh death I follow," which are Elaine's final words in her song as well.

In *Tennyson in America*, John O. Eidson notes that "it was the four *Idylls of the King* published in 1859 that opened to [Tennyson] the heart of the public and began that immense popularity which [Tennyson] never saw diminished" (148). At his death in 1892, Tennyson and his Arthurian poem were still tremendously popular in America. As Cornelius Weygandt has pointed out, "Americans all over the country heard Tennyson from the pulpit," and "his verses were on Christmas cards and calendars and in the poet's corner in newspapers and in the almanacs." His poetry would, no doubt, have been widely read by those who sought middle-class, or genteel, bearings, for Tennyson's treasured poetry was "for fifty years a parlor-table book in America" (Weygandt 109). The widespread popularity of Tennyson in the late nineteenth and early twentieth centuries suggests that it is highly probable that as a student Grimké studied Tennyson's poetry while she attended elite private schools in the North. More than likely she also taught his poetry in her English classes at Dunbar High School. Considering the nineteenth-century household in which Angelina Grimké was raised, it is probable as well that the romance of Tennyson's story poems appealed to the young, cloistered, imaginative woman that Angelina Grimké was.

The inclusion of and reliance on the Elaine-Lancelot motif displaces the much-noted emphasis on lynching that others have attributed to this play. Instead, the story becomes a romance from the nineteenth century, the period during which Grimké was educated and still lived, in a sense, under the strict controls her father set up around her.[9] Rather than a race play, *Mara* becomes a tale of newly awakened sexuality, of first love or infatuation, of unrequited love, a plot that would not be unlikely to the imagination of a young woman who lived under her father's rule, whether that young woman be Mara, the character; Elaine, the lily maid; or Angelina Grimké, the playwright.[10] These connections, as noted, cannot, however, be made without a reader's digging further into the holographs, beyond the designated "complete draft."

Aware of the variant texts that confound a simple reading of *Mara*, I question the haste with which other scholars have placed *Mara* in the category of lynching plays. Research shows that it does *not* fit neatly into this tradition. Indeed, lynching and its horrors were a concern to Grimké as is evident in *Rachel*. Still, a reading of the other version of Grimké's "other play," the alternate text of *Mara*, reveals another aspect of Grimké, her imagination, and in a sense her working out of situations in her own life about which we may never be aware.

In writing only on the "lynching" version—and in their attempts to place Grimké securely within this tradition only—these scholars do both the reader and Grimké an injustice. For readers are not told of Grimké's other play, one that can be considered as valid as the lynching version, and they are thereby limited in judging both her intentions and which play might indeed be final. Grimké, too, is given short shrift, for we are not allowed to peer into what seems to be a highly autobiographical text. Instead, readers have access only to the version on which scholars have chosen to comment. The play *Mara* did not spring from Grimké's head in a completed form. She seems to have struggled with the writing of the play. It is this struggle and the "progress of her process" to which readers are not privy if they do not hear of the play's other version. It is no doubt disappointing to some scholars of African American drama that Grimké may have written a romance rather than, or at least as well as, a lynching play, that she indulged her taste for Tennyson's poetry rather than being wrapped solely in the current concerns over lynching. Still, the romance version of *Mara* is much more provocative than the lynching version for what it reveals about the writer, her person, and about her process of composition. This other version of *Mara* is more intriguing than *Rachel* for what it reveals not about the tradition of lynching plays but about the playwright herself.

One can only wonder, as does textual critic Peter Shillingsburg, "what different conclusions the literary critic[s] might have reached had [they] started with a better-edited text and had [they] understood more about its genesis and production" (23). Shillingsburg, in the same essay, also raises a question germane to *Mara* and relevant to unpublished primary documents in general: "Should I present the work of art as a finished product or as a developing process?" (23) We might ask also whether a critic should comment only on a complete text or on both it and its versional drafts.

During the days and weeks spent attempting to unravel the various pages and scenes, I had, and continue to have, many questions, most of which are still unanswered and may always be so: Was there an event in Grimké's life that prompted her to write the romance version of *Mara*? Did she intend to have either version staged? How much does Mara, the character, reflect Grimké's life? Was the play ever completed to her satisfaction or was it still "in progress" when she abandoned it and perhaps began *Rachel*? What is the actual final draft, the version that Grimké herself intended to be the finished text of *Mara*? Can we ever know? Perhaps the only fact we can derive from looking closely at

Mara and all of its pieces is that Grimké wrote two plays, one a romance play and one a lynching play.

My greatest concern, however, is the willingness of scholars to accept the version of *Mara* that fits most comfortably into an agenda: that is, that because Grimké wrote one lynching play, *Rachel*, her other play, *Mara*, must be one as well. The critics who have written on *Mara* seem to have taken one of three paths: they have either relied on the earlier research of others for their commentary; or they have not looked beyond the manuscript designated as "complete"; or they have opted not to mention Grimké's romance version. On all counts, one text of *Mara* has been privileged and the other thereby suppressed. Unfortunately, close research continually reveals that what we might seek in the recovery of primary documents is not always what is found. Those of us who work in the recovery of primary materials have an obligation, almost a moral one, to report to our readers on all of the textual possibilities an author has left us to untangle, not only those possibilities that confirm our assumptions.

NOTES

1. A chief archivist at the library reports that the version labelled as "complete" was designated as such because it was the only draft the library could cull from the *Mara* papers. It was acknowledged that this complete version may well not be the final or only draft of the play.

2. As will be discussed, among the many pages in the *Mara* papers are the play's various texts and emendations. From these pages, two main, or "dominant" and quite different, drafts can be culled.

3. Although black men also wrote lynching plays, those by women have received the greatest attention by scholars. African-American women who wrote lynching plays include Marita Bonner, Georgia Douglas Johnson, and Alice Dunbar-Nelson.

4. James V. Hatch to the writer in a letter dated November 16, 1992.

5. In an essay on African American drama, Alain Locke pointed to Ridgely Torrence's *Three Plays for a Negro Theater* (1917) and Du Bois's *Star of Ethiopia* (1913) as being the starting points for non-musical, African American drama. He may have purposely overlooked *Rachel*, for there is evidence that Locke was miffed with Archibald Grimké. Locke's annoyance may have arisen over the choice of a genteel play, *Rachel*, rather than the folk plays Locke later advocated for black writers.

6.   A sampling of titles alone reveals how Grimké's *Rachel* and *Mara* are set apart from the usual stage fare at the time: *Strut Your Stuff* (1920), *Broadway Rastus* (1920), and *Chocolate Brown* (1921). African American William Wells Brown wrote two plays that were meant to be read, rather than performed, at abolitionist rallies: *The Escape* (1859) and *How to Give a Northern Man a Backbone* (1860?). Joseph Seamon Cotter's *Caleb the Degenerate*(1903), which promoted Booker T. Washington's philosophy, was also intended to be read.

7.   In the papers that seem to make up a third version, Mara goes mad and dies, her last word being "Daddy." Marston speaks angrily of the slavery of the old South and that of the new South: [S]ince I am only a colored man with a white ravisher's blood in my veins, I have no power on earth or in heaven to protect me and mine from redress. . . . There is no law to protect a woman of my race. Only laws carefully devised to make our women the prey of the white man's lust. . . . God permitted the black hearted scoundrel to make a play thing of my mother. He permitted him to wrest her away from me and sell her south. He permitted her heart to be broken. Mounting his horse, he cries out to his wife "Ellen, Ellen, goodbye." As the curtain falls, Ellen Marston "crumples up in a heap." In avenging Mara's death and the long-standing crime of his mother's rape, Marston will more than likely be lynched.

8.   In Tennyson's *Idylls of the King*, see "Lancelot and Elaine," and the lines 1000-1010, known as "Elaine's Song."

9.   Fortunately, Grimké's biography is not difficult to locate. As Carolivia Herron recounts in her introduction to *Selected Works of Angelina Grimké*, Grimké was born in 1880 in Boston and spent most of her life with her father, Archibald. Her mother, Frances, a white woman, cared for her for only a short time after her birth. She gave the child over to her husband to raise and left the family. In this volume of *Selected Works*, Herron has included the full text of the play *Rachel* (1916). Both Herron and Hull have written that Grimké's play *Rachel* reflects in part Grimké's relationship or lack thereof with her mother. Grimké was educated mostly in the Northeast, at Cushing Academy in Ashburton, Massachusetts, and Girls' Latin School in Boston, among others. She graduated with a degree in physical education from Boston Normal School of Gymnastics, now the School of Hygiene at Wellesley College (Herron 7). In 1907, she was a gym teacher at the Armstrong Training School in Washington briefly and then transferred to the M Street School, later named Dunbar High School, where she taught English until 1926. Mention is frequently made in the materials on Grimké that she was a lesbian; support for this assumption is found in her diary entries, poems, and letters.

10.   Similarities are found between Richard Marston and Archibald Grimké. Both men were born on a South Carolina plantation and were sons of white men and black mothers. Each man was well educated, and each had a close, nearly overbearing, relationship with his daughter.

WORKS CITED

Bornstein, George. Introduction. In *Palimpsest*. Ed. George Bornstein and Ralph G. Williams. Ann Arbor: U of Michigan P, 1993.

Eidson, John Olin. *Tennyson in America: His Reputation and Influence from 1827 to 1858*. Athens, GA: U of Georgia P, 1943.

Grimké, Angelina Weld. *Mara*. Box 38. Moorland Spingarn Research Center. Howard University.

Herron, Carolivia, ed. Introduction. In *Selected Works of Angelina Grimké*. New York: Oxford UP: 1991.

Hull, Gloria. *Color, Sex, and Poetry: Three Women Writers of the Harlem Renaissance*. Bloomington: Indiana UP, 1987.

McGann, Jerome J. "Literary Pragmatics and the Editorial Horizon." In *Devils and Angels: Textual Editing and Literary Theory*. Ed. Philip Cohen. Charlottesville: UP of Virginia, 1991. 1-21.

Miller, Jeanne-Marie A. "Angelina Weld Grimké: Playwright and Poet." *CLA Journal* 21 (1978): 513-24.

Shillingsburg, Peter. "The Autonomous Author, the Sociology of Texts, and the Polemics of Textual Criticism." In *Devils and Angels: Textual Editing and Literary Theory*. Ed. Philip Cohen. Charlottesville: UP of Virginia, 1991. 22-43.

Tanselle, G. Thomas. "Textual Scholarship" in *Introduction to Scholarship in Modern Languages and Literatures*. Ed. Joseph Gibaldi. New York: MLA, 1981. 29-52.

Tate, Claudia. *Domestic Allegories of Political Desire*." New York: Oxford UP, 1992.

Thorpe, James. *Principles of Textual Criticism*. San Marino, CA: Huntington, 1972.

Weygandt, Cornelius. *The Time of Tennyson: English Victorian Poetry as it Affected America*. Port Washington, NY: Kennicat, 1936.

Williams, Ralph G. "I Shall Be Spoken: Textual Boundaries, Authors, and Intent." In *Palimpsest*. Ed. George Bornstein and Ralph G. Williams. Ann Arbor: U of Michigan P, 1993. 45-66.

Wyman, Lillie Buffum Chase. Review of *Rachel*. *Journal of Negro History* 6 (1921): 248-54.

Black Male Subjectivity Deferred?
The Quest for Voice and Authority in Lorraine Hansberry's *A Raisin in the Sun*
Keith Clark

In my play I was dealing with a young man who would have, I feel, been a compelling object of conflict as a young American of his class of whatever racial background, with the exception of the incident at the end of the play, and with the exception, of course, of character depth, because a Negro character is a reality; there is no such thing as saying that a Negro could be a white person if you just changed the lines or something like this. This is a very arbitrary and superficial approach to Negro character.

Lorraine Hansberry, 1961 interview

What I am saying is that whether we like the word or not, the condition of our people dictates what can only be called revolutionary attitudes. It is no longer acceptable to allow racists to define Negro manhood—and it will have to come to pass that they can no longer define his weaponry.

To Be Young, Gifted and Black, 1970

Like her 1950s counterpart Ralph Ellison, Lorraine Hansberry ascended to the forefront of American and African American literati on the basis of a single work. Though not lauded in the way that *Invisible Man* (1952) has been, *A Raisin in the Sun* nevertheless holds a central place in the African American/American drama canon. Just as Ellison's *magnum opus* raises literary, social, historical, and political questions, Hansberry's masterwork also elucidates myriad issues. That Amiri

Baraka (the doyen of the Black Arts Movement and one of the country's most gifted playwrights, a major drama theorist and critic in his own right) would proclaim that "neither of these plays [his own *Dutchman* (1964) and James Baldwin's *Blues for Mister Charlie* (1964)] is as much a statement from the African American majority as is *Raisin*" (19) attests to its literary and historical importance. But Hansberry's dissection of a black family's quest for material and psychological fulfillment exposes vexing questions about her inscription of the black male subject.

The first epigraphic quotation, taken from an interview conducted in 1961 (which included James Baldwin, Alfred Kazin, Emile Capouya, and Langston Hughes), is disarmingly paradoxical. Ostensibly, Hansberry foregrounds Walter Lee Younger, Jr, as the play's "subject"—its protagonist and archetypal male questing figure in the tradition of Mark Twain's and Richard Wright's heroes. But her use of the term "object" problematizes Walter Lee's position. In portraying his desire to gain *subjectivity* in a society devoted to the erasure of the black self, Hansberry renders a disconcerting view of the black male *subject*. Indeed, I contend that the playwright's conceptualization of black masculinity undermines the "wholeness" which is proffered as Walter Lee's ultimate state. Instead of constructing a protagonist who determines his own "masculinity" and identity, Hansberry creates one who is an amalgam of imposed definitions from without rather than from within—definitions that render him more "object" in a pejorative sense than "subject."

I.

I want to begin by theorizing black male subjectivity in both literary and nonliterary contexts. Steven Cohan and Linda Shires offer a comprehensive definition of "subject," one that takes into account its dual or even contradictory meanings:

> We have used the term *subject* to signify an individual (1) who performs an action—doing, thinking, feeling; (2) who apprehends him- or herself as an identifiable agent of action, the grammatical subject of a predication; and (3) who finds a signifier of that identity in discourse, *I* as opposed to *you*. But *subject* is also a term of passivity, as when one is subject to a monarch or law, or the subject of an experiment. Falling within these two poles of agency and

passivity, *subjectivity* is the condition of being (a) subject. (136 authors' emphasis)

In my own conceptualization of subjectivity, I incorporate these authors' delineations. The notion of agency is indeed paramount, and for black male figures a number of ideas are subsumed within it: the quest for voice, the concomitant need for audience and/or community to validate that voice, the need for self-definition, and the authority to reposition the self—to move from victim to agent, from margin to center.

Certainly, the African American literary canon abounds with characters—real and imagined—vying for subjectivity: Frederick Douglass, Harriet Jacobs, Janie Crawford, and Clay Williams come to mind. The desire to contest imposed definitions of black selfhood binds these figures inextricably. But *A Raisin in the Sun* is rooted in a tradition of African American writings which equate *black* masculinity with a pathological desire to appropriate debilitating Western notions of *white* masculinity. Ultimately, *Raisin* promulgates a notion of black "manhood" that merely mimics a virulent American ethos rooted in patriarchy, a conception of manhood which by its very nature excludes the black man. By the play's denouement, Walter Lee Younger attains a counterfeit manhood, one superimposed by a mother who adopts and privileges America's hegemonic and phallocentric conception of what it means to be a "man." To paraphrase the latter portion of Cohan and Shires's definition, Walter Lee's "subjectivity" is marked by passivity, voicelessness, and marginality.

In establishing a framework for a masculinist reading of Hansberry's play, I am not so much concerned with what critics such as Harold Cruse, Darwin Turner, Helene Keyssar, and Genevieve Fabre see as her "integrationist" aesthetics—what they consider her attempts to placate white, middle-class audiences by insisting that black Americans are their "native" counterparts[1]. But I deconstruct Hansberry's play on the basis of its definition of black masculinity. Here I wish to invoke another interpretation of subjectivity before moving to an analysis of the play itself. Wendy Hollway *et al.* in *Changing the Subject*, reason that "the subject itself is the effect of a production, caught in the mutually constitutive web of social practices, discourses and subjectivity; its reality is the tissue of social relations" (117). Thus, the core question is why Hansberry's "production" centers a black male *subject* who adopts "social practices" and "discourses" which are inimical to black male selfhood and wholeness. One answer might rest in the novel that serves as Hansberry's intertext, *Native Son* (1940).

Doris Abramson, one of *Raisin*'s early commentators, perceptively noted the parallels between Walter Lee and Wright's centered subject:

> Both plays [*Native Son* appeared as a play in 1941] are set in Chicago's Southside. Bigger Thomas and Walter Younger are both chauffeurs, black men who feel caged in a white society. And they both "explode" because of a "dream deferred." (242)

Though C.W.E. Bigsby has been one of black literature's most astute critics, I strongly disagree with his contention that "Hansberry's play is essentially an attempt to turn Wright's novel on its head" (157); in fact, the converse is true. Aside from the expository similarities Abramson articulates, I question Hansberry's decision to inscribe a protagonist who, like Bigger Thomas, so slavishly inculcates the values of an unscrupulous society. Bigger and Walter Lee do in fact "explode," because they cannot *be* white men—which Walter's wife, Ruth, tellingly states in the first act.

Why was Hansberry compelled, on the eve of the Civil Rights movement and given her own exhortations for blacks to repudiate the "often ridiculous money values that spill over from the dominant culture and often make us ludicrous in pursuit of that which has its own inherently ludicrous nature: acquisition for the sake of acquisition" ("The Negro" 8-9), to privilege a black subject so wedded to a self-abnegating discourse and ideology? Like his literary predecessor, Walter Lee swallows whole not merely the dogma of the American dream—rooted in materialism, rugged individualism, and isolation—but he accordingly accepts its underlying configuration of masculinity: man as "breadwinner," man as "strong" and "silent," and, perhaps most damaging, man as marginal. Wright in effect de-voices and peripheralizes his protagonist; similarly, Hansberry saddles hers with a convoluted "manhood" that renders him impotent.

II.

Walter's quest for "subject" status takes what I consider two inherently contradictory forms: a search for an African Americanist subjectivity rooted in black oral and vernacular culture—the archetypal search for black voicedness—and an adoption of a sort of materialist, *Western* subjectivity. Berndt Ostendorf's distinction between "oral" and "literate" cultures is appropriate here: "Oral cultures are dramatic, literate cultures epistemic in their focus of attention, the first develops the resources of spontaneity, style, affective performance, and catharsis" (224). Embedded in Walter Lee's quest for selfhood is an ardent desire for what I term *oral* subjectivity: the need to find a mode of expression, an outlet for his blues which will be healing and liberating—something akin to the "spontaneity" and "affective performance" Ostendorf delineates. This is not achieved in an hermetically sealed milieu; on the contrary, Walter's urgent pleas for someone to hear and validate his story attest to his desire for community. What resonates quite loudly in this drama is his desire for both voice and audience; he needs witnesses who can respond to his call.

Often, black men comprise the community Walter Lee craves. Ernest Gaines and August Wilson are two contemporary black male writers who have articulated eloquently the curative function of black male community. Works such as *A Gathering of Old Men* (1983) and *Joe Turner's Come and Gone* (1988) accentuate the empowering effect of black male voicedness for members of the male speech community; they move from object to subject, from other to brother. Hansberry, too, is aware of the potential of the black male speech act (at least on some level), for *Raisin* possesses a distinctive oral and aural dimension.

For example, the opening scene conveys Walter Lee's unmet need for oral subjectivity. The action commences with Ruth's entreating their son, Travis, to get ready for school. But when Walter suggests that Travis awaken earlier, the following argument ensues:

> Ruth (Turning on him): Oh, no he ain't going to be getting up no earlier no such thing! It ain't his fault that he can't get to bed no earlier nights 'cause he got a *bunch of crazy good-for-nothing clowns sitting up running their mouths* in what is supposed to be his bedroom after ten o'clock at night. . .
> Walter: That's what you mad about, ain't it? The things I want to talk about with my friends just couldn't be important in your mind, could they? (14-15) [emphasis added]

The dynamics of voicedness emerge in this seemingly pedestrian husband-wife confrontation. First, Walter attempts to fashion his own voice within a collectivity of other black men. However, Ruth not only deprecates Walter, but she vehemently denigrates his companions ("clowns") and their "talk"; the black male speech act is ridiculed as "running their mouths." Not incidentally, a few lines later, Ruth tells Walter Lee to "shut up." When Walter finally bellows (in scene two) "WILL SOMEBODY PLEASE LISTEN TO ME TODAY!" (57), the urgency of his plea becomes clear. But, again, his search for audience is interrupted, when his mother, Lena, demands that Walter "talk civil to his wife" while he is in *her* house; again, the conditions for black male voicedness are contested and mediated. Therefore, the play establishes Walter Lee's need for an expressive male community and his inexorable inability to secure it.

Though his desire for voice is thwarted at home, Walter Lee does experience a sense of male community and connection, which he locates in a blues context outside his family. Frustrated by his failed attempts to be heard at home, he flees to the "Green Hat," a neighborhood bar. When he returns home and faces his mother's admonitions, he laments,

> You know what I like about the Green Hat? (He turns the radio on and a steamy, *deep blues* pours into the room) I like this little cat they got there who blows a sax. . . He blows. *He talks to me.* He ain't but 'bout five feet tall and he's got a conked head and his eyes is always closed and he's all music—

He goes on to reveal the following:

> And there's this other guy who plays the piano . . . and they got a sound. I mean they can work on some music. . . They got the best little combo in the world in the Green Hat. . . *You can just sit there and drink and listen to them three men play and you realize that don't nothing matter worth a damn, but just being there—*(86) [emphasis added]

Walter's confession constitutes one of the play's few *blues moments*, instances where black male subjectivity intersects with its most authentic mode of expression, the blues or jazz performance.

Folklorist Roger Abrahams's definition of performance is relevant here: he defines it as "a demonstration of culture, one of the products of men getting together with other men and working out expressive means of operating together" (75). That Walter Lee rejuvenates himself via the male environment the Green Hat provides reveals a nascent blues and communal voice. Indeed, Walter immerses himself within what Houston Baker might call the "expressive black community,"[2] a matrix which traverses a spoken language which others refuse to acknowledge or hear. Indeed, Walter's description of the regenerative power of the blues moment is central; other black men "talk" to him without talking and therefore censuring and editing his voice. And even though his subsequent business dealings with Willy and Bobo prove fruitless, this ersatz "blues trio" nevertheless represents a variation of what Abrahams deems the male need to construct an "expressive means of operating together."

Ultimately, however, given Hansberry's conflicted presentation of black male voice, it becomes apparent why she did not include the Green Hat "scene" in her *mise-en- scene*; instead, she relegates it to the margins of her play in the same way that characters peripheralize Walter's quest for voice. Ironically, this "imagined" scene carries great rhetorical weight in light of James Baldwin's "Sonny's Blues," a work published two years prior to *Raisin* and one that extols the value of black male performance rituals within a nurturing, sacrosanct environment—a setting reminiscent of the "Green Hat."

Walter's ephemeral "blues voice" underscores what I earlier called the binary opposite of oral subjectivity—its Western counterpart. Quite tellingly, Walter's blues voice is extinguished when his mother bestows upon him $6500 from his deceased father's insurance policy: "I want you to take this money and take three thousand dollars and put it in a savings account for Beneatha's [his sister] medical schooling. The rest you can put in a checking account—*with your name on it*" (87) [emphasis added]. This exchange represents a perverted "naming" ritual, one that equates black male subjectivity with monetary power. This scene signifies upon an earlier one in which the African character, Joseph Asagai, rechristened Beneatha "Alaiyo"—"One for Whom Bread—Food—Is Not Enough" (52). Quite the contrary, "bread" is indeed enough for both Lena and Walter Lee, as the gift of money inaugurates his rejuvenation; in the next moment, he enthusiastically seeks a relationship with his son, whom he had heretofore ignored. Apparently, money mediates and inspires black male community.

Though Hansberry sententiously decried "ridiculous money values" in her essay on the black writer's role, *Raisin* upholds those values *ad infinitum*. In her seminal essay, "Reconstructing Black

Masculinity," bell hooks offers an historical context for what I deem
Western subjectivity, or what she calls "white supremacist capitalist
patriarchy." She relates an anecdote in which her ebullient brother

> became forever haunted by the idea of patriarchal masculinity. All
> that he had questioned in his childhood was sought after in his early
> adult life in order to become a man's man—phallocentric, patriarchal,
> and masculine. In traditional black communities when one tells a
> grown male to "be a man," one is urging him to aspire to a masculine
> identity rooted in the patriarchal ideal. (87-88)

Chicago in the 1950s—the storyworld of *Raisin*—was quite
"traditional," and all of the Youngers equate Walter Lee's masculinity
with tortured notions of "patriarchy." In the same vein, sociologist
Clyde Franklin cogently delineates American masculinity, a definition
to which black men have pledged allegiance:

> The definitions of masculinities deemed acceptable have the
> following broad themes: dominance, competitiveness, violence,
> homophobia, sexism, and misogyny. Mainstream society subtly
> teaches Black males that it is manly to hold dominant roles in
> society's basic institutions (e.g., the family, the economy, politics,
> religion, and education). Those men who hold such positions are
> rewarded with status, prestige, esteem, and even more, legitimate
> power. (18)

Hansberry vitiates Walter's quest for an authentic black self by having
him—and even more so, his mother—shape himself to fit the contours
of American masculinity—a Western conception of manhood
antithetical to black wholeness.

Walter Lee's quest for Western subjectivity manifests itself
throughout the play. Some of the most revealing instances involve not
only his perversion of his nascent "blues voice" but also his desire for
what hooks called the "patriarchal ideal." George Murchison, through
whom critics such as Steven Carter argue that Hansberry "satirizes
various foibles of the black American middle class" (59), may at first
glance seem to be a "wannabe," a faux white man. But what
undermines Hansberry's "satirizing" is both Walter's desire for
Murchison's approbation and his belief in Murchison's virulent
classism and paternalism.

During his drunken African "tour de force," Walter exhorts Murchison to hear Jomo Kenyatta,

> Telling us to prepare for the greatness of the time—(To George) Black Brother! (He extends his hand for the fraternal clasp) George: Black Brother, hell! (66)

George's malediction recalls what post-colonialist scholar Frantz Fanon says about the "colonialist bourgeoisie": "Brother, sister, friend—these are words outlawed by the colonialist bourgeoisie, because for them my brother is my purse, my friend is part of my scheme for getting on" (47). But Walter doesn't limit his "fraternal" designs to the scion of the Murchison fortune; he shifts his quest for "brotherhood" to the chimeric patriarch himself, George Murchison, Sr.:

> How's your old man making out? I understand you all going to buy that big hotel on the Drive? Shrewd move. Your old man is all right, man. I mean he knows how to operate. I mean he thinks *big*, you know what I mean, I mean for a *home*, you know? But I think he's kind of running out of ideas now. I'd like to talk to him. Listen, man, I got some plans that could turn this city upside down. I mean I think like he does. *Big*. Invest big, gamble big, hell, lose *big* if you have to, you know what I mean. It's hard to find a man on this whole Southside who understands my kind of thinking—you dig? Me and you ought to sit down and talk sometimes, man. Man I got me some ideas. . .
>
> Murchison (With boredom): Yeah—sometimes we'll have to do that, Walter. (70)

This exchange elucidates Walter Lee's devotion to a flawed conception of masculinity, one rooted in voracious materialism and ownership; the senior Murchison becomes the black counterpart of "Mr. Arnold," the white man for whom Walter "open[s] and close[s] car doors all day long" (60). Equally salient is the audience Walter desires. Just as Ruth opened the play by denigrating Walter's male counterparts, he himself now discounts his native "community" in lieu of having the chimeric "father Murchison" validate his voice. Walter Lee attempts to remake himself in the Murchisons' image; instead of being the offspring of "Big Walter," who toiled for whites until he

"sagged like a heavy load," he craves lineage in a line of capitalists—
"G.M." being the apogee of American business and industry. As
Fanon's comment suggests, finances determine fraternity.

Perhaps the most resonant aspect of Walter Lee's "performance"
with young Murchison is the emergence of his problematic definition of
manhood (his obsession with it surfacing through his copious use of the
word "man"). Walter Lee upbraids him for attending college instead
operating in the "real world" of investments:

> Filling up your heads—(*Counting off on his fingers*)—with the
> sociology and the psychology— but they teaching you how to be a
> man? How to take over and run the world? They teaching you how to
> run a rubber plantation or a steel mill? Naw—just how to talk proper
> and read books and wear white shoes. . . (71)

Reminiscent of both hooks's and Franklin's definitions of American
patriarchy and masculinity, Walter Lee imagines "manhood" as
testosterone run amuck—ownership and control being its core
determinants. Ironically, his allusion to a rubber plantation is relevant,
vis-a-vis a history of colonialism in which indigenous African cultures
were implacably deracinated in the name of profits. Furthermore,
Walter Lee's earlier signification on George's costume—"Why all you
college boys wear them fairyish-looking white shoes?" (69)—further
elucidates his construction of masculinity. A native son of the 1960s
black nationalists whom he precedes by a mere year, he voices a
homophobia which the cult of true American manhood sanctions.

That Walter Lee harbors atavistic conceptions of Western or
American male subjectivity in and of itself would be less troubling had
Hansberry explored the inherent contradictions of his philosophy.
Ostensibly, Hansberry's *Raisin* could be placed into a subcategory of
"anti-business" American plays such as Arthur Miller's *Death of a
Salesman* (1949) and David Mamet's *Glengarry, Glen Ross* (1983);
these works launch an unmitigated assault on the unscrupulous business
world and how it produces a deformed conception of masculinity.
Indeed, Hansberry's observations about Walter Lee in "An Author's
Reflections: Walter Lee Younger, Willy Loman, and He Who Must
Live" reify what I consider the play's promulgation of Western
subjectivity. She writes,

> For if there are no waving flags and marching songs at the barricades
> as Walter marches out with his little battalion, it is only because the
> battle lacks nobility. On the contrary, he has picked up in his way,
> still imperfect and wobbly in his small view of human destiny, what I
> believe Arthur Miller once called "the golden thread of history." He
> becomes, in spite of those who are too intrigued with despair and
> hatred of man to see it, King Oedipus refusing to tear out his eyes, but
> attacking the Oracle instead. He is that last Jewish patriot manning
> his rifle at Warsaw; he is that young girl who swam into sharks to
> save a friend a few weeks ago; he is Anne Frank, still believing in
> people; he is the nine small heroes of Little Rock; he is Michelangelo
> creating David and Beethoven bursting forth with the Ninth
> Symphony. (qtd in Carter 51-52)

But Hansberry's own "membership" in what might be considered a
white male drama "community"—her own racial and gender "anxiety
of influence"—further problematizes her configuration of the black
male subject. As the aforementioned quote attests, Hansberry situates
her protagonist on a continuum of primarily white Western male
"heroes" (the inclusion of women such as Frank notwithstanding).
Therefore, I contend that the play poses a dual conception of
subjectivity and ultimately sanctions the most debilitating one.

If Walter Lee's dreams of buying a liquor store and his fervent
complaints about wanting to be in "cool, quiet looking restaurants
where them white boys are sitting back and talking 'bout things" (60)
represented the play's self-reflexivity—its critique of the "ridiculous"
and meretricious money values inherent in white capitalist patriarchy—
then one might conclude that the playwright was "satirizing" the black
"bourgeoisie." But Walter is not primarily the one who sanctions these
foreign values; his mother and, less clearly, his father, have shaped
them. Indeed, Lena, the character who is ostensibly the play's moral
center and whose attitude comes closest to the author's own ideology,
becomes the *sine qua non* in the discussion of how Hansberry inscribes
black masculinity.

III.

Thus far, I have proffered a configuration of black male subjectivity
which is filtered through and mediated by a conflicted and limiting
notion of American masculinity. Gender theorist Peter Middleton in

The Inward Gaze: Masculinity and Subjectivity in Modern Culture provides a succinct definition of the "decentered subject": "Poststructuralism has presented a decentered subject, a kind of subjectivity-less subject: interpellated by ideology, constructed by discourses, constituted by the desire of the other" (117). Walter Lee Younger, as Hansberry has conceived him, constitutes an archetypal decentered black male subject: he is consumed with the desire of the "other" (whites), and he exists in a "subjectivity-less" realm that renders him more "object" than subject. In essence, Walter Lee is the aggregate of ideologies or "fictions" which others generate and impose.

In terms of dramaturgy or the "well-made" play, Lena ("Mama") Younger represents Walter Lee's foil. Trudier Harris's topology of the "strong" black woman in African American literature offers an instructive configuration that captures Lena's essence:

> Historically, African American women have been viewed as balm bearers, the ones who held a people together against assaults from outside as well as from within the community. They were towers of strength against the degradation of slavery. Theywere towers of strength against the abuse of husbands and the demands of children. They were towers of strength in taking care of their families—usually through domestic work. And they formed the pillars that supported the black churches that in turn demanded a tremendous strength from them. (109)

Indeed, Lena's life adheres staunchly to Harris's outline. She extols the virtues of hard work—she continues to work as a domestic for whites—and religion—she slaps Beneatha when the precocious daughter challenges the existence of God. But she is far from Walter Lee's ideological opposite; on the contrary, she corroborates the conflicted form of masculinity that he desires. By the end of the play, she "converts" her only son, conferring upon him *her* patriarch-based conception of manhood.

Earlier, I mentioned the Christianity-capitalism nexus in defining American manhood. The archetypal Western male subject has traditionally combined a fervent belief in professed "Christian principles" and an ardent desire to succeed monetarily. Cultural critic hooks, alludes to the dynamics of this paradigm vis-a-vis the black family historically:

The image of the patriarchal head of the household, ruler of this mini-state called the "family," faded in the 20th century. More men than ever before worked for someone else. The state began to interfere more in domestic matters. A man's time was not his own; it belonged to his employer, and the terms of his rule in the family were altered. In the old days, a man who had no money could still assert tyrannic rule over family and kin, by virtue of his patriarchal status, usually affirmed by Christian belief systems. (93-94)

The Younger family represents an erstwhile version of the black American family, one ruled by the philosophy of the "old days," where the father maintained inalienable sovereignty over the home in spite of his devalued economic status. Lena is the purveyor of this configuration of the black family, as she frequently calls upon the ghost of "Big Walter" to buttress her attempts to meld their son. W.E.B. Du Bois's critique of Booker T. Washington's enslavement to a "gospel of work and money" reverberates in this play as Lena's *raison d'etre*, for her Christianity is rooted in a religion that de-forms the black male subject.

Big Walter, a veritable invisible man, haunts the play much like Toni Morrison's or August Wilson's apparitional characters pervade their works. He is significant because Lena, the surrogate for his voice and authority, makes him *present* despite his palpable *absence*. She becomes the mediator for his voice, representing a variation on what I have called the de-voiced black male subject; Big Walter attains subjectivity only through his wife. According to her, he was the black Western patriarch incarnate:

Crazy 'bout his children! God knows there was plenty wrong with Walter Younger—hard-headed, mean, kind of wild with women—plenty wrong with him. But he sure loved his children. Always wanted them to have something—be something. That's where Brother [Walter Lee] gets all these notions, I reckon. Big Walter used to say, he'd get right wet in the eyes sometimes, lean his head back with the water standing in his eyes and say, "Seem like God didn't see fit to give the black man nothing but dreams—but He did give us children to make them dreams seem worth while." (33)

Lena becomes Big Walter's amanuensis; her articulation of her dead husband's *modus vivendi* becomes a sort of "drag" performance, with Lena affecting and emoting his voice and mannerisms.

Aside from the rhetorical significance of this speech, it upholds the play's core tenets about male self-definition and patriarchy; as Carter flatly states, "it is clear that while he was living, Big Walter was the head of the house" (53). In (re)presenting Big Walter, Lena articulates the same pernicious conception of manhood which sociologist Franklin posited as the foundation of American masculinity such as a domineering, even sexist relationship with women and a general self-absorption. He "loves" his children only because they represent possibilities for attaining the "American" pie which was denied him; in and off themselves they could be as valueless as the women with whom he is "wild." Big Walter's apotheosis signifies the play's flawed ideology, for he engendered the de-formed archetypal black male protagonist who has populated the canon: he failed to comprehend that his privileged definition of manhood was inapposite vis-a-vis black male subjects.

Inasmuch as Big Walter is a hybrid of what hooks deemed "white supremacist capitalist patriarchy" and "fierce phallocentrism,"[3] I think it significant to articulate the conception of manhood Big Walter bequeaths his son, a conception mediated and imposed by Lena; indeed, the play posits a cosmic link between patriarchal ancestor and male progeny with "Mama" as human umbilical cord. This connection surfaces in a number of ways, primarily when Lena attempts figuratively if not literally to inseminate Walter with his father's voice and authority. After revealing (against Ruth's wishes) the possibility that her newly pregnant daughter-in-law is considering an abortion because of the family's financial exigencies, Lena declares,

> Well—Well (Tightly)—son, I'm waiting to hear you say something . . . I'm waiting to hear how you be your father's son. Be the man he was . . . (Pause) Your wife say she going to destroy your child. And I'm waiting to hear you talk like him and say we a people who give children life, not who destroys them—(She rises) I'm waiting to see you stand up and look like your daddy and say we done give up one baby to poverty and that we ain't going to give up nary another one . . . I'm waiting.

Upon Walter's silence, she castigates him further:

If you a son of mine, tell her! (Walter turns, looks at her and can say
nothing. She continues, bitterly) You . . . you are a disgrace to your
father's memory. Somebody get me my hat. (62)

One can certainly argue that "Lena Younger's function in the play is
not so much to create values and to impose her will on her children as it
is to interpret for them Walter Senior's values and to mold them into
the kind of people he would have them to be" (Cook 170). Lena installs
herself as Big Walter's mouthpiece, authorizing the terms of their son's
speech act. Nevertheless, Lena's attempted transubstantiation of Walter
Lee into patriarch perpetuates a venal conception of masculinity that
her son ultimately accepts.

Ostensibly, one could make the same claim for Big Walter's
subjectivity that Paul Carter Harrison adduces in establishing Troy
Maxson's omnipotence in August Wilson's *Fences* (1985). Like his
dramatic antecedent, Troy has led a "blues life," one mired in back-
breaking physical labor with intermittent attempts to ameliorate it with
liquor and extramarital affairs. Harrison reads him as the archetypal
heroic "baad nigger" reincarnated:

Troy—in response to a phallocentric legacy from [Yoruba trickster
figure] Eshu—engages in sexual excesses with impunity. The birth of
a daughter out of wedlock, and his resolve to care for her, is a
testament to his procreative force, a fecund issue that demonstrates
his cosmic role as progenitor in the recurring cycle of personal
immortality. When Death catches up with Troy, it is less a tragic
defeat for him than a reinvention of his vitality, more like the
transcendental passing of a redeemer. (305)

Just as Troy's life was a testimony to his ability to "finger the jagged
grain," Lena's recreation of Big Walter's life becomes a paean to his
blues legacy that passes from wife to son. But Big Walter's
omnipotence is vitiated by disturbing comments about his life.

Often ignored in assessments of Big Walter's life is how his
adoption of Western conceptions of male subjectivity represented a
form of self-erasure. The most telltale comments about Big Walter's
reality occur when his son squanders the balance of the insurance
money the Youngers received upon the patriarch's death. First, Walter
Lee "wildly" emotes, "That money is made out of my father's flesh"

(108). Subsequently, Lena delivers an elegy on her husband's debilitating life:

> I seen . . . him . . . night after night . . . come in . . . and look at that rug . . . and then look at me . . . the red showing in his eyes . . . the veins moving in his head . . . I seen him grow thin and old before he was forty . . . working and working and working like somebody's old horse . . . like somebody's old horse . . . killing himself . . . and you— you give it all away in a day . . . ("August" 109)

Lena's description of Walter's disintegrating black body—a literal body in pain—belies the notion of "pride" and manhood that she extols. Big Walter's physical de-formation results from his unequivocal acceptance of America's culturally biased definitions of masculinity; on the contrary, he represents a denuded *object* far more than he could ever symbolize a *subject*, speaking or otherwise. I think Carter accurately suggests that Big Walter's life became a form of "protracted suicide" (23). To be sure, Big Walter, Lena, and their son represent a strange triumvirate: though Hansberry uses Langston Hughes's "Harlem" as the play's epigraph, perhaps a more appropriate one would have been "Mother to Son" because *Raisin* privileges the passing of an ascetic, debilitating set of "values" from Lena to Walter.

Though the dead patriarch is corporeally absent throughout the drama, Hansberry provides an even more suitable "husband" for Lena in the character of Lindner. Just as George Murchison represents one of the play's one-dimensional characters, Hansberry depicts Karl Lindner (read: Marx on "lender") as a straw man, a white bogey man who would extirpate the Youngers' hopes. But through the patina of Lindner's "racist" message shines an ideology which aligns him with Big Walter and Lena. For instance, his comments about the Clyburne Park residents' attempts to dissuade the Youngers from moving mirror the Youngers' own dogma: "They're not rich and fancy people; just hard-working, honest people who don't really have much but those little homes and a dream of the kind of community they want to raise their children in" (97). This banal comment is indistinguishable from Lena's presentation of her husband's solemn platitudes about "dreams."

Furthermore, Lindner embodies the conception of Western male subjectivity that Lena—and by extension Big Walter—sanctions: a view that ownership, control, and domination signify manhood. Lena seeks to buy both Walter Lee's manhood (in the aforementioned "renaming" of him with a bank account) and the family's self-respect via purchasing the "plain little old house" (78) in Clyburne park. Lindner immediately provides a counteroffer: "Our association is prepared, through the collective effort of our people, to buy the house from you at a financial gain to your family" (98). Lena and Lindner, the superficial gender and racial differences notwithstanding, are "mirror opposites": they both endow money with the power to (re)define self and with the power to coerce and control; it is not a coincidence that Lena speaks so passionately about "measuring" Walter Lee in the third act, for this is the same empiricist, business-ese of the dominant patriarchal establishment. Though Walter Lee admonishes his mother for purchasing the house and "butch[ering] up a dream of mine" (80), his resentment results from Lena's ability to negotiate in and with the white society on its terms; she has the financial currency to remake herself into the *material* subject her late husband could only "dream" of becoming.

Because they are so ideologically matched, I contend that Lindner becomes the white reincarnation of Big Walter, the white male subject whose aphoristic but conflicting conceptualization of self conforms to the one Lena worshipped in her late husband. Not coincidentally, Beneatha hints at the "conjugal" relationship between black "matriarch" and white "patriarch," informing Lena of Lindner's visit jokingly: "You had a caller, Mama" (99); subsequently, Lindner refers to Walter Lee as "sonny" (126). Indeed, the sexual subtext of these comments suggests a familial (though not necessarily sexual or propinqual) bond. And the family's re-naming of Lena as "Mrs. Miniver" and "Scarlet O'Hara" "consummates" the marriage: Lindner as surrogate father, Lena as imitation white "mistress" and conduit for Western male subjectivity.

In "Visions of Love and Manliness in a Blackening World: Dramas of Black Life from 1953-1970," Darwin Turner asks perspicuously, "Has Walter Lee actually converted to a new ideal, or does he believe that he is submitting to his mother's will?" (87). Assuredly, the answer involves both questions: Lena converts him to her will. Thus, the "manhood" which Lena confers in the play's denouement is counterfeit, one which conforms to the highly flawed conceptualization of masculinity which the play sanctions. Walter Lee's manhood becomes suspect, as Lena remakes him in the image of her deceased and "living" husbands. Ironically, the link between the denigrated "manhood" Lena and Walter Lee espouse is hinted at throughout the play: Lena demands that he "be the man" Big Walter was (62); and later, Walter Lee calls to accept the offer (to keep the Youngers out of Clyburne Park) from Lindner, whom he derides as "the [white] Man" (120).

A watershed moment in Lena's reinvention of Walter Lee comes after the revelation that he has squandered the remaining $6500: Hansberry's stage directions read,

> Mama stops and looks at her son without recognition and then, quite
> without thinking about it, starts to beat him senselessly in the face.
> Beneatha goes to them and stops it. (109)

Lena's violent act should not be ignored, for she literally beats her conception of "manhood" into her native son. But this beating harkens back to the white society's maiming and disfiguring of her husband's body; it evinces Lena's belief in the power of physical violence to restrict and eviscerate the black man's attempts to resituate himself as subject. Lena's act and Lindner's attempts to bribe Walter Lee into staying out of Clyburne Park become symbiotic gestures which have the same ends—to continue the pattern of "beatings," physical and psychological, which have abrogated the black protagonist's quest for subjectivity.

Thus, when Walter ultimately "finds his voice," it is one that has been edited, mediated, and melded by exogenous forces: a white "father" and a black mother who presume to speak for the deified black patriarch. Harrison unwittingly exposes the play's sanctioning of a Western masculinist framework when he rhapsodizes about Lena's decision to entrust the money to Walter Lee: "And when money exerts its force, threatening to split up the family, she [Hansberry] has the mother Nommo the *male principle* forward into its rightful, symbolic position in the family by giving her son, Walter Lee, the money from an insurance policy, the spiritual legacy of the dead father" (*The Drama* 201, author's emphasis)[4]. Quite assuredly, the play's "male principle" is rooted in Euro-American conceptions of hegemony. Thus, when Lena ruminates poignantly about Walter's subsequent decision to reject Lindner's offer and lead the family into the white neighborhood ("He finally come into his manhood today, didn't he? Kind of like a rainbow after the rain . . ." [130]), Hansberry's disfigured portraiture comes into focus. Lena's decree becomes the countersign for her son's regeneration, a blessing which marks his rebirth. But Walter Lee, as Turner's question suggests, speaks in the m/other's tongue; the fact that

Hansberry denotes that "Walter's voice has risen in pitch and hysterical promise. . ." (89) when Lena bequeaths him the money marks his embracing of the play's *female principle*, which has at its core a phallocentrically spurious construction of masculinity.

IV.

Hansberry's configuration of the black male subject is especially problematic given her grasp of the difficulty of writing "across" gender lines: "But I am altogether certain that in regard to the inner truths of characters, the woman character will always partially elude the male writer" ("The Negro" 97). If her assessment of the female subject's "elusiveness" with respect to the male author is taken to its logical conclusion, then her flawed portraiture of Walter Lee Younger corresponds to her own dictum. In addition, Walter Lee's function in the context of the play's other black male figures makes the author's inscription of the black male subject more "elusive" and blemished. Upon closer exploration of the play's other male figures, one finds that Walter's presentation is synechdochical; it represents a larger contextual difficulty in Hansberry's figuration of the male subject, as she paints a preponderance of black men with the same brush.

Earlier I indicated how George Murchison, ostensibly a "parody" of white patriarchal values, invariably demonstrates how the play sanctions such values. However, characters such as Joseph Asagai emerge from a similar matrix, for he engenders the same "alien" values of the play's other male characters. It first appears that Hansberry intends for the Nigerian-born idealist to be an alternative to the debilitating Western ethos of imperialism and domination. Though he rhapsodizes about a post-colonialist Africa, one where he can be "respected and esteemed" in his "new nation" (115), the underpinnings of his "Afrocentric" discourse are disconcertingly close to Walter Lee's own fantasies about transforming himself from object to subject.

Asagai's dreams of self-transformation are congruent with the patriarchal ideology the play extols. For instance, his sexism makes him the African counterpart of Big Walter. The most egregious example of this occurs in the first act, when he and Beneatha are discussing changes in contemporary gender dynamics. After she asserts that sex should not be the *sine qua non* in male-female relationships, Asagai rejoins, "Between a man and a woman there need be only one kind of feeling" and that "for a woman it should be enough" (50). Indeed, his *modus operandi* replicates the visions of manliness that the play promulgates: his proclamation marks the marriage of two symbiotic discourses—patriarchy and its twin scourge, sexism. When Carter adduces that "after all, it is Asagai, not Lena, who comes closest to being Hansberry's spokesperson in the play" (35), he is only partially right. Just as Lindner and Lena espouse starkly similar constructions of manhood, so too do Lena and Asagai mirror each other in their tainted conceptualization of black male subjectivity. Modeled on Hansberry's uncle, William Leo Hansberry, who taught African civilization and culture at Howard University, Asagai is ultimately a "faux" Fanon whose post-colonialist homilies fortify the play's conflicted conception of male subjectivity. Hansberry's distorted male mosaic is completed by her characterization of two seemingly marginal characters, Willy and Bobo.

Much like the romantic realists/naturalist American playwrights of the 1940s and 1950s, Hansberry also invests minor or even "absent" characters with great rhetorical significance; she forthrightly speaks of the similarities between her literary aesthetics and those of Arthur Miller, Eugene O'Neill, and Tennessee Williams. Just as Big Walter, Walter Lee, George Murchison (junior and senior), and Joseph Asagai form a constellation of "Westernized" black men, Bobo and Willy carry thematic weight in terms of the author's black male paradigm.

Though their names recall the duo at the center of Beckett's existentialist agon, Willy and Bobo are finally much less remarkable than Didi and Gogo. Taken together, they merely complete Hansberry's dubious composite of black male subjects. Bobo, who briefly appears to quell Walter Lee's capitalist designs, stammers and plods about the stage; ultimately, he delivers the fateful news that Willy has fled with money that was earmarked for the liquor store. The other half of this unremarkable duo, Willy, is the worst type of miscreant, one who would bamboozle fellow blacks without leaving a trace; in essence, he is a perverted version of the ruthless capitalists the George Murchisons represent—and the type Walter Lee aspires to be. I think James McKelly's simple yet trenchant comment cuts to the core of one of the play's messages: "In Hansberry's world, the only bad business which Walter Lee is guilty of practicing is entrusting his investment to another black man" (88).

What is so disquieting about Hansberry's black male rubric is that a natural response would be to flee such no-count ne'er-do-wells, which is exactly what Walter Lee does. The prospect of entering a nurturing black male community is foreclosed, and, by default, he elects to lead his family into Clyburne Park. Genevieve Fabre is one of several critics who have faulted the play's apparent "integrationist" philosophy: "The ghetto is a place to leave, and the most worthy can escape it" (34). Ironically, on the eve of the civil rights and Black Aesthetic movements—both of which were inexorably devoted to communal action—Walter Lee is left community-less, unlike the black women in the play or the denizens of the panacean Clyburne Park, who seem to form a close-knit (if close-minded) community. Given such limited choices, Walter Lee forfeits potential community when his mother decides to install him as the titular patriarch. Taken together, Hansberry's presentation of black men is at best problematic and at worst hideously distorted. I would take exception to Carter's classification of her men as "multidimensional figures" (58). On the contrary, both major and minor male characters emerge from a hyper-masculinized framework, where agency is equated with the most pejorative traits of Western materialist subjectivity.

Robert Stepto has written eloquently about the black male's quest—both real and fictional—for selfhood. His discussion of Frederick Douglass's Herculean attempts to locate his authentic black voice is particularly appropriate. In speaking of abolitionist William Lloyd Garrison's introduction to Douglass's 1845 *Narrative*, Stepto elucidates the arduous negotiations Douglass undertook to speak for himself: "We might be tempted to see Garrison's 'Preface' at war with Douglass's tale for authorial control of the narrative as a whole" (18). Though Stepto deemphasizes this struggle somewhat, I think a similar one ensues between the black female playwright and her male subject in *A Raisin in the Sun*. That Walter Lee adopts a model so contrary to black male subjectivity ultimately raises questions about Hansberry's aesthetics. Appropriately enough, his marginalized status portends that of Alton Scales, the only black character in Hansberry's Bohemian fantasy, *The Sign in Sidney Brustein's Window* (1964); a progeny of Walter, he forsakes black men *and* black women, ensconcing himself in a "hip," all-white Greenwich Village milieu. Given her privileging of Western definitions of subjectivity, I would agree with Harrison's salient comment that *A Raisin in the Sun* is "burdened with the familiar sociological formulations on the black experience" which ultimately stifle its "*blues voice*" ("August" 299, author's emphasis). Though the play possesses blues *moments*, the lack of a coherent outlet for black male voicedness—and identity defined in opposition to the debilitating construction of masculinity which the dominant culture superimposes on the black male self—renders the constellation of black male figures spatially and psychologically adrift. Hansberry's monolithic black men worship an alien ethos, and black male subjectivity becomes the dream deferred, regardless of whether it sags or explodes.

NOTES

1.   See Cruse's *The Crisis of the Negro Intellectual: A Historical Analysis of the Failure of Black Leadership,* Turner's "Visions of Love and Manliness in a Blackening World: Dramas of Black Life from 1953-1970," Keyssar's *The Curtain and the Veil: Strategies in Black Drama,* and Genevieve Fabre's *Drumbeats, Masks and Metaphor: Contemporary Afro-American Theatre.* Cruse's protracted, sometimes *ad hominem* attack on Hansberry is widely acknowledged among critics of black drama. He raises issues surrounding the intersection and possible contradictions between Hansberry's literary aesthetics and her life: "It is significant that radical leftwing sponsorship (rather than her own class) paved the way for Miss Hansberry's literary development, demonstrating the leftwing's role as the political surrogate for the social *aims* of the Negro middle class over the social *necessities* of the Negro working class" (269, author's emphasis). But such points are vitiated by the relentlessness of Cruse's criticism of both the playwright's art and life, such as when he makes the hyperbolic claim that, "*A Raisin in the Sun* demonstrated that the Negro playwright has lost the intellectual and, therefore technical and creative, ability to deal with his [sic] own special ethnic group materials in dramatic form" (281).

2.   Houston Baker configures a unique paradigm he labels "rites of the black (w)hole," in which he synthesizes anthropological and astronomical discourses on initiation rituals and "black holes," respectively. Baker charts the transformation of the black self "under erasure" to one made "whole" through his or her interaction with other blacks: "What is possible is *entry* into the singularity at the black (W)hole's center. This *singularity* consists of an initiated, expressive black *community* that has 'gotten the [white world's] picture,' used it to fuel retreat, found the center of its own singular desire, and given expressive form to a new and meaningful *Black (W)holeness*" (154, author's emphasis). With respect to Walter Lee Younger, his relationship with the "black expressive community" remains tenuous, ending with his pending immersion into a *white* community which has historically impeded black "wholeness."

3. In her essay "Reconstructing Black Masculinity" in *Black Looks,* bell hooks expounds upon these concepts: "This work [scholarly work on black masculinity] conveyed the message that black masculinity was homogeneous. It suggested that all black men were tormented by their inability to fulfill the phallocentric masculine ideal as it has been articulated in white supremacist capitalist patriarchy" (89). She goes on to assert that, "With the emergence of a fierce phallocentrism, a man was no longer a man because he provided care for his family, he was a man simply because he had a penis" (94). For my analysis of black masculinity, I modify these concepts slightly: I read "fierce phallocentrism" as a Western construct which some blacks have appropriated in constructing black masculinity; I don't think the Youngers use, for example, sexual prowess as the sole barometer of Walter Lee's "manhood," though Ruth's impending pregnancy and Lena's suspicion that Walter Lee may be cheating on his wife suggest that "phallocentrism" is part of the play's masculine matrix.

4. Though Harrison doesn't spell out a denotative definition of "Nommo" in *The Drama of Nommo,* his context provides its meaning. Drawing upon African anthropological and cultural studies to construct a model for African American dramatic aesthetics, he delineates "Nommo" as "the power of the word—spoken or gesticulated—which activates all forces from their frozen state in a manner that establishes concreteness of experience" (xx). In a larger context, "Nommo" suggests a spiritual, cosmic force (which Harrison also calls "mojo") which exists diametrically opposed to the dictates of Western culture.

WORKS CITED

Abrahams, Roger. "Folklore and Literature as Performance." *Journal of the Folklore Institute* 9 (1972): 75-94.

Abramson, Doris E. *Negro Playwrights in the American Theatre, 1925-1959.* New York: Columbia UP, 1969.

Baker, Houston A., Jr. *Blues, Ideology, and Afro-American Literature: A Vernacular Theory.* Chicago: U of Chicago P, 1984.

Baraka, Amiri. "A Critical Reevaluation: *A Raisin in the Sun's* Enduring Passion." *A Raisin in the Sun* (Expanded Twenty-fifth Anniversary Edition) *and The Sign in Sidney Brustein's Window.* Ed. Robert Nemiroff. New York: New American Library, 1987. 9-20.

Bigsby, C.W.E. *Confrontation and Commitment: A Study of Contemporary American Drama, 1959-66.* Columbia: U of Missouri P, 1968.

Carter, Steven R. *Hansberry's Drama: Commitment and Complexity.* New York: Meridian, 1993.

Cohan, Steven, and Linda M. Shires. *Telling Stories: A Theoretical Analysis of Narrative Fiction.* New York: Routledge, 1988.

Cook, William. "Mom, Dad and God: Values in Black Theater." *The Theatre of Black Americans.* Ed. Errol Hill. New York: Applause, 1987.

Cruse, Harold. *The Crisis of the Negro Intellectual: A Historical Analysis of the Failure of Black Leadership.* New York: Quill, 1984.

Fabre, Genevieve. *Drumbeats, Masks and Metaphor: Contemporary Afro-American Theatre.* Trans. Melvin Dixon. Cambridge: Harvard UP, 1983.

Fanon, Frantz. *The Wretched of the Earth.* Trans. Constance Farrington. New York: Grove, 1963.

Franklin, Clyde W., II. "Men's Studies, the Men's Movement, and the Study of Black Masculinities: Further Demystification of Masculinities in America." *The Black American Male: His Present Status and His Future.* Eds. Richard G. Majors and Jacob U. Gordon. Chicago: Nelson-Hall, 1994.

Hansberry, Lorraine. "The Negro Writer and His Roots: Toward a New Romanticism." *Black Scholar* 12 (1981): 2-12.

———. *A Raisin in the Sun.* New York: New American Library, 1966.

———. *To Be Young, Gifted and Black: Lorraine Hansberry in Her Own Words.* Adapted by Robert Nemiroff. New York: New American Library, 1970.

———, et al. "The Negro in American Culture." Interview. *The Black American Writer, Volume I: Fiction.* Ed. C.W.E. Bigsby. Baltimore: Penguin, 1969.

Harris, Trudier. "This Disease Called Strength: Some Observations on the Compensating Construction of Black Female Character." *Literature and Medicine* 14 (1995): 109-126.

Harrison, Paul Carter. "August Wilson's Blues Poetics." *Three Plays.* By Wilson. Pittsburgh: U of Pittsburgh P, 1991. 291-318.

———. *The Drama of Nommo: Black Theater in the African Continuum.* New York: Grove, 1972.

Hollway, Wendy, *et al. Changing the Subject: Psychology, Social Regulation and Subjectivity.* London: Methuen, 1984.

hooks, bell. *Black Looks: Race and Representation.* Boston: South End, 1992.

Keyssar, Helene. *The Curtain and the Veil: Strategies in Black Drama.* New York: Burt Franklin, 1981.

McKelly, James C. "Hymns of Sedition: Portraits of the Artist in Contemporary African- American Drama." *Arizona Quarterly* 48 (1992): 87-107.

Middleton, Peter. *The Inward Gaze: Masculinity and Subjectivity in Modern Culture.* London: Routledge, 1992.

Ostendorf, Berndt. "Black Poetry, Blues, and Folklore." *Amerikastudien-American Studies* 20 (1975): 209-259.

Stepto, Robert. *From Behind the Veil: A Study of Afro-American Narrative.* Second edition. Urbana: U of Illinois P, 1979.

Turner, Darwin T. "Visions of Love and Manliness in a Blackening World: Dramas of Black Life from 1953-1970." *Iowa Review* 6 (1975): 82-98.

The Desire/Authority Nexus in Contemporary African American Women's Drama

Lovalerie King

Scholars of African American theater have characterized the period of the 1960s and 1970s as a time when black playwrights exhibited a conscious effort to turn away from white paternalism, from a "white" aesthetic, and from a dependence on white patronage.[1] Generally speaking, it was a time of discovery and heightened consciousness, a time to confront, critique, and reflect reigning authority because it was inadequate for the task at hand. New avenues of information emerged, coinciding with renewed assertions of black pride. The academic community acknowledged the need for African American studies programs. It was indeed a time of accelerated social evolution.

A microcosm of the larger awakening society, the black theater community reflected a renewed consciousness and racial pride in plays about the African American experience. Discussing drama written between 1959 and 1969, Clinton F. Oliver and Stephanie Sills note in their introduction to *Contemporary Black Drama* (1971),

> the novelty lies in point of view or the vantage point of interpretation, wherein black writers, totally disenchanted with outside interpretations and appraisals, insist upon sizing up themselves, "doing their own thing"—black writers presenting black materials, played and directed by black artists mainly for black audiences with the unmistakably important purpose of defining and redefining the meaning of black lives historically and in terms of the twentieth-

century American and modern worlds. Particularly is this true of the
revolutionary black community theaters which as part of the Black
Arts Movement consciously regard themselves as the cultural wing of
the social and political assertions of the black revolution. (23)

The shift toward the expression of a strong identity centered in black
experience made the notion of "authority" central to the drama of the
period as well as to the drama immediately preceding and following.
Characterization and plot reveal a preoccupation with relocating
authority in order to fulfill long-held desires. Desire is synonymous
with longing, wanting, and coveting, but such yearning is either
fulfillable or unfulfillable. Unfulfillable desire functions as a
debilitating phenomenon that can work against self-actualization.
Fulfillable (or feasible) desire is the more likely road to self-
actualization. Understanding the difference between the two types of
desire affords the ability to exploit the growth possibilities desire
creates.

The plays discussed in this essay have in common their attention to
the necessity for a shift in the locus for authority and its connection
with a change in the nature of desire. Playwrights Adrienne Kennedy,
Lorraine Hansberry, Ntozake Shange, and Alice Childress demonstrate
to varying degrees the quest for an acceptance, re-affirmation, or
celebration of the African American subject—both male and female.
bell hooks's analysis of Isaac Julien's film, *Looking for Langston*, is
helpful here. She highlights the importance of resurrecting the buried
histories of gay black men in order to "un-silence" Langston Hughes's
sexuality, observing that:

> Footage of the Harlem Renaissance, of the jazz age, of blues singers
> gives voice to the past. And what those images say has more to do
> with the forms desire takes when it is not openly and directly
> declared, or when its declarations are mediated by the pain of
> internalized racism, shame about skin color, oppressive color caste
> hierarchies, and the inability of many black men then and now to
> mutually give each other the recognition that would be truly
> liberating. . . . The seeker must confront a desire that has no end, that
> leads him to situations where he is acknowledged and abandoned, yet
> he must continue to search. ("Seductive Sexualities" 199)

The film, says hooks, exposes the depth of longing, "of the need for a history that will name and affirm black gay identity." It acknowledges the need to "claim forefathers, to rescue them from nameless burial" (199). Alice Walker displayed a very similar need in her search for Zora Neale Hurston's burial site in *In Search of Our Mothers' Gardens*. Walker begins her volume with a quote from Vincent van Gogh who, during his lifetime, sold only one painting. Van Gogh committed suicide six months after lamenting in writing the lack of appreciation for artists, saying "I am suffering under an absolute lack of models" (4). Van Gogh's desire to be recognized for his artistry went unfulfilled in his lifetime. His suicide epitomized self-negation and was the ultimate assertion of disconnectedness with the world. Walker explains:

> What is always needed in the appreciation of art, or life, is the larger perspective. Connections made, or at least attempted, where none existed before, the straining to encompass in one's glance at the varied world the common thread, the unifying theme through immense diversity, a fearlessness of growth, of search, of looking, that enlarges the private and the public world. (5)

In her search for Hurston's burial site, Walker acknowledges the same need for models that characterizes van Gogh's statement, as well as Julien's statement in his film about Langston Hughes. Contemporary African American dramatists, such as those discussed in this essay, have demonstrated similar concerns in their works. They create characters and dialogue that call attention to the notion that the search for fulfillment of present longing for self-actualization must be grounded in the recognition of a valued past where authority is located in the experiences of black men and women. This essay focuses on the relationship between desire and authority in four representative plays written during three decades of intense social and political transformation in the United States. Abandoning linearity, I will begin with Adrienne Kennedy's 1964 tale of fatal schizophrenia, *Funnyhouse of a Negro*.

Oliver and Sills note that drama written between 1959 and 1969 was "deeply involved in what we have come to call an identity crisis" (23). The date of Kennedy's play is significant because it places the drama squarely in the midst of a critical period in this country's own identity crisis, one being played out in most extreme and fatal terms. Kennedy wrote *Funnyhouse* at a time of escalating violent confrontations, during a decade that culminated in the deaths of (among others) Martin Luther King, Jr., his mother, Malcolm X, the Kennedy brothers, and four young girls in a Birmingham church. Death was everywhere, and often at issue was the matter of race and whether there was room in this country for black subjects.

Sarah, the doomed protagonist in Kennedy's play, is symbolic of America's "melting pot." Her ancestry reflects British, European, Christian, and African heritages. Werner Sollors observes,

> In the play Kennedy has taken the contemplation of "Sarah" to the breaking point at which the central character is split into several antagonistic aspects which collide dramatically. Such a dramatic strategy is especially suited to shed light on a social world in which human beings belong to more than one community. Kennedy focuses on the moment when different modes of identifying are in sharp, deadly conflict. She portrays her character not as unified or whole but as a collage of multifaceted and contradictory selves (who are not only black and white, or male and female, but also father's daughter and mother's daughter, ruler and martyr, stoic and revolutionary, dead and alive, carnal and spiritual, young and old, hairy and bald, glamorous and humble, or proper and lascivious). (509)

Kennedy's relatively short play is rife with allegorical complexity; however, the overwhelming statement is of the destructive potential of a unit divided against itself. The play, early on, makes apparent Sarah's obsession with shedding all traces of the African self (Patrice Lumumba, killed in 1961). She battles against any assertion of the African aspect of her schizophrenic mind, even to the point of committing suicide by the time the play ends. She cannot articulate a feasible desire, such as acceptance of her African heritage, or acknowledgment of a place for black subjectivity. Such acceptance or acknowledgement would have to be based on the knowledge that within her African heritage, there was something worth honoring; her madness precludes the possibility for any such rationalization.

Christian (Jesus), European (Duchess of Hapsburg), and British (Queen Victoria)[2] aspects of Sarah's personality exhibit distress about the situation. The Belgian Duchess voices the sources of Sarah's crisis:

> Yes, yes, the man's dark, very dark skinned. He is the darkest, my father is the darkest, my mother is the lightest. I am between. But my

father is the darkest. My father is a nigger who drives me to misery. Any time spent with him evolves itself into suffering. He is a black man and the wilderness. (198)

Sarah is the tragic mulatta with a twist, clearly placing the blame for her suffering at the feet of the blackness which relentlessly taints not only an otherwise all-white ancestry but also any foreseeable progeny. Sarah asserts a mad preference for non-being over any acknowledgement of the black presence:

> As for myself, I long to become even a more pallid Negro than I am now, pallid like Negroes on the covers of American Negro magazines; soulless, educated and irreligious. I want to possess no moral value, particularly value as to my being. I want not to be. I ask nothing except anonymity. (194)

Sarah wants to repress knowledge of all things black. The longing phrased in terms of an objection to any essential aspect of blackness is fulfillable only in death because the black self cannot be sacrificed apart from Sarah's other selves. With classic racist reasoning, the non-black selves proclaim, "We of royal blood know, black is evil and has been from the beginning. Even before my mother's hair started to fall out. Before she was raped by a wild black beast. Black was evil" (194).

No one is sane in this play, but in a lengthy monologue, Sarah's landlady provides the information that Sarah's father had begged the Sarah for forgiveness. He had asked that she embrace him, and he had told her that "his existence depended on her embrace." He wanted her to "return to Africa, find revelation in the black" (202). The information is suspect, however, because the landlady is not necessarily aware of Sarah's schizophrenia. Nevertheless, Kennedy makes it very difficult to overlook the confluence of madness, irrationality, and racism. The murder of the black self takes place within Sarah's divided mind after Jesus—in missionary fashion—leads Sarah's various white selves to the jungle in a murderous quest to annihilate blackness. All four voices engage in one monologue as they carry out the murder:

> He is there with his hand out to me, groveling, saying—forgiveness Sarah, is it that you will never forgive me for being black. Forgiveness, Sarah. I know you are a nigger of torment. . . .You will never forgive me for being black. Wild beast. Why did you rape my

mother?. . . He is in grief from that black anguished face of his. Then at once the room will grow bright and my mother will come toward me smiling while I stand before his face and bludgeon him with an ebony head. Forgiveness, Sarah, I know you are a nigger of torment. (202)

The torment of unfulfillable longing ends in suicide, a powerful statement about the potential for self-destruction inherent in a unit divided against itself. Sarah's subjectivity is denied.

Lorraine Hansberry explores the quest for black subjectivity in the form of African American manhood in her 1959 play, *A Raisin in the Sun.* An Afro-philosophical concept suggests that things absorb essence in meaning from other things that are close in proximity. Bringing into harmony things which are close in proximity creates the possibility for the whole to become greater than the sum of its parts. *A Raisin in the Sun* eloquently bears this out. Clearly, a certain amount of discord exists among the Younger family members as the play opens, and the tension increases toward a climactic confrontation between Walter Lee and Lena Younger. The cause of the discord is tied directly to Walter Lee's longing to be a full-fledged capitalist, a role that he equates to manhood. He expresses a hint of that longing when he says, "This morning, I was lookin' in the mirror and thinking about it—I'm thirty-five years old; I been married eleven years and I got a boy who sleeps in the living room—and all I got nothing to give him, nothing but stories about how rich white people live—" (43). Walter Lee asserts a profound poverty as a working-class African American whose only positive role models are rich white capitalists. Ruth offers an alternative vision when she says, "There are colored men who do things." Walter Lee counters, "No thanks to the colored woman," and a few pages later he "disses" all blacks collectively by saying that they are "the world's most backward race of people and that's a fact" (43, 46). Finding no value in African American experience, Walter Lee locates authority for his manhood in white patriarchal capitalism. He, not unlike Kennedy's Sarah in *Funnyhouse*, is a classic example of Carter G. Woodson's mis-educated Negro. Woodson explained in 1933 how America breeds such blacks:

The same educational process which inspires and stimulates the oppressor with the thought that he is everything and has accomplished everything worth while, depresses and crushes at the same time the spark of genius in the Negro by making him feel that his race does not amount to much and never will measure up to the standards of other people. (xiii)

Though Woodson's remarks clearly targeted America's formal education process, they are appropriate here in a general sense because the informally educated Walter Lee is also a product of institutionalized American racism.

Walter Lee articulates a desire to own a liquor store, but Hansberry's text discloses that his real search is for his manhood. Manhood is elusive for Walter Lee because his only "models" are rich white men. bell hooks points out that Walter Lee's "longing for money, goods, power, and control over his destiny made him symbolic of the black American underclass in the fifties and sixties" (2). Walter Lee can never "be" white, but he can certainly aspire to "live white." As author of Walter Lee's life, Hansberry will not allow him to fulfill that particular desire through the enterprise of alcohol distribution with its potential for destruction in the black community. hooks observes of Walter Lee:

> [His] desire to take the insurance money and buy a liquor store links consumer capitalism with the production of a world of addiction. With visionary foresight, Hansberry suggests the possibility that substances (alcohol, drugs, etc.) and substance abuse threaten black solidarity, acting as a genocidal force in the black community. (2)

Lena Younger, representing African American tradition and experience, saves Walter Lee from the perils of engaging in an endless search for manhood. Lena is the embodiment of a valued past which has served as the foundation for the family's continued survival. She reminds Walter Lee that money is not life. As hooks observes, "The play promises that the traditional black folk culture and value system epitomized and expressed by Mama will be maintained in the new location" (2). Ultimately, the quality of the relationships among the Younger family members carries them beyond the nadir at which they learn that Willy has conned Walter Lee out of most of the $10,000 insurance check. The texture of the relationships among the Younger family becomes far more important than the structure of the family's very modest living conditions.

Still, in this play and the other plays discussed here, it is Walter Lee's yearning for something more that creates the possibility for progress toward self-actualization. Before that possibility can be realized, however, the nature of the protagonists' desire must change and for Walter Lee this occurs when authorization for his manhood is no longer located outside his own experiences and traditions. Walter Lee must finally face down Lindner, the representative from Anglo America, whose duty it is to tell the Younger family where they may live in the country built with the blood and sweat of his ancestors. Walter Lee's speech begins on a tentative note and gains strength and resolve as it progresses:

> What I am telling you is that we called you over here to tell you that we are *very proud* and that this is—*this is my son and he makes the sixth generation of our family in this country* and that we have all thought about your offer and we have decided to move into our house *because my father earned it for us, brick by brick.* . . . (He looks the man absolutely in the eyes.) We don't want your money. (He turns and walks away from the man). (118) [emphasis added]

Hansberry's parenthetical instructions are critical here, dealing a final blow to patriarchal capitalism in word and deed. Walter Lee declares his manhood by looking Lindner directly in the eye, and he indicates his refusal to submit to Lindner's assessment of him by turning down the money and turning away from the man. Walter Lee rejects the identity Lindner attempts to force on the Younger family. He expresses hope for future generations of Youngers by proudly presenting his young son and including him in the speech to Lindner. Within this scenario, family harmony is restored, and Walter Lee "becomes" a man without becoming white, rich, or capitalist. His greatest desire is fulfilled when he locates authority and finds pride in African American tradition and experience.

An unwavering sense of self is equally important in Ntozake Shange's *for colored girls who have considered suicide / when the rainbow is enuf,* written in 1975 during the waning moments of two decades of dramatic social, political, and cultural upheaval, at the end of the Nixon and Vietnam eras. Black women had suffered denigration in a number of spheres, from the perpetuation of negative myths about their sexuality (in word and deed), to The Moynihan Report, to exploitation by their fellow revolutionaries in both the women's and civil rights movements. African American women realized that neither black men nor white women provided adequate models for expressing black female subjectivity. Publications such as Toni Cade Bambara's *The Black Woman* (1970) and organizations such as the Combahee River Collective (which began meeting in 1974) symbolized their growing political awareness. Neal Lester has elaborated at length on this developing consciousness and its relationship to the rainbow metaphor in the play's title:

Shange's conventional use of the rainbow symbolizes a movement toward ideals

> for these suffering black women. It represents discovered self-worth after a series of metaphorical storms, the reasons these women or any woman might consider suicide. The rainbow as a symbol works as a visual manifestation of women's spiritual beauty and eventual self-actualization. That a rainbow is not monochromatic by definition affirms the diversity of black females' experiences socially, culturally, and individually. Only in her awareness of the complexity of her experiences can a black girl realize positive self-hood. (16)

Shange's play arrived at a most momentous time and played to rave reviews. The play employs the simultaneous occurrence of words, music, and dance to present a story of transformation. Shange "rejects standard English in favor of black vernacular and profanity and declares open war on the patriarchy by creating her own rules of spelling, punctuation, capitalizations, word usage, and even syntax" (Lester 4-5). Her colorful ladies clearly engage in a ritualistic transformation from being other-defined to being self-defined. Shange's colored girl longs to be loved for herself.

As in Kennedy's play, a form of schizophrenia is apparent. In Shange's play, schizophrenia has been induced by the internalization of the negative self-image reflected where maleness and whiteness are valued, and the multi-voiced protagonist possesses neither quality. Shange uses the multi-voiced woman of color to demonstrate a range of negative life experiences stemming from the same cause, the neglect of self, the inability to find honor and value in the black female experience. Under such circumstances, it is impossible to assert a strong black female self or identity. Together, the colorful personalities articulate their greatest pain in describing inadequate responses to their desire to receive love and respect from the men in their lives. In her own way, each lady has a tale of unfulfilled desire. The folowing monologue of lady in red is a representative sampling of their collective longing:

> without any assistance or guidance from you/i have loved you assiduously for 8 months 2 wks & a day/i have been stood up four times/i've left 7 packages on yr doorstep/forty poems 2 plants & 3 handmade notecards i left/town so i cd send to you have been no help to me/on my job/you call at 3:00 in the morning on weekdays/so i cd drive 27 1/2 miles cross the bay before i go to work/charmin charmin/but you are of no assistance/i want you to know/this was an experiment/ to see how selfish i cd be/if i wd really carry on to snare a possible lover/if i waz capable of *debasin my self for the love of another*/if i cd stand *not being wanted/when i wanted to be wanted/*& i cannot/so/with no further assistance & no guidance from you/i am endin this affair. (13-14) [emphasis added]

Lady in red acknowledges her conscious decision to seek love. She then reveals the self-denigration that results from her unfulfilled longing, and finally, she realizes the futility and ends the affair. In turn, the ladies recite tales of perpetual suffering as Shange's choreopoem unfolds amid music, dance, and poetry that only a colored girl's heart can express. Their collective suffering is portrayed in a number of ways, including the death of children, "necessary" abortions, and the exploitative actions of fickle, lying lovers. Lady in green declares that "somebody almost walked off wid alla my stuff" (49). And, lady in yellow laments her "dependency on other livin beins for love" and addresses the ridiculous question of choosing between race and gender:

> I survive on intimacy & tomorrow/that's all i've got goin & the music waz like smack & you knew abt that & still refused my dance waz not enuf/& it was all i had but bein alive & bein a woman & bein colored is a metaphysical dilemma/i havent conquered yet/do you see the point my spirit is too ancient to understand the separation of soul & gender/my love is too delicate to have thrown back on my face. (45)

Lady in yellow, through her poetry, learns and expresses the value of her own love. The remaining ladies echo her sentiment:

> my love is too beautiful to have thrown back on my face
> my love is too sanctified to have thrown back on my face
> my love is too magic to have thrown back on my face
> my love is too saturday nite to have thrown back on my face
> my love is too complicated to have thrown back on my face
> my love is too music to have thrown back on my face. (46-47)

An air of ritual is inherent in the dialogue, music, and movement, characterized by a cyclical rhythm that becomes increasingly perceptible and then fades away until the ladies give voice to the final refrain. The chant, "i found god in myself and i loved her/i loved her fiercely" (63), states a profound awareness of the empowering capacity of locating authority for black female subjectivity within black female experience. The seven voices speaking a singular refrain at the play's end are the antithesis to Adrienne Kennedy's doomed protagonist and her monologue of madness during the suicide scene in *Funnyhouse*. The seven ladies in Shange's play learn to privilege and value their experiences as African American women. Underlying the final refrain is the understanding that their unfulfilled desires resulted from misplaced authority.

Misplaced authority is clearly apparent in the opening scenes of Alice Childress's 1955 play, *Trouble in Mind*. The play-within-a-play format allows consideration of an assortment of complex issues confronting the African American theater in this era. Like Hansberry's play, *Trouble* also explores black manhood, and two male types surface in the course of the play: John Nevins, a novice actor who begins as a "yes man" but eventually asserts himself; and Sheldon Forrester, the veteran actor who, notes Elizabeth Brown-Guillory, "has been worn down and perceives that it is futile for a black man to try to function as a man in American society" (230). Brown-Guillory adds,

> Sheldon defines his manhood in terms of success at projecting that he is not a man among white men. He brags that his denial of self has helped him to survive in the world and says that blacks ought to "take low" in order to keep whatever jobs are issued out to them (230-31).

In the opening moments of the play, the protagonist, Wiletta, seems to share Sheldon's resolve. She adjusts her reactions and temperament in chameleon-like fashion to accommodate white authority, and she tells John to "Laugh! Laugh at everything [whites] say, makes 'em feel superior" (297). Sheldon and Wiletta support each other's complacency in the following exchange:

> *Sheldon.* Do, Lord, let's keep peace. Last thing I was in, the folks fought and argued so, the man said he'd never do a colored show again . . . and he didn't!

> *Wiletta.* I always say it's the man's play, the man's money and the man's theater, so what you gonna do? . . . You ain't got a pot nor a window. Now, when you get your own . . . (300)

The black cast members are either so preoccupied with the need to accommodate white authority, or so mired in double-consciousness, that any possibility for group consensus is seriously undermined. Thus, when Wiletta finally confronts white authority, it must be a solitary effort.[3]

During Act 1, Manners, the white director, shakes Wiletta from her mask of complacency by forcing her into an extremely uncomfortable situation. Judy, the sole white woman in the play, while rehearsing a scene for *Chaos in Belleville*, bends to pick up a piece of paper that the director drops onto the stage. Manners tells Judy to hold her position, and he directs Wiletta to pick up the paper. When John and Sheldon start for the paper, the following exchange occurs:

> *Manners.* I asked Wiletta! (Catches Wiletta's eye.) Well?

> *Wiletta.* (Shocked into a quick flare of temper.) Well, hell! I ain't the damn janitor! (Trying to check her temper.) I . . . well, I . . . shucks . . . I . . . damn.

> *Manners.* (Even though he was trying to catch them offguard, he didn't expect this.) Cut! Cut! It's all over. (Everyone is surprised again) What you have just seen is . . . is . . . is fine acting. (He is quite shaken and embarrassed from Wiletta's action.) (307)

The director tries to cover up his embarrassment by saying that the whole episode was a trick, but Wiletta begins to watch him with a sharp eye from that point on. Prior to the paper incident, Wiletta and Manners had been engaged in a masquerade of mutual admiration based on Manners's ability to maintain control and Wiletta's ability to accept with a smile her "place" in the theater. Wiletta's reaction to Manners's command to pick up the paper betrays, therefore, a deep-seated resentment of the subservient roles into which she has been forced on the stage. By the end of Act 1, she declares her desire:

> Henry, *I want to be* an actress, I've always *wanted to be* an actress and they ain't gonna do me the way they did the home rule! *I want to be* an actress 'cause one day you're nineteen and then forty and so on . . . *I want to be* an actress! Henry, they stone us when we try to go to school, the world's crazy. . . .Where the hell do I come in? *Every damn body pushin' me off the face of the earth! I want to be* an actress . . . hell, *I'm gonna be* one, you hear me? (She pounds the table.) (318-19) [emphasis added]

Wiletta wants to end white circumscription of her acting ability. She wants to control the messages/images she projects through her acting— subject, rather than object. Childress had been an actress in the American Negro Theatre Company, and as Samuel A. Hay points out in his historical and critical analysis of African American theater, Wiletta's role is somewhat autobiographical. Childress often complained that, as an actress, she received the same type of treatment from the white theater establishment and white audiences that she addressed in her plays. Stock charaters and recycled roles denied her the opportunity too "display the full range of her considerable acting talent" (Hay 26).

After such an emphatic assertion, Wiletta can no longer participate passively in the production of a play that undermines the assertion of herself as a versatile and talented actress. In Act 2, she questions the substance of *Chaos*, much to the director's growing irritation. The character Wiletta portrays is the mother of a young black male bound for the lynch mob. The white male author of the play wants Wiletta's character to utter the words which deliver the son into the hands of his killers. Wiletta feels that such an action is both unnatural and unjustifiable. She suggests instead, "Wouldn't it be nice if the mother could say, 'Son, you right! I don't want to send you outta here but I don't know what to do. . .'" Manners replies, "Darling, darling. . . no." Wiletta suggests further, "Or else she says 'Run for it Job!', and then they catch him like that. . . he's dead anyway, see?" Losing patience, Manners tells her, "It's not the script, it's you. Bronson does the writing, you do the acting, it's that simple" (336). Manners clearly

wants Wiletta to accept white authority without question, and after this
exchange, Wiletta gives John Nevins just the opposite advice that she
had given him in Act 1: "John, I told you everything wrong 'cause I
didn't know better, that's the size of it. No fool like a old fool. You
right, don't make sense to be bowin' and scrapin' and tommin'. . . . No,
don't pay no attention to what I said" (336). Nevins and the other two
black cast members, Sheldon and Millie, eventually voice concerns
about the logic of *Chaos* and its depictions of blacks, but Wiletta is the
only cast member willing to risk everything to confront, critique, and
displace white authority. She demands that the director listen to her:

> You been askin' me what I think and where things come from and
> how come I thought it and all that. Where is this comin' from?. . .Tell
> me why this boy's people turned against him? Why we sendin' him
> out into the teeth of a lynch mob? I'm his mother and I'm sendin' him
> to his death. This is a lie. (340)

The exchange continues, with the initially bemused director gradually
realizing that Wiletta poses a real threat to his authority.

Significantly, Wiletta bases her concerns with the "logic" of the
play on insights received during a discussion with Mrs. Green, herself a
choir and drama director in a most traditional of African American
institutions, the church. Mrs. Green's uncle actually experienced the
sharecropper lifestyle depicted in *Chaos*. Manners, of course, does not
want to hear what Wiletta has to say, and the confrontation between
them reaches a critical point when Manners finally suggests to Wiletta
that she thinks she knows more than the author. Wiletta retorts by
calling Manners "a prejudiced racist" (341). Manners, caught
completely off guard by Wiletta's assertion, forgets his manners, drops
his mask, and lets loose with a recitation of his perceptions of
American reality to which even the "impotent" Sheldon temporarily
reacts:

> The American public is not ready to see you the way you want to be
> seen because, one, they don't believe it, two, they don't want to
> believe it, and three, they're convinced they're superior . . . . Get it?
> Now you wise up and aim for the soft spot in that American heart, let
> 'em pity you, make 'em weep buckets, be helpless, make 'em feel so
> damned sorry for you that they'll lend a hand in easing up the
> pressure. (342)

A disillusioned John decides that it is time to give notice. Millie, the other black actress/character, shows that she is willing to continue to compromise when she says, "I know what's right but I need this job" (344). She also reminds Wiletta that proper procedure dictated that the group should have first discussed any proposed challenge to Manners. Sheldon resorts to his old survivor's logic, wondering if they are fired, telling Wiletta she must apologize, and in general continuing with a litany of excuses for remaining prostrate. At this point, Wiletta's is the only revolutionary mind among the black cast members.

Wiletta's challenge to white authority, indeed her attack on that authority, renders uncertain her immediate employment. Sheldon's warning, "When you kick up a disturbance, the man's in his rights to call the cops" (344), combined with Childress's notation that a police siren can be heard in the background, suggests that Wiletta may lose more than her job. No doubt, she is aware of this possibility because she has been involved in theater for some twenty-five years. Wiletta tells them, "There are times when you got to be alone. *This is mine*" (345). She decides, shortly thereafter, to take the stage and be the actress she has longed to be, telling Henry, "I've always wanted to do somethin' real grand . . .in the theater . . . to stand forth at my best . . . to stand up here and do anythin I want" (346). She takes the stage, standing tall, and, finally, she is able to perform lines of her own choosing in the manner that she chooses. She becomes author, director, actor, subject.

Wiletta undergoes heroic self-transformation during the course of the play, eventually realizing that she must locate the basis for self-authentication where it feels natural, logical and in tune with her experience as an African American woman. Equally as significant as the economic factor in this play is Wiletta's juxtaposition of the school desegregation issue with her own dilemma in the white-controlled theater world. Written during the infant years of the civil rights movement in the wake of the *Brown* decision and the murder of Emmett Till, *Trouble* symbolizes the struggling black theater community, striving to take those first tentative steps toward becoming. Clearly, Wiletta sees the big picture, and her solution is to craft an active black female subject. Under the circumstances, it was a revolutionary action. Such actions in the public sphere were taken at great risk. As would become clear in the 1960s, an independent African American theater required a willingness to risk or forego the monetary rewards which maintained compliance by forcing blacks to adapt to the demands of a colonizing authority.

Black theater insists that certain Black Aesthetic standards are valid and valuable, and the playwrights discussed in this essay include that message in their works. In the space where subjectivity is desired, authority for that subjectivity must be rooted in the experiences of the desirer. Otherwise, desire remains an unquenchable longing. If institutionalized racism oppresses blacks as blacks and women as women, it forces a double burden of oppression upon African American women. Ultimately, the struggle must be for the freedom to be fully human. In Ntozake Shange's 1979 play, *spell # 7*, a giant minstrel mask hanging over the stage symbolizes society's oppression of both men and women, black actors who must contend with being stock characterizations, mere stereotypes in the white imagination, with professional limitations imposed on their talents by outside authority. Shange proposes in her subtitle a spell or a fixative to help these men and women deal with the contradictory nature of existence for blacks in the diaspora, subtitling the play a *geechee jibara quik magic trance manual for technologically stressed third world people*. Only in the familiar, more intimate black world do the characters in *spell # 7* shed their masks and their mechanical performances to become real, multifaceted people (Shange 243).

A recurring theme in these dramas is the need to relocate authority and to build strong identities, a necessary first step toward fulfilling the desire to be active subjects in the world. Kennedy, Hansberry, Shange, and Childress have exhibited an acute awareness of the need for the development of pride rooted in African American heritage.

NOTES

1. See, for example, Mance Williams, *Black Theatre in the 1960s and 1970s: A Historical-Critical Analysis of the Movement* (Greenwood,1985); Sandra Hollin Flowers, *African American Nationalist Literature of the 1960s: Pens of Fire* (Garland, 1996); Genevieve Fabre, *Drumbeats, Masks, and Metaphor: Contemporary Afro-American Theatre* (translated by Melvin Dixon, Harvard UP, 1983); Tejumola Olaniyan, *Scars of Conquest / Masks of Resistance: The Invention of Cultural Identities in African, African-American, and Caribbean Drama* (Oxford UP, 1995); Elizabeth Brown-Guillory, *Their Place on the Stage: Black Women Playwrights in America* (Greenwood, 1988);

and Samuel A. Hay, *African American Theatre: An Historical and Critical Analysis* (Cambridge UP, 1994).

2. Mance Williams provides an interesting analysis of the significance of the various components of Sarah's mind, especially that of Jesus as the primary locus for all of Sarah's fragmented selves.

3. Childress wrote an alternative ending to the play which has the black cast membes unite and continue the production. Doris Abramson discusses this alternative ending in *Negro Playwrights in the American Theatre* 1925-1959. New York: , 1967. 201-204.

WORKS CITED

Brown-Guillory, Elizabeth. "Black Women Playwrights: Exorcising Myths." *Phylon: The Atlanta University Review of Race and Culture* 48 (1987): 229-233.

Childress, Alice. *Trouble in Mind. Black Drama in America: An Anthology.* Ed. Darwin T. Turner. Washington, D. C.: Howard UP, 1994. 291-346.

Hansberry, Lorraine. "A Raisin in the Sun." *Contemporary Black Drama.* Ed. Clinton F. Oliver and Stephanie Sills. New York: Scribner, 1971. 27-120.

Hay, Samuel A. *African American Theatre: An Historical and Critical Analysis.* Cambridge: Cambridge UP, 1994.

hooks, bell. "Liberation Scenes." *Yearning.* Boston: South End, 1990. 1-13.

———. "Seductive Sexualities: Representing Blackness in Poetry and on Screen." *Yearning.* Boston: South End, 1990. 193-201.

Kennedy, Adrienne. "Funnyhouse of a Negro." *Contemporary Black Drama.* Ed. Clinton F. Oliver and Stephanie Sills. New York: Scribner, 1971. 187-206.

Lester, Neal A. *Ntozake Shange: A Critical Study of the Plays.* New York: Garland,1995.

Oliver, Clinton F., and Stephanie Sills, eds. *Contemporary Black Drama: From A Raisin in the Sun to No Place to Be Somebody.* New York: Scribner, 1971.

Shange, Ntozake. *for colored girls who have considered suicide / when the rainbow is enuf.* New York: MacMillan, 1975.

——— *spell # 7: geechee jibara quik magic trance manual for technologically stressed third world people. 9 Plays by Black Women.* Ed. Margaret B. Wilkerson. New York: Mentor, 1986.

Sollors, Werner. "Owls and Rats in the American Funnyhouse: Adrienne Kennedy's Drama." *American Literature* 63 (1991): 507-32.

Walker, Alice. "Saving the Life That Is Your Own: The Importance of Models in the Artist's Life." *In Search of Our Mothers' Gardens*. San Diego: Harcourt, 1983. 3-14.

Woodson, Carter G. *The Mis-Education of the Negro*. Washington: Associated Publishers, 1933.

Celebrating the (Extra)Ordinary
Alice Childress's Representation of Black Selfhood
E. Barnsley Brown

> Writers, be wary of those who tell you to leave the past alone and confine yourselves to the present moment. Our story has not been told in any moment.
>
> Alice Childress, "The Negro Woman in American Literature"

> The very act of a black woman telling her story, speaking her truth, can be perceived as an act of resistance to oppression; the real power in her exercise of artistic freedom is the casting of her own image by her own hand.
>
> Sydné Mahone, "Seers on the Rim"

As part of a survey of African American writers published in the January 1968 issue of *Negro Digest*, Alice Childress asserts, "There is no artist among us whose individual success will free the rest of us. There is no substitute for human rights . . . not even art" (86). Although Childress clearly rejects art as a replacement for social and political equality, she has used it as a vehicle for social protest throughout her writing career. Since she is a writer who has written plays and had them produced for well over four decades, she is quite familiar with the challenges and struggles the literary marketplace presents for writers in general. Furthermore, as the only African American woman whose plays have been written and professionally produced for nearly half a century (Brown-Guillory, "Alice Childress" 66), Childress is a trail blazer who testifies to the alarming lack of accurate representations of

African Americans, especially African American women, in the American theater.

Indeed, Childress is committed to representing and revising the notion of what is "ordinary." She reports that as a child she was encouraged to write papers about successful African Americans rather than those for whom "life ain't been no crystal stair."[1] She avers, "I turned against the tide and to this day I continue to write about those who come in second, or not at all . . . the intricate and magnificent patterns of a loser's life" ("A Candle" 112). To focus solely on the "successful" blacks, those few who have "made it," would be to deny the many deferred dreams of those who have suffered irreparably from racism and sexism in their various social and economic forms.

In effect, to reclaim the "ordinary" is thus to situate the experiences of African Americans within a real socio-political context rather than to suggest that all African Americans should follow or even have the opportunity to follow the example of the "accomplishers." As Childress maintains, "I concentrate on portraying have-nots in a *have* society, those seldom singled out by mass media, except as source material for derogatory humor and/or condescending clinical, social analysis" ("A Candle" 112). Childress does not blame the "losers" for their failures but instead embraces them as integral aspects of the African American experience. She asserts, "Black writers cannot afford to abuse or neglect the so-called ordinary characters who represent a part of ourselves, the self twice denied, first by racism and then by class indifference" ("Knowing" 10). In her commitment to conveying the "ordinary" or "little" people, Childress represents with accuracy and precision those who would not otherwise be represented and asserts their importance to a comprehensive understanding to the repercussions of prejudice.

In her commitment to depicting the lives of such people, Childress also stakes out a territory in spite of the white marketplace in which writing by blacks is not considered "universal" or applicable to the entire American experience. She observes, "That [white] measure of 'universality' and 'common experience' places shackles on a writer's pen" ("A Candle" 113). Yet Childress escapes these shackles by celebrating the very ordinariness of the characters she constructs. Of her own aesthetic she states,

> My writing attempts to interpret the "ordinary" because they are not
> ordinary. Each human is uniquely different. Like snowflakes, the

> human pattern is never cast twice. We are uncommonly and
> marvelously intricate in thought and action, our problems are most
> complex and too often, silently borne. ("A Candle" 112).

She refuses the notion of a single all-encompassing "black experience"
and, instead, conveys a multiplicity of selves and experiences as part of
the universal human condition.

Childress's rejection of stereotypical constructions of blackness is
evident even in her first play, *Florence,* first produced at the American
Negro Theatre in Harlem in 1949.[2] Like many of her black female
predecessors, Childress chose the one-act format for this play[3] and
streamlined the number of characters to highlight the clash of black and
white. The play is essentially a dialogue between a middle-aged black
woman, "Mama," and Mrs. Carter, a well-dressed white woman. That
"Mama" represents the stereotype of the black matriarch is suggested
by the fact that she is only referred to by her proper name twice at the
end of the play and never in Childress's notes; instead, she is identified
solely by her role as the mother of Florence, a young actress trying to
succeed in New York City. Mama's lack of importance except in
relationship to Florence is emphasized by the play's title; Childress
constructs Mama so it is solely her matriarchal role, her literal and
figurative ability to mother, that defines her at the beginning of the
play. In that respect, Mama fulfills one of the major criteria for the
matriarch stereotype.[4]

Mama's desire to protect Florence from white prejudices also
reveals yet another aspect of the black matriarch stereotype. As the play
opens, Mama is waiting for a train to go visit her daughter in New York
City and to bring her back home to the South where she belongs.
Florence is ambitious, but as her sister, Marge, explains, "She got
notions a Negro woman don't need" (111). In fact, Marge proclaims,
"She must think she's white!" (112). Marge resents the fact that
Florence's ambitions to be an actress are costing the family, especially
when, "them [white] folks ain't gonna let her be no actress" (112).
Mama, too, doubts that Florence can make it as a black actress and
wants to shield her from failure by bringing her safely back home. Yet
it is clear that Mama is also extremely proud of Florence. She argues
with Marge's criticism that Florence's aspirations are futile by
asserting, "But she was in a real play" (111). Mama is similarly proud
when the black porter tells her his brother saw Florence in a Colored
moving picture (113). Mama obviously yearns for her daughter to

succeed but is fearful that it will not happen in the white-controlled American theater.

Childress further complicates Mama's conflict by dramatizing the separation between blacks and whites in the Jim Crow South. The stage space itself is divided in two with one side labeled "White" and the other, "Colored."[5] Although Marge crosses the low railing to the white side and flippantly remarks, "Don't feel a damn bit different over here than it does on our side" (112), the entire play attests to the immensity of the difference.

In effect, this difference is symbolized by the rest room doors on the stage, two of which are marked "Colored men" and "Colored women" and two of which are marked "White ladies" and "White gentlemen"; thus, to be white is to have the wealth, power, and prestige of the title, "lady" or "gentleman," whereas to be black is to be defines solely in terms of gender, of biological makeup. Even then, Mama is symbolically de-feminized when the porter advises her, "If you go to the rest room, use the Colored men's . . . the other one is out of order" (114). By the "other one," the porter is obviously referring to the Colored women's rest room rather than the white ladies' rest room; not only does Mama lack any right to use the "ladies'" rest room, but she is also symbolically divested of her womanhood by having to use the men's room.

In addition to being de-feminized, Mama is also de-humanized by her interaction with Mrs. Carter. Mrs. Carter obviously regards Mama as being at her disposal, demanding her attention by claiming, "I've simply got to talk to someone" (115). At first, Childress shows Mama in a faithful "Mammy" role to Mrs. Carter; Mama gives Mrs. Carter her attention like a devoted servant. Yet as the dialogue continues, it becomes evident that Mrs. Carter and Mama are speaking in radically different languages, or, in Bakhtinian terms, "social dialects."[6] Mrs. Carter's social dialect arises from an ideology of friendly racism in which she maintains, "I'm not a southerner really" (114), implying that she is not racist. However, she refers to the porter as "Boy," in classic racist fashion and introduces herself grandiosely to Mama without ever inquiring about Mama's own name. Although Mrs. Carter converses with Mama and monopolizes her attention, she still constructs a symbolic railing between Mama and herself when she laments, "You know, I try but it's really difficult to understand you people" (117). Mrs. Carter's social dialect insists upon a "you people" versus "my people" distinction in which her people are undoubtedly superior.

Childress emphasizes the racism of Mrs. Carter's social dialect at two key points in the play. In the first, Mrs. Carter discusses her brother's latest novel about a mulatta who has "this deep shame." When Mama asks, "What shame has she got?", Mrs. Carter replies, "It's obvious! This lovely creature . . . intelligent, ambitious, and well . . . she's a Negro!" (115). Mama, speaking in a social dialect in which being black is never a source of shame, continues to wait for the explanation of the character's reason for shame. When Mrs. Carter recounts that the heroine jumps off a bridge and drowns herself because she is part black, Mama's response illustrates the fundamental ideological difference in their social dialects. Indeed, Mama's simple question, "Why?" reveals the glaring difference between her social dialect and that of Mrs. Carter.

Mama's simple question is also significant because it signifies her rejection of the tragic mulatta stereotype.[7] Mrs. Carter believes that the novel's protagonist commits suicide because "She can't face it! Living in a world where she almost belongs but not quite" (116). However, Mama knows, "That ain't so! Not one bit it ain't!" (116). Although Mama's language heretofore has been very polite and respectful, at this point, it shifts dramatically, and Childress actually shows the conflict between Mama and Mrs. Carter through their clashing social dialects. While Mrs. Carter has previously invaded Mama's space by insisting upon Mama's participation in their conversation, now Mama symbolically moves one foot over onto the "white" side and stands "face to face" with Mrs. Carter. She counters Mrs. Carter's flimsy construction of the tragic mulatta with concrete examples of real people who could pass for white but are proud to be black. Ironically, here Childress is deconstructing the literary figuration of the tragic mulatta within a dramatic context that purports to be real.

Childress also deconstructs the tragic mulatta by showing that Mama resists the stereotype not only through her verbal responses to Mrs. Carter's presuppositions but also through strategic silences. After Mama realizes that Mrs. Carter is not really hearing what she has to say, she begins to use silence, paradoxically, to voice her rage and resistance. Childress writes silence into the scripts four times in the space of just one-third of a page, suggesting that silence is yet another language that figures in Mama's social dialect. As Peter Hitchcock explains, "Subalternity produces not only voices but strategic silences, the gaps in communication themselves signal a disabling of the traditional modes of 'speaking' the other, and this too must be figured in the dialogics of the oppressed—silence itself as a 'language' of trangression" (xvii). Mama's withdrawal from the dialogue builds a protective wall around her but also enables her to resist Mrs. Carter's monologic discourse that would attempt to speak (for) her.

In effect, Mama is resisting the racist ideology embedded in Mrs. Carter's statement about her brother, "He knows the Negro so well" (117). This statement assumes that all blacks are the same and attempts to establish a monologic black identity or black experience, a project which Childress uses her characters to undercut at every possible moment. As Childress states, "There is no such thing as *the* Black experience" ("A Candle" 115-116). To explode stereotypes that suggest such a generalized experience is thus to open up new ground for accurate and multi-faceted constructions of blackness.

Therefore, Childress depicts Mama as moving from the traditional subservient role of the "Mammy" to a more militant role. In the second key section of the play, the difference between the social dialects of Mama and Mrs. Carter is again made apparent, but this time, Mama opts for a more active resistance to Mrs. Carter's prejudice than silence. When Mama explains that Florence is an aspiring actress and asks if Mrs. Carter could possibly help her find a job, a long interchange ensues in which Mrs. Carter considers which of her many contacts and friends might be able to help Florence. Only after a long exchange does Mrs. Carter reveal that she is thinking of Florence for domestic work; it does not even cross her mind to consider her for acting jobs. When Mama finally realizes what Mrs. Carter intends, she takes control and warns, "You better get over on the other side of that rail. It's against the law for you to be over here with me" (120). Mama thus uses the laws meant to restrict her to establish a safe distance from this woman whose racist politics insult her daughter's talents and abilities. In this climactic moment, Mama tears up the paper with Florence's address on it, asks the porter for a stamp, and mails Florence a letter that says, "Keep trying" (121). She realizes that Florence's aspirations are symbolic of the aspirations of African Americans to be treated as equal citizens in a society that has established whiteness as its norm and standard of value.

At this same moment, Mama is referred to by her proper name for the first time in the play. Symbolically, she ceases to be "Mama" or the doting Mammy and instead becomes "Mrs. Whitney," an interesting choice of names on Childress's part since "Whitney" appears to be "Whitey" with the negative French "ne" inserted within it, linguistically suggesting "not white." In addition, the black porter is named at this time and his name is even more obviously symbolic: "Mr. Brown." This striking use of names in the play seems to suggest that in rejecting Mrs. Carter's stereotypes of blacks and her resultant attempt to fix Florence's fate as a domestic, Mama succeeds in securing her personal identity as well as that of other African Americans. Indeed, one can hear Childress's own voice echoing as Mama asserts, "She [Florence] can be anything in the world she wants to be! That's her right!" (120).[8] Like Childress herself, Mama rejects and revises stereotypical constructions of blackness and claims her human right to do and be anything she desires.[9]

While Childress primarily revises the stereotype of the Mammy in *Florence*, her rejection of a number of stereotypical constructions of blackness is formally emphasized by her metadrama, *Trouble in Mind* (1955). Borrowing the device of the play within a play from Shakespeare, Childress politicizes it to reveal and debunk the racist ideology that perpetuates stereotypes. As Mae King contends, "Racial stereotypes are the reformed, more sophisticated techniques used by moon-age America for maintaining the essence of both the slave and caste systems, i.e. white domination of blacks by the exercise of power on a racist basis" (5). Childress uses the microcosm of the American theater depicted in *Trouble in Mind* to suggest the macrocosm of American society in which stereotypes are perpetuated to advance a racist ideology of white supremacy and black inferiority.

Childress's major spokeswoman in the play is Wiletta, a middle-aged actress who has experienced the pervasive racism of the white-controlled American theater and resists it with a cynical attitude and dry wit. When she meets John, the young, educated black actor who will play the lead in the play within the play, she challenges him, "Why you want to act? Why don't you make somethin' outta yourself" (139). As a veteran of the theater, Wiletta proclaims, "You don't have to take what I've been through . . . don't have to take it off 'em." And yet she counsels John, "Laugh! Laugh at everything they [whites] say, makes 'em feel superior" (139). Wiletta shifts between a militant discourse that challenges the white-controlled system and a subservient discourse that perpetuates racist stereotypes such as the Uncle Tom or devoted servant.

These stereotypes become very evident in *Trouble in Mind* when Wiletta and another black actress, Millie, discuss the sorts of roles they are used to playing. Millie comments that *she* would like to be the heroine in the play, and Wiletta scoffs, "Ha! That'll be the day!"

Instead, the play's heroine is Miss Renard, the white daughter of the boss, who fights her father because of the way he treats the blacks. In racist fashion, the white daughter is valorized for standing up for the black tenant farmers while the blacks are cast as ignorant, passive workers.

Millie's description of her theatrical costumes is also significant. She grumbles, "Also wish I'd get to wear some decent clothes sometime. Only chance I get to dress up is offstage. I'll wear them baggy cotton dresses but damn if I'll wear another bandanna" (141). In addition, Wiletta makes fun of the stereotypical names given to black Mammy figures in the white theater, grumbling further, "She's played every flower in the garden" (141), while Millie jokingly retorts, "And you've done the jewels . . . Crystal, Pearl, Opal!" (141). As the women break into laughter, they diffuse the power of this "Master" script and the stock theatrical roles for blacks it proffers. Indeed, humor is a powerful tool for Childress as a playwright since it makes her message palatable to a white audience and uplifting to a black one. John O. Killens explains, "Childress's humor is in the profoundest tradition, i.e., humor with a political vengeance" (131). Or, in Bakhtinian terms, Childress's humor is often carnivalesque in nature, signifying a temporary overthrow of authority,[10] in this case, the authority of the "Master" script.[11]

Childress exposes the Master script not only through the stereotypes the African Americans are meant to play in the drama but also through the language they are scripted to use. For example, Sheldon, who is to play the Uncle Tom figure, stumbles over his lines when he reaches the word, "iffen" (142). Not understanding this inaccurate depiction of African American dialect, he pauses, and Millie sardonically comments, "Iffen." Indeed, most of Sheldon's lines are variations of "Yes, sir" and "Thank you, sir," so Millie mockingly remarks, "Iffen you forget one, just keep shakin' your head" (142). By conveying the reactions of Sheldon and Millie to this contrived black dialect, Childress is able to show how ridiculous both the dialogue and Sheldon's role really are.

The dialogue is made all the more unbelievable by the fact that the action of the play, *Chaos in Belleville*, is supposed to be transpiring in 1957. Sheldon assumes that the dialect signals the play is set long ago, "in them days," but Manners, the white director, corrects him: "The time is now, down south in some remote little county, they say those things . . . now" (147). Manners is convinced that they play will be a hit because "this is *now*, we're living this" (14). His statement is particularly ironic since the racist assumptions present throughout the play show that the Master script, the socio-linguistic order of the slave holder's ideology, still prevails even in the middle of the twentieth century.

While the Master script is evident throughout the play, it is most obvious in the speech of Mr. Renard, the white boss. Renard speaks publicly because some of the Negroes in Belleville plan to vote for the first time and he voices the opposition to their voting:

> Let us weigh our answer very carefully when the dark-skinned Oliver Twist approaches our common pot and says: 'Please, sir, I want some more.' When we say 'no,' remember that a soft answer turneth away wrath. . . . If we are superior, let us show our superiority! (155)

Thus, Renard justifies refusing to grant blacks the right to vote as a means of confirming white superiority.

It is no wonder that Childress describes the rendition of Renard's speech by the white actor, Bill O'Wray, as "masterful" (155). As O'Wray represents the white master figure in the play within the play, so the white director, Manners, represents the master in the framing play. His racist social dialect is evident in the play when he calls Millie "gal" (144) and the black lead, "boy" (168). He also commands Wiletta to pick up some trash on the stage (146) and attempts to intimidate her in a "game" of word association (152), all under the guise of wresting a convincing performance from her. Yet Wiletta maintains from the start, "I know exactly what you want" (151). She knows the stereotypical role she is supposed to play, that of the spiritual-singing black matriarch who is devoted to the whites for whom she works. Wiletta refuses to develop any motivations for this character because it is a standard formula she knows well and has probably played dozens of times.

As the rehearsal progresses, however, Wiletta realizes that she cannot consent to play such a role because it is demeaning. In fact, Childress shows Wiletta challenging Manners about the third act of *Chaos in Belleville*. In this act, her character's son, Job, is killed because she tells him to turn himself in. Wiletta declares, "I don't see why the boy couldn't get away," and Manners condescendingly responds, "We don't want to antagonize the audience" (164). His comment reveals that the audience for this Broadway-bound show is predominantly white since a black audience would want Job to escape, especially since he does not deserve any sort of punishment.

Not only does Wiletta refuse to categorize Job's attempt to vote as a crime, but she also refuses to believe that her character would send him out to a lynching mob. She challenges, "I'm his mother and I'm sendin' him to his death. This is a lie." As she shifts into militant discourse, Wiletta reveals what had been obscured by Manners's insistence that this is an anti-lynching play: "The writer wants the damn white man to be the hero—and I'm the villain" (169). Wiletta comprehends that not only does *Chaos in Belleville* cast the blacks in stereotypical roles that are inaccurate, but that these roles are also quite deleterious.

By acting in the play, Wiletta realizes that she is contributing to the propagation of negative images of African Americans, and she rebels.[12] Here we see Childress rewriting Wiletta's character since Wiletta advises John at the start of the play that, "White folks can't stand unhappy Negroes . . . so laugh, laugh when it ain't funny at all" (139). Near the end of the play, however, Wiletta addresses Manners directly and declares, "You are a prejudiced man, a prejudiced racist" (170). The rest of the company is shocked by her comment until Wiletta eggs Manners into revealing his bigotry. She presses him with questions such as, "Would you send your son out to be murdered?" (171) until Manners is angered and retorts, "Don't compare yourself to me! What goes for my son doesn't necessarily go for yours! . . . Don't compare him [Job] with my son, they've got nothing in common . . . not a goddam thing!" (171). When Manners unveils his own Master script, his own racist social dialect, the members of the cast simultaneously become aware of the Master script in *Chaos in Belleville*. Childress makes it clear that the play within the play as well as the framing play evince the pervasive racism of American society.

Manners explains that, "the American public is not ready to see you the way you want to be seen" (170) and thus exhorts Wiletta to conform to stereotypes of African Americans that are acceptable to a white audience. However, Wiletta realizes that these stereotypes are more debilitating than helpful. She protests, "I'm sick of people signifyin' we [African Americans] got no sense" (171). Although Sheldon accepts his role in typical Tommish fashion and urges Wiletta to apologize to Manners, Childress has Wiletta maintain the militant discourse she has adopted during the play. Wiletta threatens, "I'm playin' a leadin' part and I want this script changed or else" (172). Her rejection of the Master script and call for its revision and/or replacement articulate Childress's own project as a black woman playwright who strives to create accurate depictions of black selfhood.[13]

In *Wedding Band* (1966), Childress not only shows the importance of creating accurate representations of black selfhood but also of taking pride in the African American heritage. Indeed, the tragic flaw of Julia, the heroine in the play, is her perception of herself as separate and alienated from her people. In the words of Catherine Wiley, "Julia's problem throughout the play is less her white lover than her reluctance to see herself as a member of the black community" (188). Hence, the subtitle of the play, "A Love/Hate Story in Black and White," underscores not only the strained relationship between Julia and her white lover but also between Julia and the black community at large.

The subject matter of the play was, of course, dangerous at the time it was written. In the late '60s, the play was slated to begin the Atlanta Municipal Theatre's season but kept being moved to later in the season until there was no funding left to produce it. Evidently, the board of directors had no intention of letting the play run since it concerned an interracial couple and, "white folks were not ready to deal with that issue" (Molette 32-33). However, Childress points out that black audiences were equally uncomfortable with the play:

> Black critics felt that the character I based on Miss Julia should not have wanted to marry a white man, no matter that this situation often occurs in real life. The black audience would have been more comfortable if Julia had rejected her white lover. (Betsko and Koenig 65)

Even Childress herself was not enamored with the subject matter of the play, yet she stuck with it, probably because it was so real to her. Based on a true story her grandmother had told her when she was a child, the play was unusual in that it courageously dealt with the still-taboo topic of miscegenation while depicting a usually ignored epoch in history. Childress created the play to serve as "a remembrance of the intellectual poor" (Betsko and Koenig 62), those folk she was raised with and by in Harlem; she thus succeeded in truthfully and poignantly representing a slice of life that had hitherto been devalued or ignored altogether.

Set in 1918 in South Carolina, the play concerns what Childress calls "anti-woman" laws as well as anti-miscegenation laws in the post-Reconstruction South. Childress comments in an interview:

> *Wedding Band* dealt with a black woman and a white man, but it was about black women's rights. I took Herman [the white man] as an understanding, decent human being. But he could not give her [Julia, the black protagonist] protection in a society where the law is against them. . . . The play shows society's determination to hold the black woman down through laws framed against her. (qtd. in Curb 59)[14]

Given the play's restrictive socio-political setting, one can comprehend why it is one of Childress's most serious and tragic plays.

Even in the beginning, the play has a serious tone as Julia's landlady, Fanny, attempts to pry into her new tenant's life. Fanny urges Julia, "Tell me 'bout yourself, don't be so distant" (80), but Julia maintains, "I'm not much of a mixer" (81). The irony in Childress's wording here is, of course, that Julia's "beau" is white. Because she is involved in an illegal and clandestine mixed relationship, she cannot safely mix with other African Americans who might divulge her secret. Not only is Julia the Other in her relationship with Herman, a white baker, but she is also the self-imposed Other within the African American community since she chooses surreptitious involvement with a white man.

When a traveling salesman, "The Bell Man," appears at Julia's new abode, he threatens to disclose her secret and taunts, "Move a lot don'tcha?" (85). He follows Julia into her house where she has gone to fetch money, proceeds to sit on her bed in spite of her protests, and implores her to have sex with him: "Sister, Um in need for it like I never been before. Will you 'comodate me? . . . Wouldn't take but five minutes. Um quick like a jack rabbit. Wouldn't nobody know but you and me" (86). Julia orders him to leave her house, but the scene illustrates that the Bell Man assumes she will be his concubine because she sleeps with another white man. He cannot even conceive of a committed relationship between a black woman and a white man; his social model for such a liaison would still be that of the white slave master and his black mistress.

Once the Bell Man departs, Julia comments, "I hate those kina people," and Lula, another tenant, automatically assumes she means white people, as shown by her response: "You mustn't hate white folks" (87). However, Childress never actually has Julia refer to color and thus suggests that Julia does not treat people differently according to their race. In Julia's words, "There are days when I love, days when I hate" (87). As this echo of the subtitle of the play suggests, her love and hate are not directed towards particular ethnic or racial groups but rather towards those who are prejudiced in general.

Ultimately, Childress uses the play to show that prejudice is not solely a matter of color, of black and white. For example, since Herman and his family are German Americans at the end of the first World War, ethnic slurs are painted on the side of their house. In spite of their first-hand experience with prejudice, however, Herman's mother and sister cannot overcome their own racism. Julia recalls, "Your mama's own words . . . I'll never forget them as long as I live. Annabelle [Herman's sister], you've got a brother who makes pies and loves a nigger" (96). Although at least Herman's mother concedes that he does indeed love Julia, like the Bell Man, she cannot even conceive of an equal romantic partnership between a black woman and white man.

Childress reveals that this prejudice is not unusual but rather a sharp reminder of the period in which the play is set. And just as prejudice is directed from Herman's family to Julia, it is also directed from the black community to Herman as well as to Julia. In one of the most important parts of the play, social and racial divisions are made readily apparent. In this first scene, Mattie, one of the tenants, approaches Julia about reading a letter from her husband who is away at war. That Mattie trusts Julia enough to read the letter suggests that Julia is being offered friendship and a place in the community. However, as Julia reads the letter, she feels more and more different from Mattie.[15] Mattie's husband writes, "Two things a man can give the woman he loves . . . his name and his protection. . . . The first you have, the last is yet to someday come" (90). Even though Julia avows, "I know how much a woman can love" (90), her statement reaches far beyond a recognition of woman-to-woman comradery, and she realizes that Herman can offer her neither his name nor his protection. Paradoxically, the simple gesture of reading a letter, a gesture intended to make Julia feel included in the community, results in even greater feelings of alienation for her.

In an attempt to assuage these feelings, Julia confides in Mattie and Lula, "My friend is white and that's why I try to stay to myself" (91). Childress emphasizes the prejudices of Mattie and Lula in their responses to Julia's admission. Lula disdains, "A white man is somethin' else. Everybody knows how that low-down slave master sent for a different black woman every night . . . for his pleasure," and Mattie adds, "And right now today they're mean, honey. They can't help it; their nose is pinched together so close they can't get enough air. It makes 'em mean" (92). Julia tries to assure them that she and Herman are just like an African American couple; however, both Mattie and Lula cannot comprehend why Julia has betrayed her racial heritage by taking up with a white man. Indeed, they cannot conceive of a relationship between a white man and a black woman in which the woman is not degraded and objectified.

The overall play does suggest at some level that Julia is, in fact, degraded by her interracial relationship, if not directly by Herman. On their tenth anniversary when Herman gives Julia a ring, it is not simply a wedding band but instead "a wedding band . . . on a chain" (97). Certainly, the chain serves to hide the ring from the general public who would see it if it were worn on a finger. Yet the double meaning of chain suggests that Julia is trapped in this relationship, much like the slave mistress of old. When Childress writes in the stage directions, "She fastens the chain around her neck" (97), it is as if Childress, too, is implicating Julia for choosing a white man.

When Herman falls sick with influenza at Julia's house, the perils in their relationship are highlighted. A doctor cannot be called since, "It's against the damn law for him [Herman] to be layin' up in a black woman's bed" (104). When Herman's mother and sister are called to the scene, Julia is forced to meet them for the first time. Herman tries to introduce Julia to his sister, Annabelle, but Annabelle refuses to talk with Julia. Herman's mother's racism is even more blatant, and she demands that Julia return Herman's money and possessions, implying that Julia stole them. In her opinion, Julia is to blame for the relationship, a relationship that goes against both the laws of nature and of man since, "There's something wrong 'bout mismatched things, be they shoes, socks, or people" (117). Her greatest blow to Julia comes when she declares, "He's better off dead in his coffin than live with the likes-a you . . . black thing!" (119). She objectifies Julia, calling her "black thing," a "dirty black bitch" and a "dirty black nigger," among other derogatory terms. Julia reacts violently to this abuse and resolves to erase any love she has had for Herman:

> Name and protection . . . he can't gimme either one. I'm gon' get down on my knees and scrub where they walked . . . .Clean the

> whiteness outta my house. . . . Free . . . Free to hate-cha for the rest of
> my life. When I die I'm gonna keep on hatin' . . . I don't want any
> whiteness in my house. (120)

As Julia ends her tirade, she yells, "Stay out. . . . and leave me to my
black self!" (120). Instead of having Julia go up North to marry Herman
in a state where mixed marriages are legal, Childress has her determine
to stay home. As a self-reliant, strong woman who embraces her
blackness, Julia represents a new image of black womanhood, an image
Elizabeth Brown-Guillory identifies as "the evolving black woman"
("Black Women" 234).[16] Instead of having Julia continue to play the
stereotypical role of "the depreciated sex object" (King 7), Childress
creates a new and more dynamic role for Julia at the end of *Wedding
Band*.

At the end of the play, Childress has Julia symbolically reach out
to her people. Julia gives Mattie her wedding band and chain as well as
the tickets and affirms, "You and Teeta [Mattie's daughter] are my
people . . . You and Teeta are my family. Be my family" (132).
Childress suggests that by asking to be accepted by Mattie and her
daughter, Julia assumes her rightful place in the African American
community, and this new sense of belonging strengthens and upholds
her. When Herman's mother and sister return to take him home to die,
Julia threatens, "Nobody comes in my house." Childress writes in the
stage directions, "She [Julia] is going through that rising process
wherein she must reject them [Herman's mother and sister] as the
molders and dictators of her life" (132). This time, Childress shows that
Julia withstands the racist onslaught of Herman's family with aplomb
because she has claimed her "black self," her identity as an evolving
black woman.

In actuality, the majority of Childress's lead female characters—
Florence, Mama, Wiletta, Millie, Irene, Julia, and others—can be
considered representations of the evolving black woman. However,
Childress' most vivid representation of this figure is Tomorrow Marie
in *Wine in the Wilderness* (1969). Janet Brown classifies this play as a
feminist drama;[17] however, the play is simultaneously much more.
Indeed, it is a call for action for African Americans, especially African
American women, to reject white representations of black selfhood and
to take control of depicting the African American socio-cultural
heritage with pride and precision.

While Childress dramatized the theme of representations of black selfhood using the play within a play device in *Trouble in Mind*, she now draws attention to this theme through the visual medium of painting. *Wine in the Wilderness* opens in the middle of a 1964 riot in Harlem as Bill Jameson, a struggling African American artist, prepares to meet a woman his friends have selected to model for his current painting. Bill is painting a triptych which contains three representations of black womanhood. The first he calls "Black Girlhood" and it depicts "a charming little girl in Sunday dress and hair ribbon" (125). The second is his obvious favorite and the one for which he has named the entire triptych, "'Wine in the Wilderness' . . . Mother Africa, regal, black womanhood in her noblest form" (125). This example of what Bill calls "perfect black womanhood" is actually little more than an idealized illusion, a commercialized image of the stereotype of the exotic black female.[18] As Childress describes the image in her stage directions, "She is cold but utter perfection, draped in startling colors of African material, very 'Vogue' looking" (125). That Childress describes the painting in terms of a magazine that usually features Euro-American models is quite revealing since it points to the falsity of the representation.

While Bill believes that this African queen is the central focus of his triptych, he has reserved the third unpainted canvas for "the messed up chick" whom he describes as the following:

> The lost woman, . . . that the society has made out of our women.
> She's as far from my African queen as a woman can get and still be
> female; . . . She's ignorant, unfeminine, coarse, rude . . . vulgar . . . a
> poor, dumb chick that's had her behind kicked until it's numb . . . and
> the sad part is . . . She ain't together, you know, . . . there's no hope
> for her. (126)

Aside from the obvious misogyny in Bill's description, he also arrogantly plans to use the painting to disparage black women in general. He asserts, "The queen, my black queen will look down from the wall so the messed up chicks in the neighborhood can see what a woman oughta be . . . and the innocent child on the side of her and the messed up chick on the other side of her . . . MY STATEMENT" (126). That Bill insists on the triptych being *his* statement is noteworthy for as the play progresses, he is left with only a blank canvass.[19] Childress thus metaphorically implies that black womanhood outstrips categorization.

Indeed, as the play progresses, Tomorrow Marie becomes a real embodiment of "Wine in the Wilderness." In her own words at the end of the play, "Bill, I don't have to wait for anybody's by-your-leave to be a 'Wine in the Wilderness' woman. I can be if I wanta, . . . and I am. I am. I am" (148). Here, theatrical enactment, the very presence of characters interacting on stage, insures that Tomorrow's image will live on in the spectator's mind since she becomes not simply a passive object represented on canvas but rather a speaking (and "cussin' and fightin'") subject who inscribes herself, her "I am," in discourse.

At first in the play, Tommy is concerned about what Bill thinks about her and asks his friend, Cynthia, "What's wrong with me?" Cynthia, an educated African American social worker, counsels Tommy to give up being a black matriarch, to sacrifice her strength and independence in order "to let the black man have his manhood again" (134). However, Childress points out that it is Bill who needs to change. In fact, Childress uses the play to laud Tommy's strength as an evolving black woman whose matriarchal qualities have enabled her to survive on her own.

Obviously, Childress admires the strength that black women, and especially black matriarchs, have exhibited throughout history. She affirms, "Facing the world alone makes a woman strong" ("The Negro Woman" 19). Childress elaborates further, "It seems a contradiction for a woman to be degraded by law, and by popular opinion which was shaped and formed by that law, and yet also take her rightful place as the most heroic figure to emerge on the American scene, with more stamina than that shown by any pioneer" ("The Negro Woman" 19). The stamina and strength of the African American woman, qualities nourished by the matriarchal role she has often had to play, thus distinguish her as a true American heroine.

Although Tomorrow Marie is ordinary—she is no idealized African queen—her courage and strength are truly extraordinary. When she discovers that Bill intended for her to pose as "the messed up chick," she accuses him of not liking "flesh and blood niggers" (146). Tomorrow realizes that although Bill declares, "Black is beautiful" (139, 143), his love of blackness is merely academic. He has no real understanding of or appreciation for his cultural heritage, a heritage embodied in the ordinary folk whom Bill's friend condescendingly refers to as "the masses" (147). In fact, Bill's painting of a supposed

African queen conforms to white rather than black ideals of beauty. Tomorrow thus does Bill and his friends a service by showing them that blackness is not an accessory, "Somethin' you add on or take off." She stresses, "The real thing is takin' place on the inside . . . that's where the action is. That's 'Wine in the Wilderness,' a woman that's a real one and a good one. And yall just better believe I'm it" (148).

As her name suggests, Tomorrow is the hope for the future because she celebrates her blackness "because she is rooted in and proud of her cultural heritage, because she is an ordinary woman who has absorbed and passes on the oral history of her people" (Shinn 153). Childress thus valorizes Tomorrow's (extra)ordinariness since her identity cannot be limited by Bill's artistic attempts to stereotype her as the third example of Black Womanhood in his triptych. In fact, Tomorrow stands as one of the best examples of Childress's commitment to constructing characters whose individualized experiences and selves do not represent an entire monologic "Black Experience."

Childress thus creates innovative representations of black selfhood within the traditional Eurocentric form of realistic drama. That she would use realistic drama to advance her agenda is understandable since it allowed her to reach a middle-class white as well as black audience,[20] and secured a place for her in the more mainstream branches of American theater. However, it also allowed her to revise and to reshape tradition from within tradition. In spite of being one of only a few African American women playwrights who have received some of the critical attention they deserve,[21] Childress has remained true to her vision. She asserts, "I've a play to write that may never be seen by any audience anywhere, but I do my thing, who has ears to hear, hear . . . all others, later" ("Can Black" D9).

By doing her thing, Childress has not only taken her rightful place as an esteemed playwright in the American theater, but she has also represented a multiplicity of black constructions of self to counter stereotypical constructions. Her thematic exploration has set the stage for the thematic as well as structural experimentation of younger African American women playwrights such as Adrienne Kennedy, Ntozake Shange, and P.J. Gibson. However, Childress's 1969 charge to both writers and critics is still applicable to today's situation:

> The Negro woman will attain her rightful place in American literature when those of us who care about truth, justice, and a better life tell her story, with the full knowledge and appreciation of her constant,

unrelenting struggle against racism and for human rights. ("The Negro" 19).

Childress's life, career, and works invite the literary and nonliterary worlds alike to claim a positive representation of the black woman as a resilient and venerable American heroine, a figure whose ordinary struggles for survival, freedom, and equality are truly extraordinary in both nature and scope.

NOTES

1. See Langston Hughes's poem, "Mother to Son" in Joel Conarroe, ed., *Six American Poets* (New York: Random House, 1991), 247.

2. In 1939, Childress helped found the American Negro Theatre and began acting there. She was actively involved in various aspects of production with the ANT for eleven years.

3. For a discussion of the appeal of the one-act play to early African American women playwrights, see page 281 of Jeanne-Marie A. Miller's "Black Women Playwrights from Grimké to Shange: Selected Synopses of Their Works" in Gloria T. Hull, Patricia Bell Scott, and Barbara Smith, eds., *All the Women Are White, All the Blacks Are Men, but Some of Us Are Brave* (Old Westbury, New York: Feminist P, 1982), 280-296.

4. In "Black Matriarchy: Portrayal of Women in Three Plays," *Negro American Literature Forum* 10.3 (1976): 93-95, Mary Louise Anderson lists four aspects of the matriarchal stereotype. She contends that the black matriarch, "regards the Black male as undependable and is frequently responsible for his emasculation, is often very religious, regards mothering as one of the most important things in her life, and attempts to shield her children from and to prepare them to accept the prejudices of the white world" (93). For our discussion of *Florence*, we will focus on the latter two aspects.

5. For a discussion of the significance of these labels as both signs and symbols, refer to Samuel A. Hay, "Alice Childress's Dramatic Structure," in Mari Evans, ed., *Black Women Writers: Arguments and Interviews* (London and Sydney: Pluto P, 1985), 117.

6. As Wayne C. Booth explains in his introduction to Mikhail Bakhtin's *Problems of Dostoevsky's Poetics,* Caryl Emerson, ed. and trans. (Minneapolis: U of Minnesota P, 1984), "We come into consciousness speaking a language already permeated with many voices—a social, not a private language. From the beginning, we are 'polyglot,' already in process of mastering a variety of social dialects derived from parents, clan, class, religion, country"(xxi).

Therefore, when I refer to Mrs. Carter's social dialect or Mama's social dialect, I am actually referring to a complex web of dialects that each character has interwoven to achieve what Booth calls "a kind of individuality" (xxi) in which the character's view of the world is represented.

7.   For excellent discussions of the tragic mulatto, consult the following: Judith R. Berzon, *Neither White nor Black: The Mulatto Character in American Fiction* (New York: New York UP, 1978), Hazel Carby, *Reconstructing Womanhood: The Emergence of the Afro- American Woman Novelist* (New York and Oxford: Oxford UP, 1987), and Barbara Christian, *Black Women Novelists: The Development of a Tradition, 1892-1976* Westport, CT: Greenwood, 1980).

8.   In effect, this quotation suggests what Samuel A. Hay considers the main idea of the play: "Black people—not white liberals—must struggle if there is to be real political and economic equality" (119). See "Alice Childress's Dramatic Structure" in Mari Evans, ed., *Black Women Writers: Arguments and Interviews* (London and Sydney: Pluto, 1985).

9.   Elizabeth Brown-Guillory asserts that Florence is an example of a positive image that appears in the plays of Childress, Hansberry, and Shange, namely the image of "the evolving black woman" (234). See "Black Women Playwrights: Exorcising Myths," *Phylon* 48.3 (1987). However, I would like to emphasize that Mama herself is the evolving black woman in *Florence* since it is *her* change, *her* evolution, that is the focal point of the play.

10.   For an analysis of carnival laughter, see pages 126-7 in Mikhail Bakhtin's *Problems of Dostoevsky's Poetics*, Caryl Emerson, ed. and trans. (Minneapolis: U of Minnesota P, 1984).

11.   *In Taking Center Stage: Feminism in Contemporary U.S. Drama* (Metuchen, NJ and London: Scarecrow P, 1991), Janet Brown summarizes theories that address how female writers have used comedy, particularly wit and irony, to subvert the patriarchy (23-25). Rosemary Curb also demonstrates how the unruliness of women, "the carnivalized feminine principle," has been used to upset the patriarchy; look at "Re/cognition, Re/presentation, Re/creation in Woman-Conscious Drama: The Seer, The Seen, The Scene, The Obscene," *Theatre Journal* 37.3 (1985): 315-16. Both discussions can help us situate the overthrow of the Master script in *Trouble in Mind* within a larger context.

12.   In effect, Childress has Wiletta change from object to subject as Gayle Austin observes in "Alice Childress: Black Woman Playwright as Feminist Critic," *The Southern Quarterly* 25.3 (1987): 52-65: "Wiletta becomes a critic/artist of the play she is performing, changing from passive object to active subject in front of our eyes" (57).

13.   As Childress asserts on page 14 of "The Negro Woman in Literature," *Freedom ways* 6.1 (1966), "The Negro woman has almost been omitted as important subject matter in the general popular American drama, television, motion pictures and radio, except for the constant, but empty and decharacterized faithful servant." Indeed, it was because of her awareness of the need for accurate images of African Americans that Childress began to write plays. See Elizabeth Brown-Guillory, "Alice Childress: A Pioneering Spirit," *SAGE* 4.1 (1987): 66-68.

14.   In her article, Curb explains that examples of these laws include those that prevented black women and their children from inheriting property rights, those that absolved black or white fathers of the children of black women from any responsibility for their progeny, and those that prohibited miscegenation and deemed the birth of a mulatto as ample proof to convict a mother of violating this law. In all cases, a woman's testimony about who had fathered the child was not even considered as evidence.

15.   See Catherine Wiley's treatment of the scene in "Whose Name, Whose Protection: Reading Alice Childress's *Wedding Band*" in June Schlueter, ed., *Modern American Drama: The Female Canon* (London and Toronto: Associated UPs, 1990), 184-197. Wiley explains, "The words Julia reads remind her of what she does not have with her lover: the social legitimation of the public bond racism denies them. Julia carries October's message to Mattie in her voice; her enactment of his text and Mattie's reactions to it reconfirm Julia's own insecurity" (191). Thus the reading and enactment of the public text force Julia to confront her private reality.

16.   The figure of the evolving black woman is best described by Rosemary Curb in "An Unfashionable Tragedy of American Racism: Alice Childress's *Wedding Band*," *MELUS* 7.4 (1980): 57-68. Curb maintains, "Through essentially solitary struggles, Childress' strong women forge through barriers not only of race and sex, but also class, education, and age which threaten to keep them poor and powerless to a recognition of personal worth" (65).

17.   In *Feminist Drama: Definition and Critical Analysis* (Metuchen, NJ and London: Scarecrow, 1979), Brown argues, "Because *Wine in the Wilderness* shows a female protagonist, Tommy, asserting her autonomy in opposition to an unjust socio-sexual hierarchy, the play can be considered a feminist drama" (68).

18.   For an excellent discussion of this stereotype, see "The Quicksands of Representations," chapter eight in Hazel Carby's *Reconstructing Womanhood: The Emergence of the Afro- American Woman Novelist* (New York and Oxford: Oxford UP, 1987).

19.   See Gayle Austin's exploration of the symbolic significance of the blank canvas in "Alice Childress: Black Woman Playwright as Feminist Critic." *The Southern Quarterly* 25.3 (1987): 53-62.

20.   For further discussion of realistic drama as middle-class drama, see Helene Keyssar, "Black Drama: Reflections of Class and Class Consciousness," *Prospects: An Annual of American Cultural Studies* 3 (1977): 263-288. Childress also chose realistic drama simply because she believed in it. She comments in a recent interview, "Some people criticize the 'well-made' play, but it is not to be knocked. If you buy a suit you want it to be well made. You don't want the tailor to experiment; we want something dependable; well, I do" (Betsko and Koenig 67).

21.   I specify "some" here since the lack of full-length studies of the work of African American women playwrights and the difficulties they continue to face in getting their work produced and evaluated from an Afrocentric perspective attest to the still pervasive racism and sexism of the American theater and academy.

WORKS CITED

Betsko, Kathleen, and Rachel Koenig. *Interviews with Contemporary Women Playwrights.* New York: Beech Tree, 1987. 62-74.

Brown-Guillory, Elizabeth. "Alice Childress: A Pioneering Spirit." *SAGE* 4 (1987): 66-8.

———. "Black Women Playwrights: Exorcising Myths." *Phylon* 48 (1987): 229-39.

Childress, Alice. "A Candle in a Gale Wind." *Black Women Writers: Arguments and Interviews.* Ed. Mari Evans. London and Sydney: Pluto, 1985. 111-26.

———. "Can Black and White Artists Still Work Together?" *New York Times* 2 Feb. 1969, sec. 2:1, 9.

———. *Florence. Wines in the Wilderness: Plays by African American Women from the Harlem Renaissance to the Present.* Ed. Elizabeth Brown-Guillory. New York: Greenwood, 1990. 110-121.

———. "Knowing the Human Condition." *Black American Literature and Humanism.* Ed. R. Baxter Miller. Lexington: UP of Kentucky, 1981. 8-10.

———. "The Negro Woman in American Literature." *Freedomways* 6 (1966): 14-19.

———. *Trouble in Mind. Black Theater: A 20th Century Collection of the Work of Its Best Playwrights.* Ed. Lindsay Patterson. New York: Dodd, Mead, and Company, 1971. 137- 74.

————. *Wedding Band. 9 Plays by Black Women.* Ed. Margaret B. Wilkerson. New York: New American Library, 1986. 73-133.

————. *Wine in the Wilderness. Wines in the Wilderness: Plays by African American Women from the Harlem Renaissance to the Present.* Ed. Elizabeth Brown-Guillory. New York: Greenwood, 1990. 110-21.

Curb, Rosemary. "An Unfashionable Tragedy of American Racism: Alice Childress's *Wedding Band.*" *MELUS* 7 (1980): 57-68.

Fuller, Hoyt T. "A Survey: Black Writers' Views on Literary Lions and Values." *Negro Digest* 17 (1968): 10-11, 36, 86-6.

Hitchcock, Peter. *Dialogics of the Oppressed.* Minneapolis and London: U of Minnesota P, 1993.

Jordan, Shirley M., ed. *Broken Silences: Interviews with Black and White Women Writers.* New Brunswick, NJ: Rutgers UP, 1993. 28-37.

Killens, John O. "The Literary Genius of Alice Childress." *Black Women Writers: Arguments and Interviews.* Ed. Mari Evans. London and Sydney: Pluto, 1985. 129-33.

King, Mae C. "The Politics of Sexual Stereotypes." *The Black Scholar* 13 (1982): 2-13.

Mahone, Sydné. "Seers on the Rim." *American Theatre* 2 (1994): 22-4.

Molette, Barbara. "They Speak, Who Listens?: Black Women Playwrights." *Black World* 25 (1976): 28-34.

Shinn, Thelma. "Living the Answer: The Emergence of African American Feminist Drama." *Studies in the Humanities* 17 (1990): 149-59.

Wiley, Catherine. "Whose Name, Whose Protection: Reading Alice Childress's *Wedding Band.*" *Modern American Drama: The Female Canon.* Ed. June Schlueter. London and Toronto: Associated UPs, 1990. 184-97.

The Discourse of Intercourse
Sexuality and Eroticism in African American Women's Drama
Janice Lee Liddell

In their insightful study of the black family, Robert Staples and Leanor Baulin Johnson make the following observations regarding patterns of sexual intimacy in the African American context:

> In looking at the painful history of race relations in America, it seems clear that much of the discrimination that African Americans have encountered is due to the existence of white American stereotypes about their moral character . . . . American society was founded on the Protestant ethic, which equated poverty with sinfulness, idleness, vice, and a belief that the poor are sexually indulgent.(72)

Sexuality, while historically important for African Americans as with all others of the human species, has often been a detriment to their social advancement. Staples and Johnson state,

> Research has done little to invalidate the earlier generalizations about Black sexual drives or to illuminate the sociocultural forces that differentiate between Black and white sexual behavior. The result has been fostering and reinforcement of stereotypes about black immorality and hypersexuality. Such false images serve to fuel the fears of those people who remain psychologically wedded to America's puritanical view of sexuality and strengthen their resistance to Black demands for equal opportunity in American life. (72-73)

With this social backdrop, early African American imaginative writers made every attempt to anesthetize the sexual image of African Americans by virtually eliminating the themes of sexuality and sensuality from their works or subverting these themes where they appeared at all. Drama scholar, Margaret Wilkerson, presents the issue more concretely in terms of its implications for African American women:

> Two stereotypes of black women—e.g. the neutered, domineering mammy who ruled the roost, or the over-sexed floozy—were particularly insidious, for they masked the vulnerability of the female to exploitation. The tragic mulatto embodied another stereotypical notion: that the "enlightened" white world is a source of fine qualities (and beauty, of course) and the "savage" black side, of unruly passions that eventually cause degradation or demise. Other stereotypes led producers to actively discourage the portrayal of genuine relationships between black men and women characters. (xv)

The sexual exploitation and subsequent, persistent derogatory images of African American women dating back to slavery were a particular motivation to black women playwrights who reacted to these degrading and disquieting stereotypes through their craft. However, as the consciousness of African Americans, particularly that of these women playwrights developed, their attempts to define their own experiences within their art evolved proportionately. These artistic experiences, of course, included much more explicit forms of sexuality and analyses of that sexuality on the playwrights' own terms. This evolution, which spanned approximately seventy years, is evidenced in two important literary anthologies, Kathy Perkins's *Black Female Playwrights: An Anthology of Plays Before 1950* (BFP) and Margaret Wilkerson's *9 Plays by Black Women* (PBW).[1]

While individual women playwrights may have been writing as early as the 1800s, what might be described as a collective of African American women playwrights did not begin to appear until the 1920s. During this early period, their plays were identified either as protest/propaganda plays or as folk plays with an overriding purpose of entertainment. The motivating impetus behind each of these genres of African American drama remained that of projecting what these writers viewed to be a more realistic and positive spectrum of the black experience than those dramas written by whites about blacks.

In effect, these nascent plays written by black women sought to dispel the myths and stereotypes perpetuated by a white racist patriarchy. To this end, these playwrights became almost obsessive in their effort to minimize even the natural sexuality of African American women. Thus, while sensuous romance fiction written by white writers was finding a comfortable niche during this period, African American writers were unable to depict serious versions of black love relationships with much veracity or verisimilitude.

Still, these playwrights were able to incorporate some of the powerful themes and tensions of black sexuality, often through a subverted and codified discourse. For example, Zora Neale Hurston's folk play *Color Struck* (1925) successfully codifies its sexual tensions through such common cultural vestments as music, dance, and food. The play focuses on the jocularity of a group of dancers on their way from Jacksonville, Florida to St. Augustine for a championship "cakewalk." The group, primarily couples, get into the mood by urging Effie, one of the singles on the journey, to "limber up." Her swing into a rapid dance step reaches a physical crescendo while the accordionist plays. The implied sexual pitch of the music/musician and dance/dancer intensifies as her dance does:

> *Wesley* (in ecstasy): Hot stuff I reckon! Hot stuff I reckon! (The musicians are stamping. Great enthusiasm. Some clap time with hands and feet. She hurls herself into a modified hoochy koochy and finishes with an ecstatic yell. There is a babble of talk and laughter and exaltation.) (Hurston 92)

The brief dance, while taking place safely in a crowded train car, is essentially orgasmic. All the participants are able to enjoy the innocent sensual experience. The subverted sexual charge of the scene permits them to do so without casting negative images on the participants.

In another scene, Hurston employs food as the erotic codification. John, another of the dancers, is with his jealous girlfriend, Emma, who sees flirtation in the actions of every woman who approaches her man. However, her interpretation of the dancer Effie's offerings may be correct. The exchange that follows, with its highly sexual subtext, is essentially a war between "sweet things":

> *Effie*: Ya'll have a piece uh mah blueberry pie—it's might nice! (She proffers it with a timid smile to Emma who "freezes" up instantly.)

Emma: Naw! We don't want no pie. We got coconut layer-cake.

John: Ah—Ah think ah'd choose a piece up pie, Effie. (He takes it.) Will you sit down an' have a snack wid us! (He slides over to make room.)

Effie: (nervously) Ah, naw, Ah got to tun on back to mah basket, but ah thaought maybe y'll maut' want tuh taste mah pie. (She turns to go.)

John: Thank you Effie. It's mighty good, too. (He eats it. Effie crosses to her seat. Emma glares at her for a minute, then turns disgustedly away from the basket. John catches her shoulder and faces her around.)

John: (pleadingly) Honey, be nice. Don't ack lak dat!

Emma: (jerking free) Naw, you done ruint mah appetite now, carryin' on wid dat punkin-colored ole gal . . . youse jus' hog wile ovah her cause she's half-white? No matter what Ah say, you keep carryin' on wid her. Act polite? Naw, Ah aint gonna be deceitful an bust mah gizzard fuh nobody! Let her keep her dirty ole pie ovah there where she is! (Hurston 94-95)

In this exchange, Effie's pie and Emma's cake both take on highly sexual overtones in the hands of the respective warring women. In addition, the two "sweet things" propose the codified sexual options as they are presented to John. But within the codification, this discourse, of course, remains innocent.

In the propaganda plays, as opposed to the folk plays, the discourse is inherently political and, therefore, more serious with the clear aim of exposing and protesting—sometimes quite subtly—the superordination/subordination dialectic of race as it is evoked through sex and sexuality. In contrast to the jocular nature of the folk plays, the subverted sexuality in the propaganda plays is never natural and joyous. Instead, any sexual union signifies the victimization of one or both engaged parties. Sandra Govan's insightful commentary is useful here:

> The specter of unholy lust, illicit sex, suppressed erotica, and
> unlicensed sexual violence, acknowledged or not, permeates both our
> history and, sadly, or society. That such themes recur in our literature
> should be recognized as necessary revelations, as psychological
> insight into individuals and the culture which produced and
> "sustains" them. (43)

These "unholy" and usually unsanctioned lustful interactions are often
manifested in these early plays through the illicit unions between white
men and black women and the horrible consequences of mere
allegations of these unions.

In noted propaganda playwright Georgia Douglas Johnson's *Blue
Eyed Black Boy* (193?), the irony of the illicit unions, one real and the
other alleged, is glaring. While the play foregrounds the
superordination/subordination of power in the racially dichotomized
south, a sexual subtext plays the dynamic out. In the play, Pauline
Waters, mother of a grown son and daughter, is central to what emerges
as the drama's sexual duality. The daughter Rebecca initially reveals
the source of the sexual tension in the play: "It's funny [Tom's] the
only one in our family's got blue eyes . . . Pa's was black and yours and
mine are black too—It certainly is strange—I wish I had em" (Johnson
48). Rebecca's observation sets the stage for the revelation that Pauline
has kept secret from everyone: the identity of the biological father of
her son. Not even the boy's father knows of his progeny. Recently
arrested for allegedly brushing against a white woman on the street,
Tom has just been "dragged to the jail house to await his lynching."
With this life-threatening charge and consequence facing her only son,
Pauline is forced to use her "trump." She gives a family friend a ring
and a message to take to the governor:

> Just give him the ring an say, Pauline sent this, she says they going to
> lynch her son born 21 years ago, mind you say twenty one years
> ago—then say—listen close—look in his eyes—and you'll save him
> (Johnson 50).

Of course, Tom is saved through the intervention of the governor, a
man none but his mother knows to be the young man's father. The
irony is that a white man has risen to the highest position in the state
subsequent to his illicit relationship with a black woman, while a black
man is sentenced, without trial, to death for only *allegedly* touching a

white woman. Even though the presence of the ring does suggest Pauline's own culpability in the illicit sexual affair, the superordination of whites remains the important thread connecting both of the sexually charged situations.

Another propaganda play, *It's Morning* (1940) by Shirley Graham, also exposes the racial superordination/subordination dialectic inherent in the American patriarchy. An impending illicit union is the indirect cause of a young girl's death on the morning of the slaves' emancipation. Cruel Massa Charles has claimed the beautiful pubescent Millie for his young mistress despite his wife's objections. His decision is known throughout the plantation community. The following dialogue ensues between two slave women lamenting the situation:

> *Phoebe:* He'd do it Kas he's cruel un'hard,
>   He's lak a beast dats scented fresh, young meat,
>   He's old—He'll suck ha blood low damp swamp ting . . .
> *Cissie:* Ah seed him lick his lips an' smile an grin,
>   Ole misie beg him wait till cotton bust,
>   An' promise im de best bales in da lot.
>   He say he wait no mo. . . He want da gal.
>   Ah seed his hands. . . dey touch huh golden breast,
>   She war so scared, she douldn't run . . .
>   An 'den she scream . . . an' missie tell huh go.
>   Ah heard him laf . . . an' spit upon da floah! (Graham 214)

This rhythmic dialogue is filled with sexual allusions and more blatant references to, as Sandra Govan puts it, the "unlicensed and unbridled sexuality deriving from pure power relationships and not from genuine human feelings" (37).

The horror of this potential affair is exacerbated in Graham's depiction of Millie's innocence. In parenthetical stage directions she explains:

> *[A] song stops as the girl reaches the door. It is Millie. Her thin dress reveals the beautifully molded lines of young womanhood as she hesitates just outside the sunshine. She is the color of burnished gold, and in her soft, wavy hair, framing the round face, are glints of copper. Her mouth is full and curves sweetly like a little child's. Her eyes are wide and know no shadows.* (217)

Graham's description evokes in the reader and audience the painful historical memory of racial and gender oppression. Young Millie is obviously ripe for the lecherous slave master. However, her mother's determination to save her from a gross indignity she undoubtedly has seen too often is absolute. She is prepared to kill her own daughter. Hence, despite the incrimination by her friends, she does so by stabbing the girl to death. While the gesture is phallic and invasive, it is committed through the knowing love of the mother and is, thus, an act of liberation. The sad irony comes on the heels of Millie's death with the arrival of a Yankee soldier that very morning who announces the emancipation of all the slaves.

As with the theme of sexuality in most of these propaganda plays, this theme in Mary Burrill's *They That Sit in Darkness* (1919), one of the earliest plays by an African American women, is also grounded in protest against sexual oppression. In so many of these early dramas, sexual violence serves as the source of this oppression; however, in Burrill's play, the source is the ignorance of those who engage in sex and the motivation of a social system to maintain this ignorance. Malinda Jasper, "a frail, tired-looking woman of thirty eight" is the tragic protagonist who has been sentenced to death by a social agency who could at any time provide her a reprieve. After ten pregnancies, Malinda has been physically weakened to the point of death; nevertheless, her social service nurse, by dictates of a state law, denies her contraceptive information. The following scene reveals her dire situation:

> *Mrs. Jasper*: (Shaking her head wearily) Ah wonder what sin we done that Gawd punish me an' Jim law dis!

> *Mis Shaw*: (Gently) God is not punishing you, Malinda, you are punishing yourself by having children every year. Take this last baby—you knew that with your weak heart that you should never have had it and yet—

> *Mrs. Jasper*: But whut kin ah do—de chillern come!

> *Miss Shaw*: You must be careful!

> *Mrs. Jasper*: But whut kin ah do—de chillern come!

Miss Shaw: You must be careful!

Mrs. Jasper: Be keerful! Dat's all you nu'ses say! You an' de one
    whut come when Tom wuz bawn an' Selena! Ah been keerful all
    Ah knows how but whut's it got me—ten chillern, eight liven'
    an' two daid! You got 'a be telling me sumpin better'n dat, Mis'
    Liz'beth.

Miss Shaw: (fervently) I wish to God it were lawful for me to do so!
    My heart goes out to you poor people that sit in darkness, having
    year after year, children that you are physically too weak to
    bring into the world—children that you are unable not only to
    educate but even to clothe and feed. Malinda, when I took my
    oath as nurse, I swore to abide by the laws of the State, and the
    law forbids my telling you what you have a right to know. (71-
    72)

The dialogue here indicates that this play, with its rather heavy-handed
approach to the issue of birth control for poor black women, is perhaps
the first literary work by an African American to touch this highly
sensitive issue. Although the theme of sexuality is not addressed
explicitly, it does remain an undercurrent concern. The Jaspers, like
other poor blacks, are sexually repressed by a racist system that negates
the pleasures and privileges of their own sexuality by denying them this
access to birth control.

    Except for the jocularity of the "folk plays" written for
entertainment, even as they projected more realistic images of African
Americans than did white dramas, the sexual mood of most of the early
dramas was generally somber and painful. The goal of these plays, of
course, was to restore morality, piety, and virtue to the black
community and more importantly to the image of black women.
Whether these early playwrights achieved this goal is beyond the scope
of this study; nevertheless, their attempts were certainly valiant. The
next era to witness what might be considered a wave of black women
playwrights was that of the 1960s and 1970s. The goals of African
American women playwrights in their depiction of sexuality underwent
a transformation that paralleled that of the new sexual mores that
Robert Staples and Baulin Johnson describe in *Black Families at the
Crossroads*:

The 1960s and 1970s gave birth to what is popularly called the sexual revolution, accompanied by a greater sexual candor in public discussion, books, film, television, art, and dress. Some sexologists claim that sexual behavior did not change—that only the attitudes toward it and the openness surrounding it were affected. However, there are indications that Americans now engage in premarital intercourse at an earlier age, with more partners and in different ways. (87)

Similar to other cultural expressions, drama in this period developed in accordance with the emerging socio-cultural mores. Hence, plays written by African American women after 1960 were generally much more liberated sexually than those of the pre-1950 era. Sexual references were much more explicit contextually and depicted sexuality as women experienced it. Moreover, under the influence of the pervading women's liberation movement, these references often sought to undermine the oppressive patriarchy that dictated so-called acceptable sexual parameters. Many of these dramas, then, were as much about sexual rights, responsibilities, and the ensuing results for the individual woman as they were about the impact of sexuality on a race. In fact, Margaret Wilkerson views the playwrights of this later period as a "new generation" who are "no longer bound by the restriction of theatrical realism and cultural inhibitions" (xxiii).

African American women, the venerated "mules of the world," had been faced with varied forms of repression within their own communities and even more so in the wider community. Responding to explicit and subtle forms of racism, intraracial discrimination, sexism, and classism, later African American women playwrights found sexuality to be a new and viable tool of rebellion. Out of this new vision of self and society (or self in society) also emerged a new political discourse on sexuality—one that is explicit and uninhibited. While this discourse is certainly new for African American women playwrights, it is remarkably similar to that which emerged in post-Franco Spain in response to the previous totalitarianism. Writing about this dramatic milieu, one scholar says,

That dramatists utilized the themes of sexuality and the erotic to express their discontent with a range of social and political restrictions . . . comes as no surprise. In the case of the Franco dictatorship, patriarchal values, machismo, and strict censorship were paramount. (Podol 257)

In the case of African American women playwrights, a similar discontent was being expressed with overt racism, sexism, and classism. In addition, these new playwrights proactively liberated their own sexuality in their drama.

The consciously liberated and liberating fulfillment of sexual desires and sexual pleasures added an exciting dimension to the scope of drama written by African American women. This new erotic force, as it emerged in the drama, did so in at least four forms: homoerotica, heteroerotica, autoerotica, and deviant erotica. This eroticism, in the hands of these new women playwrights was not only exciting but forcefully political.

Lorraine Hansberry, author of *A Raisin in the Sun*, the first widely acclaimed black drama, does more than hint at this new vision of sexuality through her use of homoerotica in the unfinished play *Toussaint*. While *A Raisin in the Sun* is perhaps the first American play to address the issue of abortion, the theme of sexuality plays only a minuscule role. However, in *Toussaint*, Hansberry's use of the theme of sexuality enables her to express discontent with American racism and raise the supremely delicate issue of homophobia. An exploitative lesbian relationship between Lucie, the unfulfilled wife of plantation manager, Bayon D'Bergier, and her slave Destine serves this purpose. While the relationship is a power-centered one, it is perhaps the first glimmer of even a latent lesbian relationship in the drama of any African American (perhaps in that of any American). The body massage ordered by Lucie evolves into a sensual encounter with Destine before they are caught by D'Bergier, and it continues after his departure.

> *Lucie*: Shut up and finish my massage—don't keep me lying here half naked! Finish! (The slave begins to smoothe the oil on . . .) Ahh . . . (with a sudden change of mood) . . . How beautiful your hands are . . .(She catches one of the hands on her shoulder and holds it and looks at it.) How lovely you are . . . (Turning to face the slave.) Your body was molded by the Gods—(She puts her hands carressingly to the sides of the other woman's body. Her husband re-enters, gets an article he had forgotten, and looks at her with disgust.)

Bayon: When you are—finished—you will please join our guests downstairs. (He turns on his heel and exits abruptly.)

Lucie: (Screaming after him.) My pleasures are mon own—monster! monster!   monster! . . . (She stares after him and at last settles back.) Oh, what does it matter, what does any of it matter . . . That's it . . . soothingly . . .caressingly. (Hansberry 65-66)

Homoerotic relationships surely occurred with no less frequency prior to the 1950s than they did after, but only during this more progressive era could such erotic tensions (though not mutually consensual) between these two eighteenth-century characters even be depicted. The climate of homophobia and racism, which Hansberry herself undoubtedly experienced, perhaps motivated her experimentation with interracial homosexuality as a vehicle of protest and permitted her to serve as precursor to the exploration of black women's homoeroticism in plays by later African American women playwrights.

P.J. Gibson's innovative and highly experimental *Brown Silk and Magenta Sunsets* also responds to the black woman's racial and gender oppression in much the same way as a number of the contemporary political Spanish plays—"through transgression of [society's] taboos by a celebration of the erotic, and more fundamentally, through a reversal of traditional values" (Podol 257). The play achieves this end through the exploration of at least three erotic forms: heteroerotic, autoerotic, and deviant erotic.

Gibson's use of obsessive heterosexual passion as the ostensible oppressive force of protagonist Lena Larsen Salvinoni parallels the extent to which black women are exploited and controlled in a patriarchal racist society. Gibson's impassioning of a black woman to such an extreme that she will transgress some of the most time-honored sexual taboos known to humanity serves as a vivid manifestation of the most extreme forms and results of gender and racial oppression experienced by African American women. While Lena's own passions seem to evidence her collusion in her oppression, one must remember she is not the actual creator of her psycho-sexual universe (nor is Gibson). This universe has already been created by the omnipotence of a racist patriarchy.

Lena is, from the beginning, a potential "ultimate victim," one who is without recourse in her total destruction. From the time she is eleven, when she is often without parental supervision, she is seduced by the sweet music of twenty-one-year-old saxophonist Roland Watts. Her destiny is, thus, prescribed. As a prospective ultimate victim, Lena is not able to alter her life course. Even her limited career options—either working in the Heinz tomato factory as her single mother has done before her or singing in a jazz band—exacerbate her victim status.

As an older woman, Lena tries desperately to recapture the passion and the ecstasy of her youth. Alcohol becomes her conduit. In her perpetually drunken state, her only intimate relationships are with the life-sized and, for her, incarnated portraits of the three individuals who themselves have been destroyed by Lena's obsessive love (Roland, her lover; Veeda, his wife; and her daughter, Fendi). It is through the memories evoked by her conversations with these figures that much of Lena's sordid sexual history is revealed:

- At seventeen she has an affair with twenty-seven-year-old Roland, with whom she has a daughter and whose wife, Veeda, has for years served as Lena's surrogate mother, mentor, and friend.

- Some years after Roland and Lena have broken up, they engage in another brief passionate union which produces a son. Lena fails to reveal the existence of this child to Roland but instead disposes of the baby on the New York black market.

- She then meets, serves as mistress to, and ultimately marries a very old but very rich white man who bequeaths her his fortune upon his death. This legalized form of prostitution, while affording her a life of opulence, brings her only more unhappiness and despair.

Towards the play's end, Lena engages in acts that can be perceived as heteroerotic, autoerotic, and deviant erotic. The incarnated Veeda and Fendi accuse Lena of sexual interest in Abel, the young delivery boy-*cum*-artist who bears a marked resemblance to Roland and is the approximate age of their abandoned son. At this accusation, Lena begins to act out an extremely passionate sexual scene with the Roland of her imagination. She is able to achieve orgasm by autoerotic stimulation as no other living person is in the room.

By the play's last scene, when Abel arrives at Lena's apartment, the ultimate victim's doom is imminent. Maternal instincts are alien to this woman ruled so completely by her passions; hence, Lena is unable to connect with the nineteen-year-old Abel, who just might be her own son, in any way except sexually. Lena achieves her ultimate victim status as the oppressive force of her own passion incites her heinous violation of one of the greatest sexual taboos—incest. With the life-sized portraits as audience, Lena engages in a passionate deviant erotic act with her apparent son.

> *Lena*: (To Abel.) You're so good! Oh baby . . . my baby . . . My sweet, sweet baby.
>
> (*Lena*: pulls *Abel's* head down to her breasts.)
>
> The strobe once again starts a slow wind-down rhythm
>
> *Lena*. (Softly to Abel.) you're so good.

The portraits, serving as both her subconscious and her conscience, motivate her sexual passions but also condemn her for them. They see the sexual union with the boy for the deviant act that it is, and their denouncement is harsh:

> *Veeda*: (To Lena) Look what you done, Lena.
>
> *Fendi*: (To Lena) Look what you done, Momma.
>
> *Roland*: (To Lena) What you do, Lena?
>
> *Veeda*: . . . Makin' it with your son gotta be one of the irreversible sins. (502-503)

Lena's suicide is not an unexpected conclusion for the ultimate victim. Her obsessive passions have already psychically oppressed her; their degeneracy to incest is her death sentence. There is neither liberation nor salvation. One so totally controlled by a patriarchal racist society *and* the deviant psycho-sexual universe it creates cannot possibly survive. Lena, ultimate victim, as Gibson demonstrates, thus, cannot survive.

Another contemporary play that utilizes sexuality and eroticism to make its point is Alexis DeVeaux's *The Tapestry*. In its implications for the African American community, *The Tapestry* is more unsettling than *Brown Silk and Magenta Sunsets*. Writing about DeVeaux's creative work in general, Wilkerson explains that it "focuses on the 'inner space of relationships' as a microcosm of community. DeVeaux is interested in presenting the black woman in relation to her Eros, her sexuality" (135). Such can be said about *The Tapestry,* where relationships are key to the exploration for the overriding theme—woman's coming into self. Moreover, acts of and attitudes towards sexuality within these relationships serve as major tensions in the evolution of the primary character, Jet. The play is about Jet's individuation into a whole woman, one capable of delicately balancing the sexual, social and political aspects of the self to achieve that wholeness.

Jet, consumed by the stress and pressures of her law exams and her boyfriend, Axis, is in the middle of the greatest personal struggle she has known. On the surface, the struggle is, of course, to pass her exams, but her deeper struggle is the identification of her true self in the midst of her various life tensions. The play opens with Jet's flashbacks to a distant past that embraces her relationships with her parents and with the religion that was so much a part of her upbringing. The importance of these relationships is not clarified until the play's end when the potential for her to become the sacrificial chicken of her nightmare looms great. Only Jet can liberate herself from the oppression of her past, a past that continuously haunts her and provides her with the necessity to reflect on the power struggles that have always been a part of her experiences. Her present plagues her with the same necessary analysis. How must she respond to the important personal relationships as she forges her own identity as woman?

The simultaneous entry into the drama of both Axis and Jet's best friend, Lavender, foreshadows the duplicity that surfaces later in the play to threaten what little stability Jet believes she has thus far achieved. While Jet seems not to privilege either of these relationships over the other, both Axis and Lavender tend to look for the supremacy of the male/female relationship, particularly its sexual dimensions. Through this perception, shared by her two closest friends, the heteroeroticism in the play assumes a pivotal role in Jet's journey to selfhood.

As Axis' name suggests, he, as male, is assumed to be the referent entity in any coordinate relationship. Further, for both Axis and Lavender, heteroeroticism is primary to the male domain of power which Axis asserts. Andrea Dworkin speaks of this display of male power: "The power of sex is manifested in action, attitude, culture and attribute is the exclusive province of the male, his domain, inviolate and sacred. . . .The woman is acted on; the man acts and through action expresses sexual power, the power of masculinity" (22-23). Dworkin's observation is particularly true of *The Tapestry*. The play is fraught with this sexual tension and sexual power play with Axis often in the middle. Lavender's philosophy concerning sexuality purports to support this male supremacy as evidenced in her advice to Jet:

> if you dont give it to him when he wants/ it and as much as he wants/ hes going to get it from somewhere honey/ that a mans nature/ he got to have his stuff/ and if you aint going to treat him right/ you cant expect him to be perfect. (DeVeaux 171)

However, her sexual encounters with married men, casual friends, and finally with Axis, ironically, also seem to demonstrate a kind of rebellion against sexual oppression. Lavender does claim for herself the traditional male rights to sexual desire and sexual pleasure. However, these seemingly liberated/ing acts are almost addictive; thus, they are ultimately reduced to complicitous acts of sexual oppression and self destruction.

On the other hand, Jet's rebellion against the display of male power moves her further towards a self possessed concept of her own womanhood. This rather aberrant display of male power and Jet's rebellion against it emerge in the following dialogue between her and her boyfriend:

> *Axis* . . . i like a woman who knows how to be woman/for a man/ knows what to do to keep him

> *Jet* . . . thats a pretty narrow damn/view of a woman/ if I ever heard one

> *Axis* . . . what?/ listen baby aint but two roles' in the universe/ male and female in that order/ everything is bullshit/you hear me?

> *Jet* . . . who elected you/ the new black Jesus?

> *Axis* . . . i tell you something serious/little girl and you make a joke of it

Jet (offended) . . . how many little girls/ you know is as serious as I
am/ about anything?

Jet's attitude is underscored when she later tells Lavender:

i want to be defined on my own terms/not somebody elses/i want to
leave my mark on the work/make it all worth something/something
more than working my way into old age and a social security check/ I
see things to be done/ so many things (170)

In these lines, we see that Jet's determination to forge her academic
success and tenacious self-definition enable her to perform some
resistance to her own sexual oppression. Though subtle, her refusal of
the domineering Axis's sexual overtures, even temporarily "might be
regarded as an exercise of stopping power" (Cryle 133).

We see that Jet resists the erotic demands of patriarchy, thereby
exerting control over her own physical body and initiating the rebirth of
her psychic self. However, the point of climactic individuation actually
occurs after Axis' and Lavender's sexual betrayal is revealed. It is
certainly no surprise by the drama's end that these two, so consumed by
the power of male-centered heteroeroticism, could engage in such a
duplicitous act almost under Jet's nose. Jet's immediate response is
painful ambivalence:

leave me alone/ leave me axis/ lavender, please don't/leave/hurt
meeee (194)

Her despair serves as catalyst for both her symbolic and actual
individuation. A galaxy of personae, including Axis and Lavender,
appear up in the final surreal scene. All of them, from both her past and
present, represent the unhealthy power-centered relationships from
which she must escape—and she does. It is a newly conscious self that
emerges "growing/pulling out/everything [she] thought was true" (194).
No longer is Jet the "sacrificial chicken." The reader knows, as does
Jet, that she is now prepared for freedom, finally prepared "to make it
worth something."

The discourse of sexuality and eroticism in *Toussaint, Brown Silk
and Magenta Sunsets, The Tapestry,* and earlier plays, is for the most
part, fiercely political. Even Zora Neale Hurston's act of codifying her
sexual themes in order to express them becomes political. Through

their plays, all of these women articulate their own yearnings—and those of other African American women, for voice, respect, and individuality. That they utilize sexuality/eroticism as a tool through which to accomplish these rather basic, but elusive, ambitions demonstrates their understanding of the power inherent—in this society, at least—in the tensions of sexuality.

Perhaps a more raw and gratuitous sexuality has found a niche in an underground dramatic movement, but "mainstream"/published plays by African American women still tend towards this political focus. Even in more recent plays written in the nineties—an era when almost anything goes sexually (if other popular African American art forms serve as a socio-cultural barometer)—the new sexuality in the drama may also be even more prevalent, and uninhibited, but generally, it is not so for its own sake.[2] This phenomenon may result from the puritanical spirit that continues to guide so much of American dramatic expressions—including that of African American women. Perhaps what may be called explicit sexuality is viewed as redeemable by an infusion of social value. More likely, however, the phenomenon remains simply a well-articulated artistic resistance to the degrading and distasteful images of African American women and, even more, against the myriad repressive and oppressive elements still encountered by those on the bottom of the social ladder. To paraphrase the words of Alexis DeVeaux's Jet, African American women dramatists see things to be done—so many things. The discourse of intercourse continues to be one viable mode by which they choose to do them.

NOTES

1. Quotations from plays written before 1950 are from Kathy Perkins's anthology. Quotations from plays written after 1950 are from Margaret Wilkerson's anthology. All quotations are cited within the essay.

2. In Sydné Mahone's provocative edited collection *Moon Marked and Touched by Sun* (1994) sexuality glaringly reaches the foreground of the drama in such works as *Sally's Rape* by Robbie McCauley, *White Chocolate for My Father* by Laurie Carlos, and *Caged Rhythm* by Kia Corthron. Nevertheless, in each work sexuality has a purpose other than existing for its own sake.

WORKS CITED

Burrill, Mary. *They Sit in Darkness. Black Female Playwrights: An Anthology of Plays before 1950.* Ed. Kathy A. Perkins. Bloomington:Indiana UP, 1989. 67-74.

Cryle, Peter M. "Gendered Time in Erotic Narrative: Finishing Power vs Staying Power." *Romantic Review* 83 (1992): 132-148.

DeVeaux, Alexis. *The Tapestry. 9 Plays by Black Women.* Ed. Margaret Wilkerson. New York: New American Library, 1986. 135-195.

Dworkin, Andrea. *Pornography: Men Possessing Women.* London: The Women's Press. 1989

Gibson, P.J. *Brown Silk and Magenta Sunsets. 9 Plays by Black Women.* Ed. Margaret Wilkerson. New York: New American Library, 1986. 425-505.

Govan, Sandra. "Forbidden Fruit and the Unholy Lust: Illicit Sex in Black American Literature." *Erotique Noire/Black Erotica.* Eds. Miriam DaCosta-Willis, Reginald Martin, and Roseann P. Bell. New York: Anchor Books/Doubleday, 1992. 35-44.

Graham, Shirley. *It's Morning. Black Female Playwrights: An Anthology of Plays before 1950.* Ed. Kathy A. Perkins. Bloomington: Indiana UP, 1989. 211-224.

Hansberry, Lorraine. *Toussaint. 9 Plays by Black Women.* Ed. Margaret Wilkerson. New York: New American Library, 1986. 41-67.

Hurston, Zora Neale. *Color Struck. Black Female Playwrights: An Anthology of Plays before 1950.* Ed. Kathy A. Perkins. Bloomington: Indiana UP, 1989. 89-102.

Johnson, Georgia Douglas. *Blue-Eyed Black Boy. Black Female Playwrights: An Anthology of Plays before 1950.* Ed. Kathy A. Perkins. Bloomington: Indiana UP, 1989. 47-51.

Mahone, Sydné. *Moon Struck and Touched by Sun.* New York: Theatre Communications Group. 1994.

Perkins, Kathy A., Ed. *Black Female Playwrights: An Anthology of Plays Before 1950.* Bloomington: Indiana UP, 1989.

Podol, Peter, L. "The Socio-Political Dimension of Sexuality and Eroticism in Contemporary Spanish Theatre." *Alec* 17 (1992): 257-70.

Staples, Robert, and Leanor Baulin Johnson. *Black Families at the Crossroads: Challenges and Prospects.* San Francisco: Jossey-Bass Publishers, 1993.

Wilkerson, Margaret, ed. *9 Plays by Black Women.* New York: New American Library, 1986.

The Nightmare of History
Conceptions of Sexuality in Adrienne Kennedy's
Funnyhouse of a Negro[1]
Carla J. McDonough

Flavius Davis:

He taught World History and was the first person whom I ever heard
say that every event was connected to every other event. And that
there was a "universal unconscious." All events are connected, he
would say. I hurried along the corridor at nine in the morning and sat
right in front of him. It was the most exciting class I'd ever had.

Kennedy, *People Who Led to My Plays* (64)

In part because she was not initially embraced as a spokesperson for the
civil rights of blacks or for feminism—two movements which
championed a number of important writers in the sixties and
seventies—Kennedy was largely overlooked by the critical community
until the 1980s, when some of the first critical articles of substance
devoted to her work began appearing. Most critics have examined her
theater for its feminist themes or for how she fits into the canon of
avant-garde writers of African American writers.[2] While each of these
approaches has its advantage, there always seems to be more that we
are all missing within her hauntingly vivid theater. In an essay collected
in the 1992 volume *Intersecting Boundaries*, Kimberly W. Benston
comments that "[w]riting about Adrienne Kennedy is not unlike being
written by her: one feels always already estranged from any clear point
of departure, though a plethora of intellectual, psychic, and political
themes suggest themselves as equally plausible centering concerns"

(113). It is this plethora that interests me. In Kennedy's plays, as in her world history class, every event seems connected to every other event. As a result, her work tends to historicize questions of identity as she melds acutely personal images and symbols (as becomes apparent when tracing the origin of some of those images in her autobiography *People Who Led to My Plays*) with widely disseminated images from historical events throughout the world. Although many of her plays deserve examination in this light, this essay will focus on her first produced play, the Obie- award-winning *Funnyhouse of a Negro*, which is still widely considered to be her best play, even though the original production was financially unsuccessful and drew some sharp criticism.

The nature of this criticism is itself revealing, in that it responds to the uncomfortable position in which Kennedy places both her heroine and her audience as she explores certain racial and gender issues. Billie Allen, who originated the role of Sarah in *Funnyhouse*, described in a recent interview how "some people got very angry about this play. Some black people, some white people, especially some black people because they felt it was denigrating of blacks" (in Bryant-Jackson and Overbeck 219). Alisa Solomon's foreword to Kennedy's *The Alexander Plays* mentions the negative response that *Funnyhouse* drew from some quarters as one reason why her theater has not received the critical support and attention Solomon believes it deserves. Even more vividly, in a 1987 interview Kennedy herself speaks of her reaction to this negative response to *Funnyhouse,* describing how

> A lot of blacks hated this particular play and said it was pretentious and imitative. . . . I remember that there was an article written in the sixties that attacked my writing specifically and said that I was an irrelevant black writer. That sort of criticism was pretty pervasive at the time, so I built up a little resistance to it. I was criticized because there were heroines in my plays who were mixed up, confused. But I knew what my alliances were . . . . (252)

Although several influential theater people such as Joseph Papp, Joe Chaikin, and Michael Kahn championed Kennedy's early work, she did not receive the publicity and critical support that rocketed to fame many of her contemporaries such as Amiri Baraka and Sam Shepard. Such a comparison forces us to realize the favored status offered certain images of Americana and denied others due in part to complex issues of race and gender. While such a comparison is fodder for a very different article than the present one, these issues of reception indicate how Kennedy's theater raises some uncomfortable challenges for its audience.

In *Funnyhouse of Negro*, Kennedy offers a wide scope of historical and cultural images surrounding the main character, Sarah. Of particular interest is the resonance Kennedy sets up between the present experiences of a young black woman in America, and the American, European, and African history of colonialism that shapes her conceptions of self. In this melding of Sarah's life with historical figures, Kennedy examines how personal identity is historically created. As Sarah explores her identity through her memories and fantasies of her parents, she also reveals how that identity is not her own due to the historical positioning that shapes and invades it. For Kennedy's character, identity and history are entangled in ways that support the idea that the personal is political, and that indicate the complex matrix of power issues that comprise black and white identity in the colonial and postcolonial age. No wonder Kennedy's heroines are often "mixed up and confused." They try to make sense of themselves using historical paradigms that usually provide them more paradoxes than answers. Far from being a traitor to the cause of social justice for blacks, Kennedy's play offers a vast historical canvas upon which her character, "The Negro," plays out her life, acknowledging the link between history and identity, while subtly undermining the white supremacist ideology that Sarah embraces.

The play's main character tells the story of her life through the voices of her alternate selves: Queen Victoria, the Duchess of Hapsburg, Patrice Lumumba, and Jesus. Using her own voice and those of these characters, Sarah engages in the act of self-interpretation as she recounts the significant events of her life and of her parents' lives. Her version of that history is shaped and selected by her personal ideology which itself has been shaped by the historically precarious position of a mulatto poised between two cultures—white and black. As she tells the story of her life and of the lives of her mother and father, we are led to consider what it means to write a history and what it means to be written into history. For as much as Sarah is the narrator of events she both witnesses and imagines, she is also guided and shaped by an inherited ideological stance regarding how to interpret these events.

Sarah prefaces her explorations of her origins and family history with the need to "maintain a stark fortress against recognition of myself" (6). Thus, her odyssey into self-examination is paradoxically framed by the desire to escape self. The action of the play can be interpreted as the fortress she puts up—returning to a specific version of events and resisting any retranslation or reinterpretation of it. She is unable to see herself as integrated and whole and instead sees herself as segregated into many parts, all of which, though, tell similar stories. That story is of her dark-skinned father and light-skinned mother who fell out of love in Africa as the father pursued his mission—given him by his mother—to uplift the race in Africa by taking Christianity there. In Africa, the mother refused to interact with the father or with Sarah, turning away from them both and ultimately becoming insane. It is in Africa that Sarah is conceived—the product of the rape of her mother by her father to which Sarah constantly refers. From Africa, the story shifts to America where Sarah's mother is in an insane asylum; Sarah attends school and wants to write English poetry like Edith Sitwell, and the father pursues Sarah even though he is dead. His death is the result either of having hung himself upon hearing of the death of Patrice Lumumba, or of having been killed by Sarah herself. The story, in the multiple parts and versions told by the characters, changes only subtly as Sarah's multiple selves repeat it. However, the story itself is less important than the way it is told. Sarah's selves place all blame for Sarah's confusion and insanity (represented by the loss of her hair) on the father and, in contrast, idolize the mother. The source of this interpretation of events is evidently the result of received ideas about the value of blackness and of whiteness, which are associated with the father and the mother, respectively. In her first monologue, Sarah herself tells us of her longing to be white, explaining, "As we of royal blood know, black is evil and has been from the beginning" (5).

Given the above lines, it is understandable that some black viewers of this play initially considered Kennedy to be a traitor to the cause. Sarah's obvious hatred of her blackness certainly stands in direct contrast to the widely-heralded tenet, "black is beautiful." She buys whole-heartedly into the idea that blackness is "evil" and that only in embracing whiteness, in trying to be white, can she be whole. However, to assume that Sarah's desire to be white condemns blackness is to overlook the complexities of Kennedy's play. All of Sarah's comments are part of her "stark fortress against recognition of [her]self" (6). The majority of the play's stories of Sarah's origins and family, the world that Kennedy describes as the "funnyhouse" of this Negro girl, can be read as Sarah's method of building that fortress against self-recognition. The question is begged, however, as to why Sarah believes that she, "like all educated Negroes," must deny herself (6). It is impossible to experience this play without wondering why Sarah needs such an elaborate fantasy/funnyhouse. What are the cultural and social dynamics that make such a funnyhouse not only possible but seemingly, for Sarah (who is notably described as "the Negro"), necessary and inescapable? In this question resides the crux of the play and the complexity of Kennedy's position regarding the racial ideology her character both replicates and undermines.

Kennedy's Sarah sees herself as a racist white society would have her see herself: as evil, ugly, and bestial because of her blackness. This is the recognition of self that she longs to fortify against. As her praise of her mother who "looked like a white woman" (3) and her hatred for her father whom she describes as a "wild black beast" (3) indicate, she despises her blackness and longs to be white. Yet this image of self does not issue from an objective mirror but from the warped and distorted "funnyhouse" mirror of the racist society that shapes Sarah's world. In examining the funnyhouse world of Sarah's consciousness, Kennedy examines the forces that create and shape that funnyhouse. How does Sarah, a young black woman in America, come to grips with a history that posits her as a victim without getting lost in its victimization? This victimization is presented by the self-negation Sarah embraces in trying to make herself white. How does she escape her role as victim without positing herself in the role of victimizer? This role is apparent in Sarah's betrayal of and physical or psychological murder of her father who represents her own blackness. Perhaps this dilemma of being both victim and victimizer is what has led to the multiple stories Sarah tells of her own immediate ancestors—her mother and father—and of their relationships to the other selves in the play.

Sarah's fracturing of her psyche, caused by this dilemma, leads viewers to the immediate assumption that Sarah is crazy and the play nothing but insane ramblings of little consequence. If Sarah is crazy, we need to know what constitutes sanity in this world. Much as Michel Foucault sought to define the age of reason by studying its definitions of madness, so too, we need to examine which of Sarah's ideas constitute her abnormality in order to understand what is considered to be normal in this world. Which of her beliefs or desires can we label as insane? That she wants to be white in a culture that valorizes whiteness? That she desires to escape blackness in a culture that despises blackness? What, according to the values of her society, is mad about these desires? The desire itself is a logical continuation of the belief that black is evil and white is good. Yet, since Sarah herself is black, her culturally-created desire stands in contrast to her physical reality. There is no place for "Negro" Sarah to acquire the positive values associated with whiteness—beauty, worth, goodness. Precisely by following or internalizing the values of her society which have caused her to deny her "Negro" self, Sarah's madness is created. She is fractured by the ideology of a culture that seeks to control, shape, and warp her self-image, a warping very like the images created by fun-house mirrors.

Sarah is an excellent example of this country's cultural wars in which culture is largely defined and certainly shaped not only by race but also by class. She longs to be not only white, but of the ruling class—a queen or duchess, one "of royal blood" (5). She has bought into a version of the events in her life that reflects the preferences of a racist and classist white culture, an ideology which she voices in her opening monologue: white is good, black is evil, a mix of the two is not to be tolerated; art and interior decor should reflect the taste of the (white) moneyed upper classes. But to understand the workings of Kennedy's play, we must recognize that these values are ultimately implicated, in Sarah's world, with sexuality. Exploring how her sexual terrain replicates racial dynamics makes the historical resonances of her dilemma apparent.

Sarah obviously longs to be white, "to become even a more pallid Negro" (5). She dreams of living in white rooms of European decor, eating off white tables, surrounded by white friends, but this dream as re-spoken by her father is described as "vile" (13). Sarah's desire to embrace white culture, especially as represented by both her mother and by England, is clearly portrayed as a self-denial or self-negation that is destructive, not delightful, thus contradicting the initial criticism that the play embraces white ideals for blacks. Sarah longs to be white in order not to feel, in order not to recognize herself. This embracing of whiteness connects with a flight from self that negates both power and feeling. The white rooms Sarah longs to inhabit reflect the pallor of death that clings to the "astonishing whiteness" of the statue of Queen Victoria and to the Duchess. So, although Sarah longs to be as white as the Queen and the Duchess, Kennedy clearly condemns that longing by connecting it to a numbness and a death wish that hardly glorifies or empowers whiteness. In addition to the deathliness that clings to Victoria's whiteness, insanity is associated with the whiteness of the mother. The more the mother turned away from blackness as represented both by Sarah's father and by Sarah herself, the more insane she became, until she was finally locked up in an asylum.

Given these associations of whiteness with insanity and death, Sarah's stories obviously question the equation of light skin with good and dark skin with bad, although Sarah herself refuses to see this questioning. Sarah's story shows us a dark-skinned father who wishes to connect with his daughter and a light-skinned mother who seems incapable of parental affection. The mother, whom we see at the opening of the play walking about like the figure of Lady Macbeth, is insane, hardly a positive trait; she has turned away from her daughter, refusing to answer her; she prefers the company of owls. The bird imagery throughout the play that is associated with the mother links her with the flight of those birds which fill the stage at the play's opening. This flight imagery takes on particular resonance when we consider that the mother's turning away from physical connections with her daughter or her husband can be interpreted to embody Eldridge Cleaver's description of what he terms the white, "ultrafeminine" women "of the elite" whose sexual identity relies on "flight from their bodies" (169). Even though Cleaver's description of gender relations is problematic for many feminists, it is fitting in regard to the mother's image in this play: it captures the gender dynamic that is expressed by the mother's vision of white femininity. Through her whiteness and through her "frigid" behavior, the mother suggests an emptiness of feeling and a fear of sexuality. In contrast to the "ultrafeminine" image of ideal feminine beauty associated with the mother's whiteness, Sarah's father is made into what Cleaver has described as the "brute" of the lower classes, the "supermasculine menial" engulfed in bodily sexuality. This image of black men as over-sexed brutes is one that has also been examined by feminists such as Michelle Wallace and Angela Davis. In *Black Macho and the Myth of the Superwoman*, Wallace examines the attractiveness of this image for some male leaders of the black power movement who embraced the macho image of the sexually potent black man as a cultural power for themselves. Wallace argues that in taking on this image, the black power movement played into the stereotypes of white society and ended up driving a wedge between black men and black women. Angela Davis's more recent , "Rape, Racism, and the Myth of the Black Rapist," considers how the myth of the sexually violent/aggressive black man has been used as a "deadly racist weapon" (174) and considers how racism leads to sexism through reducing individuals to sexual stereotypes. Sarah confirms how this stereotypical sexual positioning has corrupted her understanding of her parents by continuously describing her father as a "black beast" who almost mindlessly "keeps returning" to pursue Sarah (3) while she longs to imitate the "soulless" white beauty of her mother (5). Sarah's "heterosexual terror," as Rosemary Curb terms it, is that the father returns to rape her as he supposedly raped her mother. This image fits the stereotypes of sexuality in a racist and sexist society which perceives black men as sexually violent and white women as frigidly fearing sexual contact.

The terms which describe both the mother and father echo fantasy's powerful role in shaping social consciousness regarding black and white sexuality. In examining such fantasies, the play takes us into the funnyhouse not simply of Sarah's imagination but of the distorting social forces that have shaped her. The most potent social force is that of colonialism. In the American slave system, white fantasies of black sexuality shaped relations between masters and their slaves by displacing sexual appetites and sexual aggression from whites onto blacks. The politics behind the myths of the sexually submissive and promiscuous black woman and the sexually aggressive black male have been discussed in fruitful detail by such critics as Angela Davis, bell hooks, and Gerda Lerner. These studies demonstrate how such definitions of black sexuality were created by the white power structure to sanction the sexual exploitation of black women by white men and the terrorist control of black men by white men as a key tool in enforcing enslavement before emancipation and continuing to limit the social and political power of blacks after emancipation. Sarah's portrait of the sexually frigid mother is implicated in this dynamic in that the mother is seen as trying to replicate pure, white womanhood, whose chastity was protected by the supposed availability of black women and women of the lower classes to satisfy the more animal desires of the white man. By keeping white women as the ultimate sexual "prize" unavailable for the black man and by limiting the definition of "true" womanhood to that of the kept woman with soft, lily white hands, this sexual positioning seeks to deny black men a sense of their own manhood and black women a sense of their own womanhood.[3]

While the mother's story embraces this sexual positioning by equating white femininity with a chastity that becomes sexual frigidity, the story of the father replicates the positioning of black male sexuality as dangerous, aggressive, and violent. White fantasy/fear regarding the supposedly over-sexed black man, a puritan repression of fear of their own sexuality, surfaces in Sarah's fantasy/fear regarding her own father. Consider that the sexually-tinged scene between the Duchess and the Funnyman revolves around their discussion of the father. The two never speak their desire for each other, but they keep repeating the story of the father, the blackest one who keeps returning. The scene can be read as a sex fantasy. Kennedy's stage directions describe their relationship as one of implied physical intimacy, with the Duchess (her clothing in disarray) at the feet of the Funnyman (played by Raymond, Sarah's Jewish lover). Throughout the scene, the two characters seem to be enacting well-rehearsed parts in a sexual drama:

> *Duchess. (Carrying a red paper bag.)* My father is arriving and what
> am I to do?

> *Funnyman.* He is arriving from Africa, is he not?

> *Duchess.* Yes, yes, he is arriving from Africa.

> *Funnyman.* I always knew your father was African.

> . . . .

> *Duchess. (Goes on wildly.)* Yes, my father is a black man who went
> to Africa years ago as a missionary teacher, got mixed up in
> politics, was revealed [sic] and is now devoting his foolish life to
> the erection of a Christian mission in the middle of the jungle in
> one of those newly freed counties. Hide me. *(Clinging to his
> knees.)* Hide me here so the nigger will not find me.

> *Funnyman.(Laughing)* Your father is in the jungle dedicating his life
> to the erection of a Christian mission.

> *Duchess.* Hide me here so the jungle will not find me. Hide me.

> *Funnyman.* Isn't it cruel of you?

> *Duchess.* Hide me from the jungle.

> *Funnyman.* Isn't it cruel? (9-10)

Although these two characters do not discuss their relationship, sexual or otherwise, the sexual arousal, and growing excitement in the scene is unmistakable. Their only discussion is of the father, more specifically, of his "erection" of a mission in the jungle. The father is so closely associated with the wild, primeval, sexual power of the jungle that the Duchess finally even calls him "the jungle." This story emphasizes the father's blackness and his wildness from which the Duchess begs the Funnyman to hide her, clinging to his leg as she does so. One can easily imagine this scene being enacted in one of the brothel rooms of Jean Genet's *The Balcony*. Read as a sex fantasy, the Duchess and Funnyman's story of the father becomes foreplay—the drama that excites them, arouses them, and drives them together. Unable to speak their own sexual desire, they tell the story of the father, displacing the wildness and bestiality of their own sexuality—their jungle within— onto him.

Interestingly in the midst of this story of the father, the Duchess tells of having woken that morning "still shaken by nightmares of [her] mother" (10). Although the father is openly feared and despised (even as that fear seems to titillate the characters who speak it), the deeper fear that haunts both Sarah and all of her selves is that of the mother and her rejection. Yet this is the fear that will not be acknowledged. Sarah tells of how her mother "would not let [Sarah's father] touch her in their wedding bed and called him black" (14). The mother is described as constantly turning away both from the father and from Sarah. Thus, in contrast to the over-sexed image of the "black beast" stands Sarah's mother whose whiteness and whose frigidity parallels that of Queen Victoria, an image of Victorian sexual repression whose figure of "astonishing whiteness" presides over Sarah's funnyhouse.

In the face of these sexual stereotypes of white women and black men, the audience witnesses the father return not to rape his daughter but to ask for acceptance and forgiveness from the daughter who rejects him out of fear and disgust. The further connection of the father with the heroic figure of Patrice Lumumba, a martyr in the fight against colonialism in Africa, imparts heroic stature to the father as the martyr to Sarah's fears and insecurities. The story of Patrice Lumumba, assassinated by fellow Africans even as he sought to free Zaire from colonial rule, is subtly compared to the story of Jesus's betrayal by his own people. Sarah's betrayal of her own father is thus paralleled to the betrayal of both Lumumba and of Jesus. Through the connotations of these images, the father is re-figured as an heroic, noble man, struggling against the very stereotypes that Sarah's white ideology would place upon him. In the father, the stereotypes that coincide with sexual, political, and religious colonization are simultaneously imposed and questioned. The father as Patrice Lumumba is made to stand for liberation and postcolonial revolution, thus standing in sharp contrast to the other powerful political figure in the play, Queen Victoria, whose deathly whiteness carries with it the connotations of empire and colonialism.

This obvious link with political colonialism is further complicated by connections with sexual colonialism, apparent in the image of Victoria as the embodiment of sexual repression which fears the sexual aggression of the black beast. Religion's role in both political and sexual colonization is further explored in the figure of Jesus, the fourth of Sarah's selves. The image of Queen Victoria, coupled with her consort Prince Albert, is linked to God in Jesus's speech. Jesus describes how

> all my life I believed my Holy Father to be God, but now I know that
> my father is a black man. I have no fear for whatever I do, I will do in
> the name of God, I will do in the name of Albert Saxe Coburg, in the
> name of Victoria, Queen Victoria Regina, the monarch of England, I
> will. (19-20)

God, Albert, and Victoria: this triumvirate calls to mind the rallying cry of many English colonialists—for God and Country or for Queen and country—as they traveled into Africa or other hearts of darkness to bring "enlightenment" to the natives and riches to their own nation. Through the character of Jesus, political and religious colonialism are intricately linked. As aspects of Sarah's personality, both Jesus and Queen Victoria further indicate the connection between the history of a religion or of a nation and the history of an individual person that ultimately, for Sarah, plays out its dynamics through sexuality.

Despite the image of Patrice Lumumba, which Kennedy herself comments is the only positive figure in the play (Bryant-Jackson and Overbeck 4), Sarah's inability to accept her father as anything other than a black beast indicates the historically entrapping images of black and white sexuality that have colonized Sarah's imagination. More than once, Sarah says that the father is the black beast that "haunted [her] conception" (lO, 21). Although said initially about the supposed rape that led to her birth, the term "conception" indicates that not only is her physical birth haunted by sexual and racial stereotypes, but her ability to conceive of the world around her—her thoughts—is haunted by these images as well. She is unable to conceive of a world other than the one that insists upon a hierarchal relationship between white and black.

Importantly, the images that haunt Sarah's conception are not only that of blackness as evil, but also the idea of whiteness as good. She speaks often of her father haunting her, but the play abounds with images of the mother that haunt her as well. Each image is set up in contrast to the other and remains throughout the play an integral part of the other. However, in keeping with colonial ideology, blackness is viewed as the problem or aberration while whiteness is upheld as the unquestioned norm, despite its questionable position. This pattern is upheld in Sarah's funnyhouse in that the father is questioned, blamed, and made to speak his own defense, but the mother remains silent and is championed by others. This pattern, however, also breaks down as Sarah finds herself unable to maintain such a rigid system. Even as Sarah's stories insist on the lightness (read goodness) of the mother and the blackness (read evil) of the father, the play reveals the father's passionate fight for his people and for his daughter's acceptance and the mother's betrayal of both her husband and her daughter. The actions of the characters would seem to belie their ideological positioning. To say that Kennedy's play simply replicates the selfhatred that the black power movement of the sixties was trying to overcome is to refuse to see the complex layers that Kennedy is exploring through Sarah's story. Even as it is clear that Sarah's world is shaped by racist tenets that cause her to replicate the image of blackness as horror, as ugly, as worthless, the play also calls those tenets into question by the actions of the mother and father and by the images of insanity and death associated with whiteness.

While Sarah's longing to be white and Kennedy's condemnation of that desire in *Funnyhouse of a Negro* call to mind the dangers of assimilation that were such crucial issues in many plays by African Americans in the 1960s, Kennedy's Sarah cannot be so easily answered with an either/or proposition of assimilationism or nationalism because she is not easily classified as either white or black. Thus, Kennedy's play reflects a heightened sense of complexity regarding race issues that, in many ways, could not be "seen" until after the more clear-cut battles against the overt discrimination of black and white lunch counters and water fountains had been fought. In a decade where we are still struggling with the more pervasive and more elusive prejudices of not the letter of the law but the spirit, Kennedy's play offers an excellent model of internalized racism. This internalized racism is a result of cultural associations regarding the worth of whiteness and the worthlessness of blackness.

Sarah not only hates blackness but sees herself as the mistake that a society which fears miscegenation would have her see herself. Her mistake, however, indicated by the mise-en-scene of the play, is embracing the deathly whiteness represented by her mother instead of embracing the blackness of her father. She tears herself apart by accepting the image of blackness as horror that dominant white culture would have her accept. Fearing violence from her father, as a white racist society would have her fear black men as violent, she instead embraces the more likely violence from whites (for instance the legacy of white masters raping their black female slaves)[4] that could easily be the reason for her mother's whiteness. Sarah's fear of blackness also reflects what Frantz Fanon has described as the struggle of the mulatto not to slip back into blackness (*Black Skin* 54). However, a simplistic reading of the evils of whiteness (represented by the insanity of the mother) which would have us view black as evil, is further complicated by the interdependency of these two visions of black and white which coalesce in Sarah's fantasies.

While *Funnyhouse* demonstrates how Sarah's longing to be white leads to emptiness and death, in contrast, Kennedy's autobiographical *People Who Led to My Plays,* published in 1987, demonstrates how a fascination with certain images of whiteness was a fruitful, if conflicted, part of Kennedy's childhood. This stance further complicates the images that pervade Kennedy's play as we are forced to realize that stereotypical images used to divide whites and blacks, whether along sexual or class lines, are endlessly subject to reinterpretation, or to what Henry Louis Gates has termed "re-translation" (4), even if Sarah refuses to do so. In *People*, Kennedy comments about her parents' hometown, Montezuma, Georgia:

> My mother often said that most of the white people of Montezuma's families came from England. I realized dimly that this meant some of our ancestors too had come from England, since, like most "Negro" families in the town, we had white relations as well as "Negro." I became very interested in "England." (22)

Here Kennedy acknowledges where her fascination with the white culture of England began, with a realization that England literally was related to her, part of her personal history. This realization, coupled with Kennedy's fascination with characters in books set in England—characters such as Jane Eyre and Mary of *The Secret Garden*—shows us the power literary and cultural figures exert in fertile imaginations. One interpretation of this fascination is to consider how literary images can seduce a reader into their ideology. By wanting to emulate Jane Eyre, Kennedy can be seen as being colonized by the white, patriarchal ideologies that pervade the power structures in the novel, the structures that Jean Rhys deconstructs in her reworking of the story in *The Wide Sargasso Sea*. However, Kennedy's childhood fascination with Jane Eyre connects in Kennedy's mind with the story of her own mother, who was also sent to boarding school at a young age. Since her mother was such a powerful influence on Kennedy, Kennedy can also be seen to adapt the foreign tale of Jane Eyre to her own world view—in effect colonizing the colonizers' story, appropriating it for her own psychic terrain. Although I have set these two possible interpretations side by side, I prefer to consider how they interact rather than how they contradict one another because the interaction of conflicting perspectives is precisely what drives not only Kennedy's autobiography but also her theater.

A key question raised by Sarah's fantasies of white and black history and icons is not so much which culture Sarah ought to choose but whether choice is possible. If both cultures are shaped by the same set of sexual and racial stereotypes, is either, ultimately able to escape the other? Sarah's choices are trapped within the dichotomy that to view whiteness as good is to view blackness as evil, and to view blackness as good is to view whiteness as evil. In this dynamic, one image cannot exist without acknowledgment of the other, is always implicated with the other, so, is Sarah really free to be either white or black? The two are ultimately entangled by their mutual need to be defined in contrast.

The impossibility of the either/or choice is further highlighted by the fact that Sarah is both white and black by birth—receiving her white heritage from her nearly white mother and her black heritage from both her mother and father. She cannot deny either, and yet the people and images around her insist that she cannot embrace either. The whiteness of the mother rejects Sarah, and Sarah in turn rejects the blackness of her father. Yet these rejections are ultimately connected by an agreed upon positioning of white and black sexual identity as not only separate but opposite. In contrast to this positioning, Sarah's mulatto status indicates the illogic of not allowing for multiple, simultaneous interpretations. Regardless of the historical tendency to place the two in contention, she is simultaneously white and black. The impossible union of these two supposed opposites within Sarah, which her cultural ideology will not allow her to integrate, becomes the source of her seeming insanity. She is what her culture does not want to acknowledge, yet her existence cannot be denied. She has struggled against this knowledge of self, and like Hamlet, it hath made her mad.

Returning to the issue of Sarah's madness, we confront the question of which ideologies the play embraces and which it refutes, and who is to resolve this dilemma? If Sarah's selves as part of her fractured psyche are telling us their interpretation as to the meaning of the events they repeat, whom are we to believe? Who is capable of telling us the "real" story as opposed to a fantasy or hallucination? The question of objective fact in contrast to fantasy is raised throughout the play as the audience is constantly left to question what "really" happened to Sarah's parents, and what is "really" happening to Sarah now. The real becomes the shadowy figure that haunts us with the hope that it can be found somewhere behind the hallucinations and, if found, will help to make sense of what we are seeing. We are encouraged at first to view Sarah, narrator of this play and seeming authority on the story she tells, as offering this truth. In her opening speeches, Sarah explains the strangeness of the play by establishing each of the characters in relation to herself and establishing herself, specifically her origins and her "place," as the central issue of the story to be told. She lets us know that the play will be exploring the terrain of her consciousness:

> Part of the time I live with Raymond, part of the time with God, Maxmillian and Albert Saxe Coburg. I live in my room. . . .The rooms are my rooms; a Hapsburg chamber, a chamber in a Victorian castle, the hotel where I killed my father, the jungle. These are the places myselves exist in. (5-7)

But as the play progresses, we are forced to consider whether or not Sarah herself, the "authority" on her own experience, is able to answer the questions or resolve the dilemmas her story raises. Sarah's fracturing of her consciousness places her sanity in doubt for the audience and so serves to counter-act the audience's ability to accept her interpretation of events. We find ourselves looking for saner points of view in the characters of the Landlady and Sarah's lover Raymond, whom we are initially encouraged to view as being outside the funnyhouse. Indeed, when the Landlady first speaks, we find ourselves responding to her seemingly rational explanation of the cryptic and imagistic ramblings we have just witnessed. The Landlady tells us,

> Ever since her father hung himself in a Harlem hotel when Patrice Lumumba was murdered she hides herself in her room. Each night she repeats: He keeps returning. How dare he enter the castle walls, he who is the darkest of them all. . . . I tell her: Sarah, honey, the man hung himself. It's not your blame. But no, she stares at me: No, Mrs. Conrad, he did not hang himself, that is only the way they understand it . . . . (8)

The Landlady's speech gives us an explanation we can follow. Traumatized by the suicide of her father, Sarah has lost her grip on reality and slipped into a psychosis in which she believes she has murdered her father and is now haunted by his ghost. The Landlady also exchanges dialogue with Raymond, Sarah's boyfriend, as the two seemingly stand outside of Sarah's funnyhouse world and comment on it.

Yet this comforting sense of an objective voice lending reason and order to an insane world is obscured by the question of whether or not either Raymond or the Landlady ever stand outside of the funnyhouse of Sarah's consciousness. After all, Raymond becomes the Funnyman of the funnyhouse and interacts with the Duchess. His participation in the psychosis also calls into question the Landlady's objective status since she is seemingly operating on the same level of understanding as is Raymond. The final scene has the two characters speaking what seems to be a eulogy of sorts for Sarah. They agree that "she was a funny little liar," but then Raymond tells the Landlady the supposedly "real" story of the father which simply replicates the earlier fantasy of a life in a white world, living in rooms with European decor, eating off white tables (23). Raymond's closing speech sends us full circle to Sarah's opening monologue, offering a closure that seals every character in the play into the funnyhouse world as even these on-stage observers end up contributing to Sarah's story. Ultimately, none of the characters stand in an objective position outside of the funnyhouse because all of them buy into its ideology concerning blacks and whites. Although we wish to be able to distinguish fantasy from reality, Kennedy's play does not let us but instead forces us to realize that ideology is fantasy and, more particularly, that Sarah's fantasies are those of colonialism and its aftermath. If Sarah cannot reconcile history's many images, can we?

This last question leaves us with the play's overriding question: can we ever distinguish between our historical positioning and our personal identity? Can we find the one true definition of where our self-definitions break down and historically imposed ones take over? In many ways, audience discomfort with Sarah's theatrical multi-plex— running differing images of her personal history simultaneously— echoes the discomfort Hayden White chronicles during the nineteenth century's "crisis of historicism." Of this time, White writes that "The consistent elaboration of a number of equally comprehensive and plausible, yet apparently mutually exclusive, conceptions of the same set of events was enough to undermine confidence in history's claim to 'objectivity,' 'scientificity,' and 'realism'" (41). Trained to want one, "true," agreed upon version of events, historians and their followers found themselves uncomfortable when faced with differing, though nonetheless equally plausible interpretations. Kennedy's theater further confuses by indicating that the differing visions may in fact reflect each other as they rely on each other for their difference. That, in fact, all these contradictions are connected, and if they are ultimately warped or insane, then so is the culture that created them.

Funnyhouse of a Negro sets its audience adrift in a sea of images from American, African, and European history, politics, and ideology. The confusion caused by this jumble of images causes us either to want to distance ourselves from them, as Raymond tries to do when he calls Sarah "a funny little liar" (23), or to order those images—to organize them based on a pattern drawn from our ideological backgrounds of dyadic thinking. Yet, the further we explore these images, the more clearly we see them already ordered according to the sexual and racial stereotypes and fantasies by which power relationships between blacks and whites have historically been maintained since the advent of colonialism. Sarah's seemingly chaotic psyche is rigidly shaped by white power which maintains its power by displacing the "bestial," "animalistic" qualities of human nature—its sexual energy—upon black men and women. But while Kennedy's portrait of Sarah replicates that shaping ideology, it also questions this ideology by purposefully making strange what is usually so familiar that we easily overlook it. While Sarah's story ultimately plays out in an almost mythic way the history of power relations that drive the colonizing of blacks by whites, the play simultaneously questions the powerful images that haunt our conceptions of self and of each other, ultimately leading us to consider how we, like Sarah, are simultaneously the shapers and victims of our own historical positioning.[5]

NOTES

1. I would like to thank several colleagues for their advice and support in the completion of this article. Lauren Smith read several drafts and offered suggestions that helped to clarify many of the issues I was trying to discuss. In addition, an early draft was read by Deborah Geis, whose comments encouraged me to dig a bit deeper into the texture of this play. My heartfelt thanks to all.

2. For some representative works that examine Kennedy's theater from a feminist perspective, see Linda Kintz, Rosemary Curb, and Jeanie Forte. Jeanne-Marie Miller's *CLA* article, Mance Williams' *Black Theater in the 1960s and 1970s* and Paul Carter Harrison's *The Drama of Nommo* are good examples of works that consider Kennedy's theater in the context of the canon and styles of African American playwrights. The avant-garde aspect of Kennedy's work and especially her use of surrealism and expressionism have been treated by Herbert Blau, Elinor Fuchs, and William Elwood, among others.

3. Discussions of how enslavement ideology and the colonial mindset use sexual positioning to keep blacks and whites in their "proper places" is a complex issue that is only briefly touched upon here. For further study of these issues, see hooks, Davis, Lerner, and their sources.

4. For a lengthy discussion of the sexual abuses of black women under slavery, see bell hooks' *Ain't I a Woman: Black Women and Feminism.*

5. For some theoretical background regarding this positioning that has informed my reading of Kennedy, see works by Frantz Fanon and Homi Bhabba.

WORKS CITED

Benston, Kimberly W. "Locating Adrienne Kennedy: Prefacing the Subject." *Intersecting Boundaries: The Theatre of Adrienne Kennedy.* Eds. Paul Bryant-Jackson and Lois More Overbeck. Minneapolis: U of Minnesota P, 1992. 113-130.

Bhabha, Homi K. "The Other Question . . . Homi K Bhabha Reconsiders the Stereotype and Colonial Discourse." *Screen* 24 (1983): 18-36.

Blau, Herbert. "The American Dream in the American Gothic: The Plays of Sam Shepard and Adrienne Kennedy." *The Eye of Prey: Subversions of the Postmodern*. Bloomington: U of Indiana P, 1987. 42-64.

Bryant-Jackson, Paul K., and Lois More Overbeck, eds. *Intersecting Boundaries; The Theatre of Adrienne Kennedy*. Minneapolis: U of Minnesota P, 1992.

Cleaver, Eldridge. *Soul on Ice*. New York: Dell Publishing, 1970.

Curb, Rosemary K. "(Hetero)Sexual Terrors in Adrienne Kennedy's Early Plays." *Intersecting Boundaries: The Theatre of Adrienne Kennedy*. Minneapolis: U of Minnesota P, 1992. 142-156.

————. "Re/cognition, Re/presentation, Re/creation in Woman-Conscious Drama: The Seer, the Seen, the Scene, the Obscene." *Theatre Journal* 37 (1985): 302-316.

Davis, Angela. *Women, Race & Class*. New York: Vintage, 1983.

Elwood, William. "Adrienne Kennedy through the Lens of German Expression." *Intersecting Boundaries: The Theatre of Adrienne Kennedy*. Eds. Paul K. Bryant-Jackson and Lois More Overbeck. Minneapolis: U of Minnesota P, 1992. 85-92.

Fanon, Frantz. *Black Skin, White Masks*. New York: Grove, 1967.

Forte, Jeanie. "Realism, Narrative, and the Feminine Playwright: A Problem of Perception." *Modern Drama* 32 (1989): 115-127.

Fuchs, Elinor. "Adrienne Kennedy and the First Avant-Garde." *Intersecting Boundaries: The Theatre of Adrienne Kennedy*. Eds. Paul K. Bryant-Jackson and Lois More Overbeck. Minneapolis: U of Minnesota P, 1992. 76-84.

Gates, Henry Louis, Jr. "Criticism in the Jungle." *Black Literature and Literary Theory*. Ed. Henry Louis Gates, Jr. New York: Methuen, 1984. 1-24.

Harrison, Paul Carter. *The Drama of Nommo*. New York: Grove, 1972.

hooks, bell. *Ain't I a Woman: Black Women and Feminism*. Boston: South End, 1981.

————. *Black Looks: Race and Representation*. Boston: South End, 1992.

Kennedy, Adrienne. *Funnyhouse of a Negro. Adrienne Kennedy: In One Act*. Minneapolis: U of Minnesota P, 1988. 1-23.

————. *People Who Led to My Plays*. New York: Theatre Communications Group, 1987.

Kintz, Linda. *The Subject's Tragedy: Political Poetics, Feminist Theory, and Drama*. Ann Arbor: U of Michigan P, 1992.

Lerner, Gerda. *Black Women in White America*. New York: Vintage, 1973.

Miller, Jeanne-Marie A. "Images of Black Women in Plays by Black
  Playwrights." *College Language Association Journal* 20 (1977): 494-507.
Solomon, Alisa. Foreword. *The Alexander Plays.* Adrienne Kennedy.
  Minneapolis: U of Minnesota P, 1992. ix-xvii.
Wallace, Michelle. *Black Macho and the Myth of the Superwoman.* New York:
  Dial,1978.
White, Hayden. *Metahistory: The Historical Imagination in Nineteenth-
  Century Europe.* Baltimore: Johns Hopkins UP, 1973.
Williams, Mance Raymond. *Black Theater in the 1960s and 1970s: A
  Historical-Critical Analysis of the Movement.* Westport, CT: Greenwood,
  1985.

"Filled with the Holy Ghost"

Sexual Dimension and Dimensions of Sexuality in the Theater of Ntozake Shange

Neal A. Lester

. . . she and Yakubu were Black. Nobody, not even other Blacks, liked to witness such open display of sexual feelings between Black women and men, right out in public! Such shameless behavior fed into White folks' stereotypes of Blacks. Fuck white folks' stereotypes!

Calvin Hernton, "Dew's Song," 1990

She was stretched on her back beneath the pear tree soaking in the alto chant of the visiting bees, the gold of the sun and the panting breath of the breeze when the inaudible voice of it all came to her. She saw a dust-bearing bee sink into the sanctum of a bloom; the thousand calyxes arch to meet the love embrace and the ecstatic shiver of the tree from root to tiniest branch creaming in every blossom and frothing with delight. . . .She had been summoned to behold a revelation. Then Janie felt a pain remorseless sweet that left her limp and languid.

Zora Neale Hurston, Their Eyes Were Watching God, 1935

. . ./ when you filled with the Holy Ghost
every man/ in the world
can smell it/

Ntozake Shange, The Love Space Demands
(A Continuing Saga), 1991

Why do the "great love stories" in Western culture rarely involve
people of color? There's Shakespeare's Romeo and Juliet, Chaucer's
Troilus and Criseyde, Hollywood's Antony and Cleopatra, Ricky and
Lucy Ricardo, Dale Evans and Roy Rogers, Lois Lane and Clark Kent,
Barbie and Ken, even Underdog and Ms. Polly Purebread. And
American history, welfare statistics, statistics of teenage pregnancies
and unwed mothers, and other social indicators perpetuate myths of
black female and black male hypersexuality, of their raw, jungle,
animal nature—factors which allegedly exempt them from romance and
spirituality. According to what we see around us, only white people fall
in love and experience real depths of passion. Blacks remain either
invisible in the public arena of intimacy or are relegated to the racist
assessment that Mrs. Carraway, the narrator in Langston Hughes's short
story, "Slave on the Block" (1933) makes when she discovers her two
black servants, Mattie and Luther, in bed together: "It's so simple and
natural for Negroes to make love" (Hughes 27). Mrs. Carraway,
initially surprised by and shocked at this dimension of their
relationship, of their existence, appeases herself through cultural and
racial condescension. And yet the media, films, movies, music videos,
and many rappers perpetuate and capitalize on these
(mis)representations of blacks' sexual superiority, their raw animal
passion. That alleged superiority, however, contributes little to
dismantle the economic, political, and sociocultural power of whites,
generally, and of white males, particularly.

African American authors have always documented and
legitimized blacks' sexuality and sensuality as complex dimensions of
African American identity. In many cases, to present romance and
sexuality of blacks at all is to deconstruct racist mythologies and
perceptions. From Frederick Douglass, William Wells Brown, Harriet
Wilson, Harriet Jacobs, Paul Laurence Dunbar, Jean Toomer, Langston
Hughes, Nella Larsen, Zora Neale Hurston, Octavia Butler, Malcolm X,
Sonia Sanchez, Nikki Giovanni, Maya Angelou, Alice Walker, Essex
Hemphill, Hattie Gossett, to Toni Morrison, African American authors
have explored blacks' perceptions of themselves and each other in
various sexual arenas. A common task for these writers has been to
demonstrate the often-ignored complexity of African American
experience, particularly in their treatments of blacks' sexuality,
sensuality, and erotica. As Ntozake Shange posits in "Fore/ Play," her
foreword to *Erotique Noire: Black Erotica* (1992), to celebrate African
Americans' sexuality is to reject others' and our own perceptions of

African Americans as "myths or stereotypes, art forms or sex objects." She further clarifies: "We are simply folks [not simple folks] at intimate play; our fierce rhythms of desire, the exotic unencumbered by the 'other,' close and hot" (xx).

In terms of female sexuality generally and of the sexual possibilities of black women, particularly, perhaps no other writer has foregrounded her work explicitly and imagistically in the public arena of the American stage as poet-playwright Ntozake Shange. Shange simultaneously celebrates African Americans' romance and intimacy in all its rawness, its poetic lyricism, and its dangers. Daringly straightforward in her presentations of black female sexuality as simultaneously personal and political, Shange subverts racist images of blacks as animals in heat, devoid of emotion, intellect, in short, of human complexity. The black men about whom she writes are not big bucks bent on proving their manhood through intimacy with a white woman. Neither are Shange's sexually liberated black females prostitutes, sluts, or whores, despite what some men and women or society at large might have them be. They are not ashamed to "sit wif [their] legs open sometimes/ to give [their] crotch[es] some sunlight" (*for colored girls* 53), or to admit that they are not dirty because they did not douche, or to admit that they are perfectly willing and able to give themselves sexual pleasure without a man. Shange carefully takes these social (mis)perceptions of black women and redefines women's sexual possibilities in ways that create wholeness and acknowledge vulnerability. As Shange has repeatedly acknowledged, her writings are offered to "little girls coming of age" who need more than birth control information for their complete emotional and psychological development. Her presentations of sexuality generally and of female sexuality particularly are as groundbreaking and forthrightly political as her choreopoem form is innovative, her language caressing, fondling, consoling, attacking, and intimidating. With a strident feminism in her crusade against western patriarchal and social, political, and aesthetic aggressions, Shange is passionately committed to exploring and legitimizing the complex contradictions of female sexuality. With a rawness of language and imagery that at once seduces and alienates, Shange demonstrates and documents the freedoms of women, particularly black women, who realize and accept their sexuality and sensuality as fundamental signifiers of complete selfhood. In her accounts of a young woman who celebrates losing her virginity—but not her dignity—in the backseat of an old black buick on high school graduation night, to women who reminisce about "bumping and grinding" up and down the New Carver Homes en route to adulthood, Shange reveals that women who acknowledge and celebrate themselves sexually pose a threat to patriarchal social order. When a woman speaks of "laugh[ing] & [having] a good time masturbating in the shadows" just after intimacy with a male who has been duped concerning his sexual performance, or she proclaims the ignorance of some men who do not know that "machines [could] replace them & do a better job" in the bedroom, Shange demonstrates her self-professed role as a feminist "war correspondent" aggressively redefining and reclaiming for women their own sexual landscapes.

When she celebrates this reclaiming and broadening of women's sexual possibilities, Shange simultaneously launches a powerful attack on a social system that makes a woman's sexuality and sensuality social, psychological, and physical liabilities. Her observations on acquaintance rape, abortion, and female child molestation and genital mutilation recognize the contradictory life-threatening, even life-denying realities that also define and hence limit a woman's full existence.

Shange's distinctly black feminist perspective on the complexities of human sexuality is documented throughout her work. In her efforts to legitimize these experiences, she posits: "We are lost in the confusion of myths and fears of race and sex. To be a 'good' people, to be 'respectable' and 'worthy citizens,' we've had to combat absurd phantasmagoric stereotypes about our sexuality, our lusts and loves, to the extent that we disavow our own sensuality to each other" ("Fore/ Play" xix). Shange's theater pieces affirm her belief that people of color and women survive when they are in tune with their own "fierce rhythms of desire."

Ntozake Shange is not the first African American author or even the first African American female author to explore the complex connections between sexuality and female identity. Slave narratives abound with details showing black female sexuality as a survival negotiator between white male slaveowners and their black female slaves. Frederick Douglass's account of his Aunt Hester's vicious beating in *Narrative of the Life of Frederick Douglass, an American Slave* (1845) suggests that the beating derives from the master's jealousy that beautiful Aunt Hester would dare sneak away to be with Lloyd's Ned. Harriet Jacobs's *Incidents in the Life of a Slave Girl, Written by Herself* (1861) reveals the complicated landscaping of black female sexuality in Linda Brent's efforts to redefine herself and her enslavement. Jacobs's ability to master her master through acts of sexual intercourse with another man proves the uniqueness of black female position in the pre-Civil War moral and social order. Jean Toomer's *Cane* (1923) shows a kind of oneness of women's sexuality and a natural cosmic order that upsets the social order established by men. Nella Larsen, in *Passing* (1929), reveals the sexual ambiguities of female identity in the relationship between Clare and Irene, a relationship offered in blurred suggestion and implication, a relationship nevertheless perceived and expressed in heterosexual dynamics. Zora Neale Hurston's Janie, in *Their Eyes Were Watching God* (1937), is perhaps the most sexually liberated of African American heroines. Janie, masturbating to the rhythms of nature, experiences a oneness with nature that she longs to find in a relationship with a male. Only after two loveless marriages with older men is Janie able to capture that pear tree ecstacy with a younger man, Tea Cake, whom Hurston describes as "the love thoughts of women." Even Toni Morrison's Sethe in *Beloved* (1988) is not without sexual desires that make her whole despite the Beloved's threatening jealousies and seduction of Paul D.

Indeed, black female sexuality is not an issue unexplored in African American writings, particularly in fictional and autobiographical texts. Bringing that sexuality to the stage not through explicit dramatization but through narrative exploration is, however, one of the dimensions of Ntozake Shange's groundbreaking moves in American theater. Shange is not even the first playwright to present sexuality of African Americans upon the American stage. Earlier playwrights have presented dimensions of sexuality usually as a backdrop to some larger political message dealing with black and white race relations. For instance, plays dealing with the sexual myths between blacks and whites along gender lines include James Baldwin's *Blues for Mister Charlie* (1964), Amiri Baraka's *Dutchman* (1964) and *The Slave* (1964), Douglas Turner Ward's *Day of Absence* (1965), Ed Bullins's *How Do You Do* (1965), *A Minor Scene* (1966), *It Has No Choice* (1966), and *The Taking of Miss Janie* (1975). Georgia Douglas Johnson's *Blue Blood* (1927) and *Blue-Eyed Black Boy* (n.d.) and Langston Hughes's *Mulatto* (1931) consider the residual effects of slavery in the sexual dynamics between "free" blacks and whites. And plays abound that connect black manhood with sexuality, at least superficially—Louis Peterson's *Take a Giant Step* (1953), Ron

Milner's *Who's Got His Own* (1966), and Lonne Elder, III's
Ceremonies in Dark Old Men (1969). Even African American
homosexuality is treated by Baraka in *The Toilet* (1964) and by Richard
Wesley in *The Mighty Gents* (1974). Lorraine Hansberry's *A Raisin in
the Sun* (1959) implies a passion between Ruth and Walter only when
Walter feels financially empowered, and Adrienne Kennedy considers
father/ daughter incest in *Funnyhouse of a Negro* (1964). Among
others, Sonia Sanchez's *The Bronx Is Next* (1968), Martie Charles's
Black Cycle (1971), Alice Childress's *Wedding Band: A Love/ Hate
Story in Black and White* (1973), and Elaine Jackson's *Paper Dolls*
(1979) focus more on black female sexuality than other plays. But few
playwrights have presented the black female centerstage as a complete
sexual being as has Shange. In Shange's world, black female sexuality
is a cause for celebration, a vehicle of communication and
miscommunication, and a source of exploitation in relationships with
some men. Shange also presents female sexuality as a woman's weapon
when she feels otherwise powerless against masculine domination.
Responsibly, Shange writes as aggressively about sexual violence
against women and children as she celebrates the pleasures of female
sexual liberation. She also demonstrates sexuality as a power
determinant in some heterosexual intimacies. Finally, sexual
independence is an important dimension of women's selfhood as they
come to realize their ability to control their own bodies and their own
minds.

Shange's choreopoem *for colored girls who have considered
suicide/ when the rainbow is enuf* (1976) presents sexuality as one of
the reasons colored girls might consider suicide. At the same time,
sexuality is part of the rainbow that prevents their acting upon wishes to
destroy themselves. To present in a 1976 public Broadway setting
seven black women laughing and talking about a first sexual experience
was Shange's first task in redefining black female identity. That women
could and would talk openly about sexuality, that women would enjoy a
sexual encounter and not see themselves as whores and prostitutes
redefined possibilities for black women's selfhood in this first drama by
Shange. As the women narrate their own private pains and joys,
sexuality is a link that joins them in this rainbow of experiences.
Shange does not present sexuality as a liability in the choreopoem's
early moments. In fact, as the girls remember dancing on graduation
night, Shange equates slow dancing—"doin nasty ol tricks" (*for
colored girls* 8)—with sexual intercourse. The "bump and grind"

dancing and this first sexual experience on this particular night and at this particular moment of this woman's life become a kind of rite of passage as this young female moves into womanhood:

> bobby started lookin at me real strange
> like i waz a woman or somethin/
> started talkin real soft
> in the backseat of that ol buick
> WOW
> by daybreak
> i just cdnt stop grinnin.
> . . . .
> yeh, and honey, it was wonderful. (9)

This entrance into womanhood establishes the realities that threaten to make female sexuality synonymous with pain and liability—the possibilities of unwanted pregnancy, acquaintance rape, male partners' infidelities, and overall emotional vulnerabilities.

In this second phase of Shange's presentation of female sexuality, she shows a woman who celebrates sexual freedom but who accidentally becomes pregnant. In the poem, "abortion cycle #1," the young woman does not regret her sexual liberties; she is not even necessarily promiscuous. She simply forgets to take a birth control pill. As a result of human error, she becomes pregnant. Having an abortion seems this woman's way of escaping public humiliation since she is unwed. The poem is less an attack on this woman's mistake than an attack on social mores that would make a woman's sexual freedom a social liability. The imagery of this poem also highlights the ambiguity of rape and consensual sexual intercourse for women and even reminds us that any gynecological exam for women is not metaphorically far removed from rape—legs spread with steel rods and other foreign objects entering females' bodies.

That a woman's sexuality is a liability is further demonstrated in the poignant poem, "latent rapists'" where sexuality is a means of demonstrating "manhood" and power for men:

> women relinquish all personal rights
> in the presence of a man
> who apparently cd be considered a rapist (20).

Here, rape is a means of asserting men's power over women. Clearly, Shange does not call every man a rapist. However, she does alert women to the possibility that in the presence of men, they need not be paranoid but always on guard.

Female sexuality used as an instrument of revenge is detailed in the story of the Passion Flower who lures black men to her bed only to toss them out before daybreak as men have treated women, her female sisterhood. While this woman perceives her sexuality as a means of righting all the wrongs done other women, the game itself results in empty triumph as she cries herself to sleep after each encounter. The sexual passion she manufactures for her plan does not satisfy her emotional and spiritual need for a man's sincere and honest affections. Neither the Passion Flower nor Sechita, the tent dancer in the rural south who is her "cracker" male audience's would-be whore—the men toss coins toward her genitals as she performs—is a prostitute as many would argue or assume their behavior, lifestyle, and even costumes suggest. Instead, they are women trying to define their personal power on their own terms.

Sexuality is also a means by which some women try to cement relationships with selfish men. In the poem, "no assistance," a woman has made every attempt to transform a primarily sexual relationship with a man into one that is more emotionally and spiritually satisfying for her. While she admits her willing participation in this game of satisfying this man, she is ultimately able to leave this destructive relationship before she is emotionally destroyed.

While Shange's women enjoy the physical passions of heterosexual intimacy and readily admit using sexuality as a means of escaping the realities of one-sided romance, infidelities, and low self-esteem—"those scars [they] had hidden wit smiles & good fuckin" (46)—they realize that their salvation from self-destruction and from being destroyed by others lies within them:

> i know bout/ layin on bodies/ layin outta man
> bringin him alla my fleshy self & some of my pleasure
> being taken full eager wet like i get sometimes
> i was missin something. (65)

These women recognize that while sexuality and intimacy are important to their complete being, sexuality does not necessarily create or lead to a sustaining spirituality that signals peace within themselves.

Shange's choreopoem, *spell #7* (1979), while it concerns itself with establishing and maintaining a healthy African American identity in a racist society that works to fragment and to define through limitation, expectation, myth, and stereotype, also highlights black female sexuality. As a play about the debunking of racial myths and the powers of African Americans' creative imaginations, this piece attacks the professional limitations on black female actors who want to play roles other than whores and prostitutes. One improvisation involves Fay, a single mother who, while her children are away vacationing, goes out on the town to have a good time. Her good time may or may not involve having "some nice brown man . . . wind up in her bed" (*spell #7* 21), but Fay is open to such amorous possibilities. While she drinks and seems unconcerned that one of her breasts peeks from behind her halter top, Maxine, the narrator, is quick to point out that "[F]ay waznt no whore/ just a good clean woman out for the nite" (21). Even the cab driver who chauffeurs Fay to the Manhattan bar and who along the way "kisst the spaces she'd been layin open to [him]" (22) knows that Fay "waz a gd clean woman/ . . . burstin with pride & enthusiasm" for life. Maxine desires such a role on the stage but racial and gender stereotypes prohibit such an opportunity. According to Maxine who also dramatizes Fay's story, "all [white male directors] want me to do is put my leg in my face/ smile & [fuck]" (23). Indeed, socially imposed limitations on female sexuality impact upon black female artists' professional opportunities as well.

In the story of Sue Jean, Shange presents female sexual independence in a game of seduction, deception, betrayal, and self-destruction. Sue Jean, feeling no connection with anything or anyone around her, desperately wants to be a mother. Much like the Passion Flower who uses her sexuality to trap men, drain them sexually, then toss them from her space, Sue Jean manipulates a male friend in her pregnancy scheme:

> . . . there waz nothin special there/ only a hot rough bangin/ a brusque barrelin throwin of torso/ legs & sweat/ ray wanted to kiss me/ but i screamed/ cuz i didnt like kissin/ only fuckin/ . . . i waz a peculiar sorta woman/ wantin no kisses/ no caresses/ just power/ heat   & no eaziness of thrust. (28)

Sue Jean's sexuality is not a celebrated dimension of her identity. Instead, her sexual independence—her self-gratification through "masturbatin in the shadows" (29) after intercourse with Ray—is presented as a narcissistic, self-destructive act. Shange, through Sue Jean's murder of the child she conceives, illustrates the ultimate futility of sexual manipulation.

Although Shange's female characters speak openly about their sexual attraction to Bob Marley whom they imagine "knows exactly what to do" (42) to satisfy a woman sexually, they also recognize the dangers of sexuality of which even as little girls they are made aware. In another of Maxine's improvisations about growing up as a black girl, Shange shows that not only must a black girl reconcile the contradictions of racism—that blacks have polio despite the fact that they do not appear on polio posters and that black adults do molest children—she has also to learn that her move into puberty and adolescence can be as much a physical danger in the presence of men as her blackness can be in the presence of racist whites:

> when i became a woman, my world got smaller. . . . i didnt celebrate
> the [black male] trolley driver anymore/ cuz he might know i waz in
> this condition. i didnt celebrate the basketball team anymore/ cuz they
> were yng & handsome/ & yng & handsome cd mean trouble. . . .now
> trouble meant something abt yng & handsome/ & white or colored. if
> he waz yng & handsome that meant trouble. (50)

This limited existence connected with female sexuality echoes the sentiments of the adult woman in the poem, "i used to live in the world" (*for colored girls* 38), wherein a woman's independence of movement is restricted by the unimagined possibility of male sexual aggression:

> i come in at dusk
> . . . .
> praying wont no young man
> think i'm pretty in a dark mornin'
> wdnt be good
> not good at all
> to meet a tall short black brown young man fulla
>   his power
> in the dark
> in my universe of six blocks. (39)

This woman's sexuality, like Maxine's adolescent female persona, soon learns that being born female and growing into womanhood can lead to diminished freedoms and limited possibilities for complete selfhood.

Foregrounding sexuality in all its complexities and ambiguities, *a photograph: lovers in motion* (1979) is one of Shange's most complex character presentations. Specifically, the play delicately intertwines sexuality with violence, power, and gender confusion. It is also Shange's only play that deals however minimally with bisexuality and homosexuality. These characters try to use sexuality to define and clarify their dreams and illusions.

Sean David, the photographer and "leading man" of the play, is convinced that his manhood is defined by his alleged sexual prowess. He makes this connection clear when one of his female lovers challenges him to define his manhood: "i fuck you fool/ you still dont know i'ma man?" (*a photograph* 87). In fact, Sean prides himself on the number of female lovers he thinks he can juggle smoothly. Avoiding truths about his misconceptions about manhood, he also equates manhood with sexual violence against and exploitation of his female lovers. It appears that Sean's chauvinist attitudes and his physical, verbal, and emotional abuse of women are learned from his own father's example:

> ... he brought the whores home/ & fucked em
> & beat em & fought em & laughed all nite long. (88)

Sean seems aware of this pattern of male behavior but seems unable to define himself in terms other than dominance over women.

To discuss male heterosexuality, Shange reaffirms, is also to discuss female sexuality and vice versa. Sean's trio of women, Claire, Nevada, and Michael feed Sean's ego largely because they have not resolved personal tensions in their own lives. Each woman tries to convince herself that this abusive relationship with Sean is all she can or should expect from a male companion.

Claire is the exhibitionist of the trio. Willing to do whatever it takes to appease Sean, she professes an emotional independence but often consents to his exploitive sexual fantasies without protest. Her participation in Sean's love/war gaming might be traced to her own misconceptions about what it means to be female, advice interestingly that comes from her father who perceived women as objects dependent upon male approval and guidance:[1]

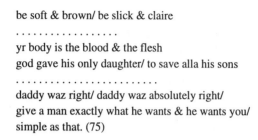

be soft & brown/ be slick & claire
. . . .
yr body is the blood & the flesh
god gave his only daughter/ to save alla his sons
. . . .
daddy waz right/ daddy waz absolutely right/
give a man exactly what he wants & he wants you/
simple as that. (75)

Claire's lessons about female-male relations have left her confused, spiritually and emotionally unsatisfied. In her effort to revise this patriarchal prescription for femininity and to demonstrate that she possesses some power in her life, she taunts Sean with talk of her multiple lovers and even implies her own bisexuality, both affronts to his own perceived manhood. Yet she herself is unconvinced that she can empower herself and consequently tumbles back into bed with the man who threatens to have her gang raped if she dares to take on other lovers.

Nevada, a lawyer with a level head about matters other than her relationship with Sean, is also a willing member of Sean's sexual harem. Nevada literally and metaphorically pays Sean for his affections; she buys him expensive camera equipment and pays his rent though he shows no special connection to her emotionally or otherwise. She accepts his emotional abuse and neglect and his parade of other lovers. Nevada's low self-esteem derives in part from a family whose wealth and social position have dictated Nevada's dreams and aspirations. And while she has achieved socially and professionally, she is emotionally desperate. Hence, she sacrifices her dignity and integrity for a man who treats her as a sexual and emotional pawn. As she awaits the fairy tale Prince to take her, caress her, and shield her from the world's evils—expectations her father gave her about her own life—she remains alone, lonely, and trapped.

Michael is perhaps the most complex character Shange presents in terms of sexual identity. Michael, whose name implies gender ambiguity, is a closet bisexual, at least to Sean, who thinks he controls every aspect of his lovers' lives. Michael perceives this secret as her power over Sean and reveals that her own father's masculinity was undermined by his female bisexual partner.

Earl is a closet homosexual. As he stands in the wings observing the performances of Sean's leading women, he imagines a secret life with Sean that is at once romantic and sexual. He wants to be what the women are to Sean and would gladly accept the same abuse Sean unleashes upon them. Earl has played the game of social conformity by hiding his homosexuality and has ended up as angry as his female competitors. His vicious threat to "fuck Claire [his former lover] til she bleeds" (106) is not far removed from Sean's threat to have her gang raped if she tries to act or think independently. Both Earl and Sean see sexual violence against women as demonstrations of their manhood, their ability to stake a territorial claim when and where they are otherwise powerless.

Through this ensemble of confused lovers trying to identify and maintain illusory gender and behavioral boundaries, Shange suggests that external forces often impact upon individuals' expectations of others and themselves in matters of romance and intimacy. Perceiving their sexuality as the only means of communication and self-empowerment, these characters are trapped in a web of abuse, confusion, and loneliness.

Moving deeper into the psychological dynamics opporating within an "all-American colored girl," Shange's *boogie woogie landscapes* (1979) presents Layla's moves toward self-knowledge racially and sexually. As she comes to accept her skin color in the face of racist threats on her spiritual and physical livelihood, she discovers dangers connected with her female sexuality. Layla's growth into womanhood makes her a target of males bent on taking advantage of her sexually. Layla's unconscious dreams remind her of women's perpetual dangers in the presence of men who define manhood and masculinity as sexual aggression and privilege.

Layla is reminded that in many parts of the world today as in ancient times, female biology predetermines her doomed destiny. In her bold challenging of social prescriptions and perceptions that make male synonymous with power and freedom and female with limitation and victimization, Shange attacks the horrific and primarily sexual ways patriarchal societies try to maintain social order ". . . infibulation, excision, clitorectomies, rape & incest are irrevocable life-deniers/life-deniers/ life stranglers & disrespectful of natural elements. . . . we pay for being born girls/ but we owe no one anything/ not our labia, not our clitoris, not our lives. (*boogie* 136)

Despite the threats that plague women at birth through womanhood—their whole lives—Shange affirms woman's rights to exist wholly, completely, and without fear. She legitimizes sexual possibilities for women despite patriarchal efforts to deny or destroy them.

Shange revises the culturally condescending notion that great romance can only occur between whites in *From Okra to Greens/ A Different Kinda Love Story: A Play/ With Music & Dance* (1985). This metaphorical love story between Okra (black female) and Greens (black male) is presented from a distinctly black feminist perspective. As such, their romance veers importantly from the mainstream's (white) boy-meets-(white) girl paper doll romance.[1] In Shange's revision, a black woman meets a black man, the black man and woman court and marry, the black man is unfaithful to the black woman, the black woman and the black man separate, the black woman and the black man are reconciled, the black woman becomes pregnant, the black woman and black man, as husband and wife, honeymoon on the beach amid nature's approving reception. Though Okra and Greens's story ends happily, at least for the moment, their relationship is not without obstacles both internally and externally. Such a presentation addresses the possibility of mutual spiritual commitment, mutual respect, and mutual sexual satisfaction in African American heterosexual romance.

Okra and Greens's relationship is one built on honesty and trust. It is also one in which lovemaking enhances their spiritual commitment to each other. Without masculine dominance or feminine deceptions, they work at open communications and are able to survive Greens's fling with another woman and Okra's ongoing romantic fantasies about Bob Marley. They bask in a passion free of social prescriptions and roles:

> *Okra.* You take my tongue outta my mouth/make me say foolish
> things

> *Greens.* You take my tongue outta my mouth/ lay it on yr skin like
> the dew between yr legs. (*From Okra* 10)

Even their language is both sensual and erotic. Their sincerity suggests that their attraction to each other makes each equally vulnerable to the powers of romance and sexuality. Hence, their lovemaking is but a manifestation of their spiritual connectedness:

> *Okra.* my body loosens for/ you. . . . . .you wet yr finger/ lay
> it to my lips that might write some more abt you/how you come
> into me

> *Greens.* how i come into you like a rollercoaster in a dip that swings
> leaves you shattered/ glistening/ rich/ screeching & fully
> clothed. (11-12)

Unlike Sean David and others like him, Greens is not concerned with a masculine identity defined by his sexual performance or by multiple sexual escapades. He is sensitive to Okra's realities as a woman living in a sexist and racist society. He even seeks a fuller understanding of her gender realities and participates fully in a recitation profiling the abusive behaviors of some men toward women, abuses grounded fundamentally in power plays around sexuality. From the "pretty man" who imagines himself bigger than he really is both in and out of bed and who turns a pleasant morning after lovemaking into a moment of threatening hostility—"suck my dick & make me some coffee" (20), to the flasher ejaculating laughter or ejaculating and laughing at a terrified and trapped female victim, to an obscene phone caller who knows his female victim, to the man who makes women sexual pawns in lieu of porno movies, to the man who tries to mask his own masculine insecurities by verbally assaulting his female lover and by coercing her to have a baby, Shange submits the outlined behavior of potentially any man who perceives his penis as a stamp of power and privilege over any woman.

A final scenario that serves to separate Greens's awareness and sensitivity as a male from the myriad of abusive males involves his and Okra's account of an initially mutually satisfying moment of intimacy that without warning or consent becomes a painful manifestation of perceived male privilege and female objectification. This man who senses the pleasure of his female partner is ultimately threatened by a woman enjoying this passionate encounter:

> *Okra.* he felt her thighs/ strong & wet her body arching like ferns
> reaching/ she was smiling & feverish with desire

> *Greens.* she felt him coming

> *Okra.* & let go all her powers.

Greens. when without warning he shot all his semen up her ass.

Okra. she kept screaming
> WHAT ARE YOU DOING WHAT ARE YOU DOING TO ME

Greens. he relaxed/ sighing
> I had to put it somewhere. it was too good to be some pussy. (25)

Greens's participation in this condemnation of male behaviors implies a human sensitivity that transcends gender boundaries. It is this sensitivity that allows Okra to forgive his transgressions and for them both to share Okra's black feminist vision. Hence, according to Shange, the complexities of romance and passion exist for African Americans as well.

Shange's celebrations of sexuality extend beyond the stage. She wrote the foreword to Robert Mapplethorpe's *Black Book* (1986), an arguable glorification of black male physicalities, and has contributed short pieces to the collection of black erotic writings, *Erotique Noire: Black Erotica* (1992). One of the collected stories, "Comin to Terms," shows the sexual tensions that derive from the dynamics of heterosexual cohabitation when other aspects of the relationship are suffering. A woman teaches her male companion to appreciate her by refusing to sleep with him and by flaunting before him her ability to pleasure herself sexually even when he is available. The other piece, "Tocame," details a pseudo-strained heterosexual relationship held together by mutually satisfying sexuality. And in her essay, "However You Come to Me," from Marita Golden's collection, *Wild Women Don't Wear No Blues: Black Women Writers on Love, Men and Sex* (1992), Shange expounds on the inevitability of power struggles between men and women even in romance and sexual intimacy. And while masculine thought continues to objectify women—women become men's "pussies" to have and to hold whenever, wherever, and however they desire—Shange makes her feminist politics clear, "Still, I have not opted for lesbian separatism or celibacy as a lifelong avocation. Why not? I like men. They're sexy, funny, exciting . . . and I enjoy sex with men" ("However" 211). This steadfast commitment to heterosexuality is one of the wedges between Shange and some lesbian feminists who insist that Shange's feminist credentials are weakened because she "sleeps with the enemy." While lesbian and gay issues are not at the heart of Shange's presentations, individual human sexuality is. And she has not turned away from this celebration of passion even in her acknowledgement of AIDS and the possibility of literally loving each other to death. Instead, her most recent volume of poetry, *The Love Space Demands (A Continuing Saga)* (1991), which was later performed as a dramatic piece starring Shange, is an exploration of new attitudes about and alternatives to dangerous loving. Among other things, the collection includes poems that exalt female masturbation for the celibate woman who

> . . . wake[s] up drippin
> with the
> spirit
> doves perch by [her] clit
> cooin with the drifters
> til the paragons & the jesters
> come/. (*The Love* 19)

The volume affords other creative options for pleasuring and being pleasured.

Shange's theater creates a space where women are empowered to realize fully and to grandly celebrate their heterosexuality without threat. In this space, Shange's women boldly challenge patriarchal ideals intended to restrict and define dimensions of their private and public existence. As a direct challenge of myths that would alter the natural landscapes of "a daughter's geography," Shange, without sermonizing, moralizing, or prescribing lifestyles other than ones of individual safety—she speaks of her partner's wearing a condom in "However You Come to Me"—shows that romance, sexuality, and raw passion, even among African Americans, are as instinctive to human existence as breathing.

NOTES

1. Similarly, in Shange's one-act play, *Daddy Says*, in Woodie King, Jr.'s *New Plays for the Black Theatre* (Chicago: Third World, 1988), a widower offers his two young daughters the following advice concerning their social roles as women: "That's what gals is s'poses to do/ have babies & keep a good house" (244). Fortunately for the daughters, the father's woman friend steps in to rewrite this patriarchal prescription in a way that challenges these restrictive gender lines as did the girls' deceased mother.

See also Alice Childress's play, *Mojo: A Black Love Story*, published in *Black World* (April 1971):54-82. Here, Childress shows the kinds of external factors that can impact upon black romance. Irene and Teddy's relationship is certainly atypical by western social standards.

WORKS CITED

Douglass, Frederick. *Narrative of the Life of Frederick Douglass, an American Slave*. New York: Penguin, 1982.

Hernton, Calvin. "Dew's Song." In *Erotique Noire: Black Erotica*. Miriam DeCosta-Willis, Reginald Martin, and Roseann P. Bell, eds. New York: Doubleday, 1992. 119-125.

Hughes, Langston. "Slave on the Block." In *The Ways of White People*. New York: Vintage, 1990. 19-31.

Hurston, Zora Neale. *Their Eyes Were Watching God*. Chicago: U of Illinois P, 1978.

Jacobs, Harriet A. *Incidents in the Life of a Slave Girl, Written by Herself*. Jean Fagan Yellin, ed. Cambridge: Harvard UP, 1987.

Larsen, Nella. *Passing*. In *Quicksand and Passing*. Deborah E. McDowell, ed. New Brunswick: Rutgers UP, 1986. 137-246.

Morrison, Toni. *Beloved*. New York: Knopf, 1987.

Shange, Ntozake. *boogie woogie landscapes*. In *Three Pieces*. New York: St. Martin's, 1981. 109-142.

———. "Comin to Terms." In *Erotique Noire: Black Erotica*. Miriam DeCosta-Willis, Reginald Martin, and Roseann P. Bell, eds. New York: Doubleday, 1992. 335-338.

———. *for colored girls who have considered suicide/ when the rainbow is enuf*. New York: Bantam, 1980.

———. *Daddy Says: A Play*. In *New Plays for the Black Theatre*. Woodie King, Jr., ed. Chicago: Third World, 1989. 233-251.

———. "Fore/ Play." Foreword to *Erotique Noire: Black Erotica*. Miriam DeCosta-Willis, Reginald Martin, and Roseann P. Bell, eds. New York: Doubleday, 1992. xix-xx.

———. *From Okra to Greens/ A Different Kinda Love Story: A Play/ With Music & Dance*. New York: Samuel French, 1985.

———. "However You Come to Me." In *Wild Women Don't Wear No Blues: Black Women Writers on Love, Men, and Sex*. Marita Golden, ed. New York: Doubleday, 1993. 203-211.

———. *The Love Space Demands (A Continuing Saga)*. New York: St. Martin's, 1991.

————. *a photograph: lovers in motion.* In *Three Pieces*. New York: St. Martin's, 1985. 53- 108.

————. *spell #7.* In *Three Pieces*. New York: St. Martin's, 1985. 3-52.

————. "Tocame." In *Erotique Noire: Black Erotica*. Miriam DeCosta-Willis, Reginald Martin, and Roseann P. Bell, eds. New York: Doubleday, 1992. 176-179.

Toomer, Jean. *Cane*. New York: Liveright, 1975. March 28, 1995.

Selected Bibliography

Abramson, Doris E. *Negro Playwrights in the American Theatre, 1925-1959.* New York: Columbia UP, 1969.

Aptheker, Bettina. *Women's Legacy: Essays on Race, Sex, and Class in American History.* Amherst: The U of Massachusetts P, 1982.

Austin, Gayle. *Feminist Theories for Dramatic Criticism.* Ann Arbor: U of Michigan P, 1990.

Beckerman, Bernard, and Howard Siegman. *On Stage: Selected Theater Reviews from the New York Times 1920-1970.* New York: Arno, 1970.

Bentley, Gerald Eades. *The Art of Drama.* New York: Appleton-Century, 1935.

Bentson, Kimberly W. "The Aesthetics of Modern Black Drama: From Mimesis to Methexis." *The Theatre of Black Americans.* Ed. Errol Hill. Vol. 1. Englewood Cliffs, NJ: Prentice Hall, Inc, 1980.

Bigsby, C. W. E. *A Critical Introduction to Twentieth Century Drama: Beyond Broadway.* New York: Cambridge UP, 1985.

Bogle, Donald. *Toms, Coons, Mulattoes, Mammies and Bucks: An Interpretation of the History of Blacks in American Film.* New York: Viking, 1973.

Brater, Enoch, ed. *Feminine Focus: The New Women Playwrights.* Oxford: Oxford UP, 1989.

Brockett. Oscar G. *Historical Edition: The Theatre.* New York: Holt, Rinehart and Winston, 1979.

Brown, Janet. *Feminist Drama: Definition and Critical Analysis.* Englewood Cliffs, NJ: Scarecrow, 1979.

Brown, Sterling A. *Negro Poetry and Drama and the Negro in American Fiction.* New York: Atheneum, 1972.

Brown-Guillory, Elizabeth. "Black Women Playwrights: Exorcising Myths." *Phylon: The Atlanta University Review of Race and Culture* 48 (1987): 229-233.

―――. *Their Place on the Stage: Black Women Playwrights in America.* New York: Greenwood, 1987.

―――. *Wines in the Wilderness: Plays by African American Women from the Harlem Renaissance to the Present.* New York: Greenwood, 1990.

Bryant-Jackson, Paul, and Lois Moore Overbeck. *Intersecting Boundaries: The Theatre of Adrienne Kennedy.* Minneapolis: U of Minnesota P, 1992.

Cameron, Kenneth M., and Theodore J. C. Hoffman. *The Theatrical Response.* New York: Macmillan, 1969.

Campbell, Paul Newell. *Form and the Art of Theatre.* Bowling Green: Bowling Green State U Popular P, 1984.

Childress, Alice. *Black Scenes: Collections of Scenes from Plays Written by Black People about Black Experience.* New York: Doubleday, 1971.

―――. "A Candle in the Wind." *Black Women Writers, 1950-1980.* Ed. Mari Evans. New York: Anchor/Doubleday, 1984.

―――. "Knowing the Human Condition." *Black American Literature and Humanism.* Ed. R. Baxter Miller. Lexington: UP of Kentucky, 1981.

Christian, Barbara. *Black Feminist Criticism: Perspectives on Black Women Writers.* New York:Pergamon, 1985.

Collins, Patricia Hill. *Black Feminist Thought: Knowledge, Consciousness, and the Politics of Empowerment.* New York: Routledge, 1991.

Cronacher, Karen. "Unmasking the Minstrel Mask's Black Magic in Ntozake Shange's 'Spell #7.' " *Theatre Journal* 44 (1992): 173-193.

Cruse, Harold. *The Crisis of the Negro Intellectual.* New York: William Morrow and Co., Inc., 1967.

Davis, Angela. *Women, Race, and Class.* New York: Vintage, 1983.

Davis, Arthur P., and Michael W. Peplow. *The New Negro Renaissance.* New York: Holt, Rinehart and Winston, 1975.

Davis, Thadious M., and Trudier Harris, eds. *Afro-American Writers after 1955: Dramatists and Prose Writers. Dictionary of Literary Biography.* Detroit: Gale, 1985.

Diamond, Ellen. "An Interview with Adrienne Kennedy." *Studies in American Drama.* 4 (1989): 143-158.

Elam, Jr. Harry J., and Robert Alexander. *Colored Contradictions: An Anthology of African-American Plays.* New York: Plume, 1996.

Esslin, Martin. *An Anatomy of Drama.* New York: Hill and Wang, 1977.

Evans, Mari, ed. *Black Women Writers, 1950-1980.* New York: Anchor/Doubleday, 1984.

Fabre, Genevieve E. *Afro American Poetry and Drama, 1760-1975*. Detroit: Book Tower, 1979.

———. *Drumbeats, Masks, and Metaphor: Contemporary Afro-American Theatre*. Cambridge, MA: Harvard UP, 1983.

Foster, Frances Smith. *Written by Herself: Literary Production by African American Women*. Bloomington: Indiana UP, 1983.

France, Rachel. *A Century of Plays by American Women*. New York: Richard Rosen P, Inc., 1979.

Gayle, Jr., Addison, ed. *The Black Aesthetic*. New York: Doubleday, 1971.

George, Kathleen. *Rhythm in Dance*. Pittsburgh: U of Pittsburgh P, 1980.

Goldfarb, Alvin, and Edwin Wilson. *Living Theatre: An Introduction to Theatre History*. New York: McGraw-Hill, 1983.

Goodman, Lizabeth. "Drawing the Black and White Line: Defining Black Women's Theatre." *New Theatre Quarterly* 1(1991): 361-68.

Hansberry, Lorraine. *To Be Young Gifted and Black*. Englewood Cliffs, NJ: Prentice Hall, 1969.

Harris, Trudier, ed. *Afro-American Women Writers Before the Harlem Renaissance*. Dictionary of Literary Biography, 51. Detroit: Gale, 1987.

———. *Afro American Writers from the Harlem Renaissance to 1940*. Dictionary of Literary Biography, 76. Detroit: Gale, 1988.

———. *Afro American Writers: 1940-1955*. Detroit: Gale, 1988.

Harrison, Paul Carter. *The Drama of Nommo*. New York: Grove, 1972.

———, ed. *Kuntu Drama: Plays of the African Continuum*. New York: Grove, 1974.

Hartigan, Karlesia V. *The Many Forms of Drama*. New York: UP of America, 1985.

Hatch, James V. *Black Image on the American Stage 1770-1970*. New York: Drama Books Specialists, 1970.

Hatch, James V., and Ted Shine, eds. *Black Theatre USA: Forty-Five Plays by Black Americans*. New York: Free, 1974.

Hay, Samuel A. "Alice Childress' Dramatic Structure." *Black Women Writers, 1950-1980*. Ed. Mari Evans. Garden City, NY: Anchor/Doubleday, 1984. 117-128.

———. *African American Theatre: An Historical and Critical Analysis*. New York: Cambridge UP, 1994.

hooks, bell. *Ain't I a Woman: Black Women and Feminism*. Boston: South End, 1981.

———. *Feminist Theory from Margin to Center*. Boston: South End, 1984.

Hornby, Richard. *Drama, Metadrama and Perception*. Lewisburg, PA: Bucknell UP, 1986.

Hunter, Frederick F. *The Power of Dramatic Form*. New York: Exposition, 1974.

Kerr, Walter. *Tragedy and Comedy*. New York: Simon and Schuster, 1967.

Keyssar, Helene. *The Curtain and the Veil: Strategies in Black Drama*. New York: B. Franklin, 1981.

———. *Feminist Theatre*. New York, Grove, 1985.

Killens, John O. "The Literary Genius of Alice Childress." *Black Women Writers, 1950-1980*. Ed. Mari Evans. New York: Anchor/Doubleday, 1984. 129-134.

King, Woodie and Ron Milner, eds. *Black Drama Anthology*. New York: New American Library, 1986.

Ladner, Joyce A. *Tomorrow's Tomorrow: The Black Woman*. Garden City, NY: Doubleday, 1971.

Lerna, Gerda. *Black Women in White America: A Documentary History*. New York: Pantheon, 1972.

Lester, Neal A. *Ntozake Shange: A Critical Study of the Plays*. New York: Garland, 1995.

Longman, Stanley. *Composing Drama for Stage and Screen*. Boston: Allyn and Bacon, Inc., 1986.

Mahone, Sydné. *Moon Struck and Touched by Sun*. New York: Theatre Communications Group, 1994.

McKay, Nellie. "What Were They Saying? Black Women Playwrights in the Harlem Renaissance." *The Harlem Renaissance Re-examined*. Ed. Victor A. Kramer. New York: AMS, 1986.

———. "Black Theatre and Drama in the 1920's: Years of Growing Pains." *Massachusetts Review* 28 (1987): 615-26.

Miller, Jeanne Marie A. "Images of Black Women in Plays by Black Playwrights." *CLA Journal* 4 (1977): 494-507.

———. "Black Women Playwrights from Grimké to Shange: Selected Synopses of Their Works." *All the Men Are Black, All the Women Are White, but Some of Us Are Brave: Black Women's Studies*. Ed. Gloria Hull et al. Old Westbury, NY: Feminist, 1982. 280-96.

Mitchell, Loften. *Black Drama: The Story of the American Negro in the Theatre*. New York: Hawthorn, 1967.

Nemiroff, Robert, ed. *Lorraine Hansberry, The Collected Last Plays*. New York: New American Library, 1972.

Oliver, Clinton F., and Stephanie Sills. *Contemporary Black Drama: From 'A Raisin in the Sun' to 'No Place to be Somebody.'* New York: Scribner, 1971.

Perkins, Kathy, ed. *Black Female Playwrights: An Anthology of Plays Before 1950*. Bloomington: Indiana UP, 1990.

Perry, Margaret. *Silence to the Drums: A Survey of the Literature of the Harlem Renaissance*. Westport, CT: Greenwood, 1976.

Phillips, Elizabeth C. *The Works of Lorraine Hansberry: A Critical Documentary*. New York: Simon and Schuster, 1973.

Richards, Sandra L. "Negative Forces and Positive Non-Entities: Images of Women in the Dramas of Amiri Baraka." *Theatre Journal* 34 (1982): 233-40.

———. "Conflicting Impulses in the Plays of Ntozake Shange." *Black American Literature Forum* 17 (1983): 73-80.

Schleuter, June, ed. *Modern American Drama: The Female Canon*. Rutherford: Fairleigh Dickinson UP, 1990.

Shinn, Thelma J. "Living the Answer: The Emergence of African American Feminist Drama." *Studies in the Humanities* 17 (1990): 149-59.

Tate, Claudia, ed. *Black Women Writers at Work*. New York: Continuum, 1983.

Timpane, John. "The Poetry of a Moment: Politics and the Open From in the Drama of Ntozake Shange." *Studies in American Drama, 1945-Present* 4 (1989): 91-101.

Toll, Robert C. *Blacking Up: The Minstrel Show in Nineteenth-Century America*. New York: Oxford UP, 1974.

Turner, Darwin. *Black Drama in America*. 2nd ed. Washington, D.C.: Howard UP, 1994.

Wilkerson, Margaret B., ed. *9 Plays by Black Women*. New York: A Mentor Book, 1986.

Woll, Allen. *Dictionary of Black Theatre*. Westport, CT: Greenwood, 1983.

———. *Black Musical Theatre: From "Coontown" to "Dreamgirls."* Baton Rouge: Louisiana State UP, 1989.

Yellin, Jean Fagan. *The Intricate Knot: Black Figures in American Literature, 1776-1863*. New York: New York UP, 1972.

Contributors

E. Barnsley Brown is Assistant Professor at Wake Forest University, where she teaches courses in Women's Studies, American Literature, and African American Literature. She is former poetry editor of *Carolina Quarterly* and presently teaches film criticism. Her recent publications appear in *Notable Black American Women* (Gale, 1992), *The Oxford Companion to Women's Writing in the United States* (Oxford, 1994), *The Oxford Companion to African American Literature* (Oxford, 1997), and poems in *Puerto del Sol, Chiron Review*, and *Kansas Quarterly*.

Keith Clark is Assistant Professor of English at George Mason University in Fairfax, Virginia. He has published essays on James Baldwin, Ann Petry, and William Faulkner. He has contributed to *The Oxford Companion to African American Literature* (Oxford, 1997). He is currently working on a study of contemporary black men's fiction and drama.

Marilyn Elkins is Associate Professor of English at California State University, Los Angeles. She is the author of *Metamorphosing the Novel: Kay Boyle's Narrative Innovations* (Lang, 1994) and editor of *The Heart of a Man* (Norton, 1973) and *August Wilson: A Casebook* (Garland, 1994). She is currently completing *Critical Interpretations of Kay Boyle* (Hall, 1997). She was the recipient of a 1994-95 Fulbright fellowship to lecture in France on African American literature.

Christine R. Gray is Assistant Professor of English at Catonsville Community College. She specializes in early African American drama and wrote her doctoral dissertation on the African American playwright, Willis Richardson. In addition, she wrote the critical introduction to the facsimile edition of *Plays and Pageants from the Life of the Negro*, first published in 1930 (UP of Mississippi, 1993). She has written other essays and reviews in *The W. E. B. DuBois Encyclopedia* (forthcoming); *American Studies International* (forthcoming); and *Theatre Survey*.

Trudier Harris is the J. Carlyle Sittersen Professor of American Literature at the University of North Carolina at Chapel Hill. She writes prolifically in African American Literature. She edited the African American Literature volumes of *Dictionary of Literary Biography* (Gale). Her most recent critical studies are *Fiction and Folklore: The Novels of Toni Morrison* (U of Tennessee P, 1991) and *The Power of the Porch: Narrative Strategies in Works by Zora Neale Hurston , Gloria Naylor, and Randall Keenan* (U of Georgia P, 1996).

LaVinia Delois Jennings is Associate Professor of English at the University of Tennessee at Knoxville where she teaches courses in American Literature and Women's Studies. *Alice Childress* (Twayne, 1995), her most recent publication is the first book-length critical examination of this prolific twentieth-century playwright and novelist.

Lovalerie King is a doctoral student at the University of North Carolina at Chapel Hill. She has written essays for *The Oxford Companion to African American Literature* (Oxford, 1997).

Neal A. Lester is Professor of English at The University of Arizona at Tempe where he teaches African American Literature. His articles and reviews have appeared in *Black American Literature Forum*; *Alabama Literary Review*; *The Journal of Popular Culture*; *African American Review*; *Diversity: A Journal of Multicultural Issues*; *Alabama English*; *Studies in American Drama 1945-Present*; *The Lion and the Unicorn: A Critical Journal of Children's Literature*. He is the author of *Ntozake Shane: A Critical Study of the Plays* (Garland, 1994).

Janice Lee Liddell is Associate Professor of English and Chair of the Department of English at Clark Atlanta University where she also teaches African American Literature, African American Women's Drama, and Africana Women's Writing. She is the author of *Imani and the Myth of the Flying Africans* (Africa World, 1994) and the co-editor of *Arms Akimbo: Africana Literature in Contemporary Literature* (forthcoming).

Carol P. Marsh-Lockett is Associate Professor of English at Georgia State University where she teaches African American Literature, African American Women's Drama, African American Women's Fiction, Caribbean Literature, and occasionally Seventeenth Century Literature. She has published essays on African American and Caribbean Literature in *CLA Journal*; *Fifty Caribbean Writers*; and *Encyclopedia of Post Colonial Literatures in English* (Routledge, 1994). She is the editor of *Decolonising Caribbean Literature* (*Studies in the Literary Imagination* 26.2, Fall, 1993) and has essays in *The Oxford Companion to African American Literature* (Oxford, 1997); *Post-Colonial African Writers* (Greenwood, 1998); and *New Critical Perspectives on Ben Jonson* (Fairleigh Dickinson UP, 1997). She is currently editing *Caliban's Turn: Critical Essays on Caribbean Literature* (forthcoming, Garland).

Carla J. McDonough is Associate Professor of English at Eastern Illinois University where she specializes in modern and contemporary drama. She has published articles on David Mamet, Sam Shepard, Christina Reid, and Timberlake Wertenbaker. She is the author of *Staging Masculinity: Male Identity in Contemporary American Drama* (McFarland and Co. Press, 1996).

Martha H. Patterson is currently a Visiting Assistant Professor of English at Grinnell College. Her work has appeared in *ATQ: 19th Century American Literature and Culture* and *Legacy* and is forthcoming in *African American Review* and *MELUS*. She is completing a book manuscript tentatively titled *Revisioning the ```New American Woman, 1895-1913*.

Index

Abrams, Roger, 92–93
Abramson, Doris, 129n.3
Africa, 57
African American:
  community, 11
  life, 10
  male agency, 11
  selfhood, 11
  sexuality, 11; **155–172; 173–192; 193–211**
  subjectivity, 90
  woman as whore, 11
  women and anger, **43–54**
Akbar, Na'im, 9
American Negro Theater Company, 125
Anderson, Mary Louise, 149n.4
anti-lynching dramas, **25–42**
anti-miscegenation laws, 142
Asante, Molefi, 9
Austin, Gayle, 152n.19
Baker, Houston, 108
Baldwin, James, 4; 80
Bambara, Toni Cade, 121
Baraka, Amiri, 87–88; 174

Baraka, Imamu, 4
  See also Baraka, Amiri
Barnett, Ida B. Wells, 26
Bhaba, Homi, 16
Berzon, Judith, 150n.7
Birth of a Nation, 74
black male subjectivity, **87–111**
black selfhood, **131–153**
black theater, 128
Bonner, Marita, 7
Booth, Wayne, 149n.6
Boston Herald, 4
Boucicault, Dion, 15
Bradford, Joseph B., 22
Broadway Rastus, 84
Brown decision, 127
Brown, Janet, 151n.17
Brown, William, Wells, 4; 84n.6
Brown-Guillory, Elizabeth, 5; 123; 128n.1; 145; 150n.5
Burrill, Mary P., 28–29; 30; 30; 35; 39; 40; **161–162**
Cane, 192
Capouya, Emile, 80

Carby, Hazel, 44–45; 150n.7;
    151n.18
Caribbean literature, 11
carnival laughter, 150n.11
Carraway, Nancy, 53n.2
Carter, Stephen, 94; 100; 102; 107
Cather, Willa, 55
Chaos in Bellville, 138; 139; 140
Charkin, Joe
Chicago InterOcean, 26
Childress, Alice, 4; 5; 10; **43–54;**
    123–128; 131–153
Christian, Barbara, 151n.7
civil rights movement, 107
civil war, 56; 57
Cleage, Pearl, 9–10
Cleaver, Eldridge, 179
Cohan, Steven, 88
Collins, Patricia Hill, 9
Cotter, Joseph Seamon, 60; 84n.6
cotton, 57
Crisis The, 7; 59; 60
Cruse, Harold, 89; 108n.1
Curb, Rosemary, 151n.16
Davis, Angela, 9; 179–180
Democrat:
    conservative politics, 14
desire, 114
DeVeaux, Alexis, **167–170**
Douglass, Frederick, 89; 107; 196
Du Bois, W. E. B., 7; 59; 68n.1;
    85n.5; 99
Dunbar High School, 81
Dunbar-Nelson, Alice, 58; 59; 67
Dworkin Andrea, 168–169
Eidson, John O. *See Tennyson in
    America*
Ellison, Ralph. *See Invisible Man*

endman, 16
Engle, Gary, 17
Esslin, Martin, 3
Europe, 57
Fabre, Genevieve, 89; 107; 128n
Fabre, Michel, 68n.1
Fanon, Frantz, 185
Fisk:
    Jubilee Singers, 15; 23n.4
    University, 5
Florence, (Childress), 46–49; 13:
    137
Flowers, Sandra Hollins, 128n.1
*for colored girls who have
        considered
suicide/ when the rainbow is
        enough,*
(Shange), 5; 63–64; 120–123; 19
    198–201
Fortune, T. Thomas:
    New York Age, 26
Foucalt, Michel, 3
Funnyhouse of a Negro, 115–118
    173–192
Gaines, Ernest, 91
Garrison, William Lloyd, 107
Gates, Henry Louis, 185
Gibson, P. J., 9; 148; **165–167**
Giddings, Paula, 9
Glory, 64
Gordonne, Charles
    No Place to Be Somebody, 4
Govan, Sandra, 158–159; 160
Graham, Shirley, **160–161**
Green, Paul, 7
Gregory, Montgomery T., 7; 8

Grimké, Angelina, 6–7; 10; 27–28; 30–31; 32;
  34–35; 39; 40; **69–85; 75**
Grimké, Archibald, 74; 83n.5; 85n.10
Hamalian, Leo and Hatch, James, 17; 22n.1
Hamlet, 20
Hansberry, Lorraine, 4; 8; 10; 32; 56; 64;
  87–111; 94; 114; 118–120; 128; 164
Hansberry, William Leo, 160
Harlem, 7
Harris, Trudier, 41n.1; 98
Harrison, Paul Carter, 101; 107; 109n.4
Hatch, James, 83n.4; and Shine, Ted, 5
  See also Hamalian, Leo
Hay, Samuel A., 125; 129n.1; 145n.5
Hemmingway, Ernest, 55
Hernton, Calvin, 193
Herron, Carolivia, 193
Holloway, Wendy, 89
homosexuality, 198
hooks, bell, 9, 98–99; 109; 114
Hopkins, Pauline, 4; 10; **13–24**
Howard University, 5; 7; 106
Hughes, Langston, 88; 114–115; 149n.1; 194
Hull, Gloria, 71
Hyers Sisters, the, 15
Independence Day celebrations, 15
interlocutor, 17
Invisible Man, 32; 87
Jackson, Elaine, 9

Jackson, Gerald, 9
Jacobs, Harriet, 89; 196–197
Jim Crow, 60
Johnson, Georgia Douglas, 7; 26; 30–31; 35–37;
  39–40; 159–160
Johnson, Leanor Baulin, 155
  See also Staples, Robert
Julien, Isaac, 114; 115
Kahn, Michael, 174
Kazin, Alfred, 88
Kelly, James, 106
Kennedy, Adrienne, 4; 5; 7; 10; **60–62**; 67; 114
  115–118; 148; **173–192**
Keyssar, Helene, 89; 108n.1; 152n.20
Klan, 20
  Ku klux Klan, 14; 52
Lerner, Harriet Goldhor, 45–46
Little Negro Theater Movement, 7
Locke, Alain, 7; 8; 83n.5
Lorde, Audrey, 44
Lott, Eric, 16
Lucas, Sam, 15
Lynching, 6; 25; 71; 81; 82n.3
  See also anti-lynching plays
Mahone, Sydne, 5–6; 131; 171
Mamet, David, 96
Mara, (Grimke), 68–85
Marston, Richard, 85n.10
McGann, Jerome, 76
Menninger Foundation, 45
middle passage, 8
Middleton, Peter, 97–98
Millet, Arthur, 96; 106
Miller, Jeanne-Marie A., 71; 149n.3

Miranda, 12
Moorland Spingarn Research
    Center, 70
    See also Howard University
Morrison, Toni, 30; 99; 197
Moynihan Report, 120–121
NAACP, 7; 26; 74
New Negro Renaissance, 71
new world, the, 57
Nommo, 104
native dramas, 7
Negro Digest, 131
Oliver, Clinton and Stephanie
    Sills, 113
O'Neill, Eugene, 7;106
Opportunity, 7
Ostendorf, Berndt, 91
Out of Bondage, 14
Papp, Joseph, 174
Passing, 197
Perkins, Kathy, 4; 5; 6–7; 30; 156
propaganda plays, 7
Prospero, 12
Rachel,(Grimke) 6–7; 32
Raisin in the Sun, A (Hansberry),
    4; 83–111;
    118–120
Rat's Mass, A, 60–69
Reconstruction, 14
Redpath's Bureau, 22n.2
Roedigger, David, 17
Republican:
    governments, 14
    sponsored civil rights bill, 14
Richards, Beah, 8; 10
Saxton, Alexander, 17
Schomburg Library, 5
Sycorax, 5

sexuality, **155–172**; **173–197**
    193–212
Shange, Ntozake, 4; 7; 63–64; 6
    114;
    120–123; 128; **193–211**
Shelton, Ruth Gaines, 7
Shepherd, Sam, 174
Shillingburg, Peter, 82
Shires, Linda, 88
Smith, Anna Deveare, 64; **65–6**
Smith, Myrtle Livingstone, 8
Solomon, Alisa, 174
Southern, Eileen, 22n.1
Staples, Robert, 155
    and Leanor Baulin Johnson, 15
    162–163
Stephens, Alexander H., 56
Stepto, Robert, 107
Stowe, Harriet, 15
Tanselle, Thomas, 70; 76;
Tennyson, Alfred Lord:
    Idylls of the King, 79; 80; 84n
    Tennyson in America, 80–81
Thorpe, James, 69
Toll, Robert, 16
Toomer, Jean:
    See Cane
Torrence, Ridgely, 83n.5
tragic mulatto, 150n.7
Trouble in Mind (Childress), 4;
    123–128; 137–141
Turner, Darwin, 5; 103; 104
Twain, Mark, 88
van Gogh, Vincent, 115
Walker, Alice, 29, 32; 115
Walker, Margaret, 29
Wallace, Michelle, 179
War, **55–68**

Ward, Douglas Turner, 4
Washington, Booker T., 84n.6
Wedding Band (Childress), 50–53;
    141–145
western:
  male subjectivity, 102
  masculinist framework, 104
White, Hayden, 189
Wiley, Catherine, 151n.15
Wilkerson, Margaret, 5; 8; 116
Williams, Ralph G., 70
Williams, Tennessee, 106
Wilson, August, 91; 99; 101
Wilson, Edmund, 55
Wine in the Childress (Childress),
    146–148
Witke, Carl, 16
Wright, Richard, 27; 88
United States, 73